Granta 3

After that is accomplished the next business in hand is getting on the right side of the Great British Public. And keep your eyebrows well pinned down. It is quite likely you may know it all and in consequence feel enormously sorry for the Great B.P. for not having enjoyed all your advantages. But the Great B.P. is not always impressed. Very frequently it is bored stiff. Silly and presumptuous of it, but there it is. Amuse it. Cheer it up. Chat to it. Bully it a little. Tickle its funny bone. Giggle with it. Confide in it. Give it, now and again, a good old cry. It loves that. But don't, for your success's sake, come the superior highbrow over it.

Editor: Bill Buford
Executive Editor: Pete de Bolla
Poetry Editor: Elaine Feinstein
Production Director: Joyce Coleman
Editorial Assistants: A.J. Close, Cathryn Gwynn and Michael Hofmann
Editorial Board: Malcolm Bradbury, Ian Hamilton, Leonard Michaels, Fay Weldon
U.S. Editor: Jonathan Levi, 3A, 25 Claremont Ave., New York, N.Y. 10027

Editorial Correspondence: Granta, Box 666, King's College, Cambridge CB2 1ST. (0223) 315290
All manuscripts are welcome but must be accompanied by a stamped, self-addressed envelope or they cannot be returned.

Subscriptions: For individuals, £5.50 for four issues; for institutions, £7.00 for four issues. For foreign subscriptions, add £3.00 per year for postage. Single copies usually £1.80 including postage.

Granta is typeset by A.G.P. Typesetting Ltd., P.O. Box 81, London S.W.6 (01) 731 3570
Printed in Great Britain by Bell and Bain Ltd., Glasgow.
Copyright © 1980 by **Granta**. All rights reserved.
Limited Edition Reprint September 1989.
Granta gratefully acknowledges the assistance of the Eastern Arts Association; the Embassy of the United States (for **Granta** 1); the George Ryland Fund of King's College, Cambridge; the Hobson Gallery; V.W. Shiel; and our many anonymous patrons.

Cover and inside illustration by John Blanche.
Quotation cited anonymously in Q.D. Leavis, *Fiction and the Reading Public*. Parts of the Introduction appeared originally in the **Bookseller**.

ISSN 0017-3231

Contents

Introduction 7

Salman Rushdie Midnight's Children 17
Angela Carter Cousins 47
Desmond Hogan Southern Birds 56
Alan Sillitoe A Scream of Toys 64
Emma Tennant Alice fell 87
Russell Hoban Riddley Walker 109

A Symposium on the British Novel
  Lorna Sage Invasion from Outsiders 131
  Chris Bigsby The Uneasy Middleground of British Fiction 137
  Frederick Bowers An Irrelevant Parochialism 150
  James Gindin Taking Risks 155
  Christine Brooke-Rose Where Do We Go from Here? 161

J.K. Klavans God, He Was Good 189

Notes on Contributors 205

Words, words, words...

from
heffers:
BOOKSELLERS
20 Trinity Street, Cambridge

Introduction

The novel has always smacked of inadequacies. It is regularly less than what is expected of it. Or, worse, it is more. But rarely the thing we had in mind, never quite settling upon an identity that it is easy to be happy about. Fifty years ago Ortega y Gasset confidently pronounced it dying. Twenty years ago, Marshall McLuhan tried hard to demonstrate that it was already dead. It wasn't, and, for some reason, isn't, still very much available as an attractive even if expensive instance of Randall Jarrell's weak apology for it: 'A longish piece of prose with something wrong with it.'

Since the war, the British novel has developed its own indigenous difficulties, or, at least, its own vernacular of complaint. When Gore Vidal remarked at the recent Edinburgh Festival that there are only 'middle class novels for middle class readers with middle class problems' he was echoing a tired charge that has become as predictable as much of the writing occasioning it. For John Sutherland, the complaint was raised to its most explicit by the best sellers list five years ago, dominated with eerie appropriateness by the publication of Jane Austen's *Sanditon*, inviting the observation that the books that are published and purchased still belong very much to that novel of sense and sensibility which has merely been written and re-written for nearly two centuries. Bernard Bergonzi's dark phrase is, in this context, ominously emblematic: the novel is no longer novel.

This vocabulary of termination has suddenly acquired a significance which has authoritatively dropped it from the theoretical to the base, real court of the marketplace. The **Current Crisis in Publishing** is, we understand from the many articles it has generated, of unprecedented proportions, and is noisy with terrible doomsday pronouncements. But it is not, in the end, the book as object which is threatened—for more are appearing (even if briefly) than ever before, although their number and kind have enlarged the image of publishing to something uncomfortably akin to the fast food industry—but the book as fiction, as an instance of literature: not the things in the window or on the railway platform, but the stuff apparently too cumbersome to consume on the run.

The implications of the present **Crisis** are obvious. It's not simply that a literature exists which many find disappointing. It's that we are being told, from now on, it can be no other way. There are reasons for it—the rising costs of this or that, the 'pound', inflation, foreign markets—and the reasons are real in a simple pocket book way. Faced with many English novels, I confess I'd rather watch television. Faced recently by their price, I see I have no choice.

In such a context, what a publisher says is important. Recently Robert McCrum, a young editor at Faber & Faber, offered his view of the **Crisis** in the *Bookseller*. A young editor at Faber is virtually a symbol, and when he enters the most prominent columns of the nation's trade magazine to say that the situation is hopeless, some scrutiny—of the **Crisis** and the institutions suffering from it—is not warranted. It is necessary.

McCrum's article is entitled 'Writing without Risk' and is written with terrible finality: current writing is bad because it is written by bad writers. Nothing could be simpler or more incontrovertible: publishers, after all, don't produce literature; they can only be ready for it when it arrives. I am starting to see matters from a vastly different perspective, and my view proceeds from a belief that since the war British publishing and bookselling have never been less ready for literature than they are today. The **Current Crisis in Publishing** I am suggesting is far worse than any of the daily newspapers are even beginning to describe.

McCrum has three complaints, the first of which is by now fairly familiar: British writers are lifeless and sapped, 'happier adding to the myths, writing about the world we have lost.' The complaint is familiar stuff: a revision of Vidal's grievance against the middle class, Sutherland's of the novel of sense and sensibility, or Bergonzi's of the dreadful droning sameness of the contemporary. The complaint, however, must be questioned. There are undeniably a great many gifted writers in Britain. There are arguably more gifted writers than in any other time in the twentieth century. But unlike most other historical periods, the problem is not simply one of number but of kind: today's interesting fiction has until recently exhibited little sense of unity, except for the superficial unity of being uneasily different from the writing usually promulgated as English: that postwar, premodern variety of the middle class monologue, with C.P. Snow on one side and perhaps Margaret Drabble and Melvyn Bragg on the other (Kingsley Amis will always be nearby providing vitriolic commentary). Now, unlike (I suspect) Robert McCrum, I have no quarrel with these writers or their readers who, for reasons still obscure to me, keep buying their books. My quarrel is with those responsible for allowing these books to crowd out the kinds of books I'd like to read.

And that grievance originates from the assumptions tucked, like bedsheets, around McCrum's second and most important complaint: 'British writing seems immune to the philosophical and intellectual fevers of the time inoculated against innovation by its native pragmatism.' The healthy (and well founded) suggestion here is that serious modern writing should be defined as much by international concerns as local ones, and it is a great convenience that ideas, unlike kinds of humour and automobiles made in Japan, are not inhibited by national borders. In the twentieth century, moreover, ideas (largely because of the book) have become extremely portable, and observation full of implications that don't seem to have been understood: the philosophical and intellectual fevers of the time are not transmitted merely by contact or proximity; no metaphor, regardless of its power, will render ideas contagious: much of the time they have to be read, and this is where the trouble begins.

We are all familiar with the complaint that English writers are, in McCrum's phrase, artistically timid, and cannot seem to carry off what the Americans keep getting away with. But the English writer's timidity is partly predetermined. The American writer's sense of experiment is largely the consequence of participating in an international dialogue. 'There is a movement of younger writers,' Charles Newman, former Editor of *TriQuarterly* observed fourteen years ago,

> to learn unselfconsciously from national literatures other than their own. There are very few promising and or young American writers today who have not been more influenced by 'foreign' writing than by any of their immediate predecessors. And the genuine merit of 'national discoveries', such as those of the new French novelists, have only become ascertainable as writers of other cultures have adapted them to their own experience, without being committed to a programmatic defense of *la méthode*.

The four most influential writers on the American fiction 'renaissance' of the sixties and seventies were foreign: Joyce, Kafka, Nabokov, and especially Borges. In 1961 Borges shared the International Publishers' Prize with Beckett. In 1962 New Directions published the English translation of *Labyrinths*. In England, *no hardback publisher ever bought the rights*. The book appeared in 1970, eight years later, four years after Newman's article, and ten years after it was written, as a Penguin Modern Classic.

Two months ago, Picador bravely (even if recklessly) published C. Cabrera Infante's *Three Trapped Tigers*, remarkable for a formal inventiveness which invites comparisons with two other 'experimental' books published this year: John Barth's *LETTERS* and Gilbert Sorrentino's *Mulligan's Stew*. Difference: *Three Trapped Tigers* was written in 1965 and translated and published in America in 1970, most probably long before *LETTERS* or *Mulligan's Stew* existed as possible ideas. Is it really surprising that a book of this sort, written over fifteen years ago, should be dismissed here—when at last it does appear—as an-oh-yes-another-one-of-those? Books, unlike the *Daily Mirror*, can confidently outlast the week, the month, or the year. But they, like the ideas they carry, must be remarkable indeed to endure the span of a decade and a half.

Translations into English are notorious money losers, but it is easy to see how the losses are continually of the publishers' own making. There can be no market for foreign literature if the books do not come out regularly enough to create it. Last spring I came across Sidgwick and Jackson's admirable publication of Mario Satz's *Sol*, the first novel of an intended trilogy. The book is big, interesting, and expensive, and arrives like a half eaten piece of food from someone else's exotic feast. Is it worth buying this book when—with the resistance to foreign literature so strong—I am certain that it is mostly a gesture, and that the remaining two volumes of the trilogy will never appear? Exactly who, to use McCrum's phrase, is approaching his or her task without risk? In the most recent *Index Translatorium* I could locate (1977), I found very few countries that translated less than Britain (for instance, Iceland and Botswana and, possibly, Uruguay). In contrast to the 486 *literary* works translated here, 1,186 appeared in France and 3,389 in Germany.

Insulation generates insularity, and the barriers are not strictly linguistic. William Gass, an American, quite possibly the most exciting practitioner of the English language, has only one book in print here (an essay). William Gaddis has none. And John Hawkes' recent novel, *The Passion Artist*, has spent 18 months circulating around London looking for a publisher. How, in such a context, can the British writer be anything but provincial? Where can one catch these 'intellectual fevers of our time'? Do publishers really believe that ideas are merely contagious? I'm afraid I'm highly suspicious of McCrum's confident assertion that 'the attics of London are not full of embryo Conrads.' If such an embryo Conrad existed would a publisher recognize him? Or worse, would a publisher encourage him to write like the *real* Conrad of nearly a hundred years ago? There are reasons why English writers demonstrate the nervous wish to be elsewhere.

Of course, it is a commonplace that what is published in the end is decided by the Great British Public. A mythic beast of extraordinary proportions—with puffy white arms, sustained by McVities Chocolate biscuits and books about the Queen Mother—this Great Public has been elevated to virtually incontestable authority. The personality requires some scrutiny if only because it seems to be determining the shape of British literature so exclusively, especially now during the **Great Crisis**. Is this Public, I'm asking, a real entity of such an incontrovertible sway or is it merely a marvellous mythology of an industry sustaining a decisively archaic practice?

The booktrade, like the items it sells, is one of the most enjoyable institutions to have survived the nineteenth century English middle class. It was of course that great, liberal, and particular public—with its one language, one education, (usually) one sex, and its one overriding determination to know things *comprehensively*—which engendered and supported marvellous intellectual periodicals like the *Edinburgh Review* and the *Quarterly* (circulations at 14,000), the *Fortnightly Review* (25,000), the *Athenaeum* (18,000), or the *Cornhill* (in 1860, 110,000). That those periodicals do not exist today and, for some very important reasons, would never survive is probably the best indication of how we in 1980 are different.

It was also that great, liberal club—wanting to know its many things—which engendered and supported the commissioning book trade, whose function was simply to keep all newly published books in stock. The assortment was fairly consistent from one shop to the next. The reading public was, after all, the same throughout the country: it could be said that its members read in the same accent.

Today's British booktrade is sweet, old-fashioned, and self-protected. It is also remarkable for the extent to which it has hardly developed throughout its history. Businesses, resisting specialization, have changed little, and the customer, pretty much like the novel he buys, is invited to remain the same. In Britain, I understand, there are roughly 2,500 bookshops. In Germany, there are 6,000. In the United States, where the population is only four times larger, there are 16,217. Something is wrong.

General bookshops sustained literary fiction because of the specific public with specifically general interests entering them. That public no longer exists, and there is no way that general bookshops can adequately sustain literary fiction today, but general bookshops unquestionably (and unquestioned) dominate. One of the many casualties has been the most ridiculous: the campus book trade. In the university town where this magazine is published, it is common for students, in numbers up to 300, to attend a lecture about a book which has sold out or was never available in the first place. The town's largest and most famous bookshop offers a window display which tacitly suggests that most of the university's students live and buy their books somewhere on the far side of the country. On the week I am writing this there was one work of fiction on display. Last week there was none.

In the United States, there are many reasons why there should be over 2,600 generically distinct campus bookshops. In Britain, there is absolutely no reason why there are not even enough to justify a statistic. I am not urging booksellers to create a 'market'. I'm saying that the market exists and has existed for some time: it's made of people not getting the books they need, and everybody—from author to reader—is suffering.

The significance of the success of Virago and the Picador series is that they have demonstrated how some publishers have been able to cultivate new markets from which, potentially, new kinds of writing—distinct from competitive market identities—can emerge. Though still terribly limited, this success (reinforced by Quartet and the Women's Press, and, in both hardback *and* paperback, by Writers and Readers, Allison and Busby, Carcanet, and others) suggests the extent to which the Great British Public takes on far too much blame far too often. It is time that publishers, distributors, and booksellers recognize that this Public is not one public, perversely homogeneous, but many publics with many needs to be served. If the adventurous novels are to be sustained—something other than the tired version of Covent Garden or the impoverished replication of *Lucky Jim* or yet another rendering of what it is like, man, to be an international television/film/journalist/play writing/jet setting/bed hopping/continent jumping/Oxbridge Personality—then it is time to secure the audience (it's there, you don't have to look far) that will buy them.

The **Current Crisis in Publishing** is revealing just how anachronistic publishing and bookselling are and just how much this society is trying to sustain its creative artists and their achievements on a system regularly incapable of performing the task it is called upon to perform. Thirty years ago the official historian of the Longman publishing house proudly announced that nothing significant had changed in publishing since 1842. His remarks today acquire a terrible pertinence: 'Those who have controlled the business during the last 107 years have provided no *new* answers. The interesting thing is that in themselves and in their policies, they have provided the old answers over and over again.' The interesting thing, now, is they continue to do so: the book, in more than one sense is a hand-made art in an economy no longer able to accommodate it.

Robert McCrum's article is, I'm sure, not representative of the person who wrote it, amounting to an instance of the high brutality of good intentions. The problem is derived from the position he argues from, a position which can only end up reinforcing the practices of an industry which is choking off the best examples of its product. And the problem is entirely unrelated to what I understand to be McCrum's central argument and third complaint—that writers and publishers take too much for granted, and are incapable of the determination and artistic integrity of those from politically repressed nations. The real censorship taking place is not political but economic, has little to do with writers and everything to do with the way their writing is produced, distributed, and sold. Hardback publishers are this culture's most influential arbiters of taste: they determine what we value if only because they determine what we will have the opportunity to judge. It is urgent to distinguish the current state of publishing and bookselling from the actual state of fiction.

In *Fiction and the Fiction Industry*, John Sutherland suggests that the literary-publishing complex, by nature inert and backward-looking, requires complete destruction of old forms as a precondition of advance; such was the case with the three decker novel in the nineteenth century and the 31 shilling novel at the beginning of the twentieth. Is the present hysteria an intimation of another revolution? Can we really believe that most publishers are going to risk publishing another Borges or another Gass or another Marquez? And do we really believe they will spot the embryo Conrad? How are we to measure silent censorship, how can we take the dimensions of a nothing? The prospect is gloomy and irritating and angering, and invokes like a banner Lawrence's anarchic phrase quite importantly revised: surgery for the way novels are made—or a bomb.

What it means to put a text in print must change. The culture in which creative prose must now make its way is obviously developing into a novelty culture, to which the busy, busy book business appears as one of its most efficient contributors. Indeed, the **Present Crisis** should be, in the end, not a cause for despair but celebration. New outlets must be developed if creative prose is to find its readers, let alone be supported by them.

The most important reason why the *Edinburgh Review, Quarterly*, the *Fortnightly Review, Cornhill*, or *Athenaeum* do not exist today is because the public who purchased them is no longer around. The alternative, however, is not in the tired continuation or uninspired variation of their format: the crowd of exhausted reviews busy with a books-in-brief or a truncated fiction chronicle or current 'hit' list merely caters to the industry's mindless pace, generating mini-ideas which, like the books they're about, exist only to be pulped. It is obvious that a new publication must come into existence which relies upon a specific, even if narrow group of readers who care not to have their intelligence insulted every time they turn the page. It must be along the lines of Charles Newman's dreams—a publication that is independent and personal and notable for the quality of its sentences. But most importantly it would respond to the culture of its time by refusing to be an instance of its worst ways, dedicated, above all, to a collaboration of writer and producer and reader. The prospect, for instance, of the reader having a definable relationship to what he reads has only been tentatively explored. Imagine a reader commissioning a writer, in the same way and for the same reasons that one commissions a sculptor. Or a group of readers commissioning a whole issue or even a series of issues. The possibilities are endless.

The present issue of *Granta* is aspiring to illustrate that today's novel is in fact far more novel than it is commonly understood to be: it is not the novel which is dying, although it may well be the old ways of its production which are, a disjunction made particularly acute by the coincidence of this **Great Publishing Crisis** and the development of a new kind of fiction. What it means to tell a story has, virtually unnoticed, taken on a new set of meanings, even if the most obvious and unfortunate one of them is that the story may never appear in hardback or, worse, never reach its potential readers.

What it means to tell, to write, to narrate, to *make up* is changing, and it is a change significant enough to be distinguished from the aesthetic concerns which have dominated the last eighty years. The twentieth century—in its modernism or its postmodernism or its literature of exhaustion—has been grounded in an attitude of opposition which is too crude and too simple and too incomplete to be viable today. The modernist precepts of Ortega y Gasset, with its dialectical rejection of the nineteenth century, was a crucial response to an entrenched bourgeois culture which is no longer the enemy because it is no longer a presence in the same way. In the art dubiously and thanklessly entitled 'postmodernist', Ortega y Gasset's precepts are elevated to a creed. But postmodernism confronts not a nineteenth century literature but a twentieth century art, not a bourgeois society but the unwieldy anonymous mass marketed twentieth century mind. Modernism was the careful collision of the permanent and the new; postmodernism has inevitably become the reckless collusion of the new and the useless: it smells of literary leftovers, with thoughts, like food, not quite digested.

Postmodernist art is important because it invites us to recognize the particular brutal emptiness of the twentieth century. But in its laboured refutation of a tradition that is increasingly difficult to identify and in its persistent depictions of the passive, vacant mindlessness readily generated by the various media around us, it is conflated with the context of its making, not transcending the problem but being an instance of it. Debilitating deconstructions dissolving into pathetic patter.

Current fiction is remarkable for its detachment, its refusal to be affiliated, its suspicion of the old hierarchies and authorities. It is not modernist or premodernist or postmodernist or of that debate, but managing nevertheless to be both arriving and departing at once. If I am right that we are moving into a different period of creative prose, it is characterized by a writing which, freed from the middle class monologue, is experimentation in the real sense, exploiting traditions and not being wasted by them. The writer today is managing to reassert the act of narration—the telling not simply of fictions but stories—not in deference to the referential workings of bourgeois realism but as an instance of the human imagination. In the work of many writers, and, here, particularly in that of Hoban or Tennant and especially Salman Rushdie, we are moving closer to the fiction of Gabriel Marquez or Italo Calvino, a magic realism, rising out of an age of technical exhaustion, where telling is at the centre of our consciousness.

The old divisions and the old generalizations are no longer usable. The fiction of today is, as Lorna Sage points out in her symposium essay, testimony to an invasion of outsiders, using a language much larger than the culture. The English novel has been characterized by the self depictions of its maker's dominance: the novel of sense and sensibility is informed by the authority of belonging. Today, however, the imagination resides along the peripheries; it is spoken through a minority discourse, with the dominant tongue re-appropriated, re-commanded, and importantly re-invigorated. It is, at last, the end of the English novel and the beginning of the British one.

Bill Buford

Salman Rushdie
Midnight's Children

The Perforated Sheet

One Kashmiri morning in the early spring of 1915, my grandfather Aadam Aziz hit his nose against a frost-hardened tussock of earth while attempting to pray. Three drops of blood plopped out of his left nostril, hardened instantly in the brittle air and lay before his eyes on the prayer-mat, transformed into rubies Lurching back until he knelt with his head once more upright, he found that the tears which had sprung to his eyes had solidified, too; and at that moment, as he brushed diamonds contemptuously from his lashes, he resolved never again to kiss earth for any god or man. This decision, however, made a hole in him, a vacancy in a vital inner chamber, leaving him vulnerable to women and history. Unaware of this at first, despite his recently completed medical training, he stood up, rolled the prayer-mat into a thick cheroot, and holding it under his right arm surveyed the valley through clear, diamond-free eyes.

The world was new again. After a winter's gestation in its egg-shell of ice, the valley had beaked its way out into the open, moist and yellow. The new grass bides its time underground; the mountains were retreating to their hill-stations for the warm season. (In the winter, when the valley shrank under the ice, the mountains closed in and snarled like angry jaws around the city on the lake.)

In those days the radio mast had not been built and the temple of Sankara Acharya, a little black blister on a khaki hill, still dominated the streets and lake of Srinagar. In those days there was no army camp at the lakeside, no endless snakes of camouflaged trucks and jeeps clogged the narrow mountain roads, no soldiers hid behind the crests of the mountains past Baramulla and Gulmarg. In those days travellers were not shot as spies if they took photographs of bridges, and apart from the Englishmen's houseboats on the lake, the valley had hardly changed since the Mughal Empire, for all its springtime renewals; but my grandfather's eyes—which were, like the rest of him, twenty-five years old—saw things differently...and his nose had started to itch.

To reveal the secret of my grandfather's altered vision: he had spent five years, five springs, away from home. (The tussock of earth, crucial though its presence was as it crouched under a chance wrinkle of the prayer-mat, was at bottom no more than a catalyst.) Now, returning, he saw through travelled eyes. Instead of the beauty of the tiny village circled by giant teeth, he noticed the narrowness, the proximity of the horizon; and felt sad, to be at home and feel so utterly enclosed. He also felt—inexplicably—as though the old place resented his educated, stethoscoped return. Beneath the winter ice, it has been coldly neutral, but now there was no doubt: the years in Germany had returned him to a hostile environment. Many years later, when the hole inside him had been clogged up with hate, and he came to sacrifice himself at the shrine of the black stone god in the temple on the hill, he would try and recall his childhood spring in Paradise, the way it was before travel and tussocks and army tanks messed everything up.

On the morning when the valley, gloved in a prayer-mat, punched him on the nose, he had been trying, absurdly, to pretend that nothing had changed. So he had risen in the bitter cold of four-fifteen, washed himself in the prescribed fashion, dressed and put on his father's astrakhan cap; after which he had carried the rolled cheroot of the prayer-mat into the small lakeside garden in front of their old dark house and unrolled it over the waiting tussock. The ground felt deceptively soft under his feet and made him simultaneously uncertain and unwary. 'In the Name of God, the Compassionate, the Merciful...'—the exordium, spoken with hands joined before him like a book, comforted a part of him, made another, larger part feel uneasy—'...Praise be to Allah, Lord of the Creation...'—but now Heidelberg invaded his head; here was Ingrid, briefly his Ingrid, her face scorning him for this Mecca-turned parroting; here, their friends Oskar and Ilse Lubin the anarchists, mocking his prayer with their anti-ideologies—'...The Compassionate, the Merciful, King of the Last Judgement!...'—Heidelberg, in which, along with medicine and politics, he learned that India—like radium—had been 'discovered' by the Europeans; even Oskar was filled with admiration for Vasco da Gama, and this was what finally separated Aadam Aziz from his friends, this belief of theirs that he was somehow the invention of their ancestors—'...You alone we worship, and to You alone we pray for help...'—so here he was, despite their presence in his head, attempting to re-unite himself with an earlier self which ignored their influence but knew everything it ought to have known, about submission for example, about what he was doing now, as his hands, guided by old memories, fluttered upwards, thumbs pressed to ears, fingers spread, as he sank to his knees—'...Guide us to the straight path, The path of those whom You have favoured...'—But it was no good, he was caught in a strange middle ground, trapped between belief and disbelief, and this was only a charade after all—'...Not of those who have incurred Your wrath. Nor of those who have gone astray.' My grandfather bent his forehead towards the earth. Forward he bent, and the earth, prayer-mat-covered, curved up towards him. And now it was the tussock's time. At one and the same time a rebuke from Ilse-Oskar-Ingrid-Heidelberg as well as valley-and-God, it smote him upon the point of the nose. Three drops fell. There were rubies and diamonds. And my grandfather, lurching upright, made a resolve. Stood. Folded cheroot. Stared across the lake. And was knocked forever into that middle place, unable to worship a God in whose existence he could not wholly disbelieve. Permanent alteration: a hole.

The young, newly-qualified Doctor Aadam Aziz stood facing the springtime lake, sniffing the whiffs of change; while his back (which was extremely straight) was turned upon yet more changes. His father had had a stroke in his absence abroad, and his mother had kept it a secret. His mother's voice, whispering stoically: *'Because your studies were too important, son.'* This mother, who had spent her life housebound, in purdah, had suddenly found enormous strength and gone out to run the small gemstone business (turquoises, rubies, diamonds) which had put Aadam through medical college, with the help of a scholarship; so he returned to find the seemingly immutable order of his family turned upside down, his mother going out to work while his father sat hidden behind the veil which the stroke had dropped over his brain...in a wooden chair, in a darkened room, he sat and made bird-noises. Thirty different species of birds visited him and sat on the sill outside his shuttered window conversing about this and that. He seemed happy enough.

(...And already I can see the repetitions beginning; because didn't my grandmother also find enormous...and the stroke, too, was not the only...and the Brass Monkey had her birds...the curse begins already, and we haven't even got to the noses yet!)

The lake was no longer frozen over. The thaw had come rapidly, as usual; many of the small boats, the shikaras, had been caught napping, which was also normal. But while these sluggards slept on, on dry land, snoring peacefully beside their owners, the oldest boat was up at the crack as old folk often are, and was therefore the first craft to move across the unfrozen lake. Tai's shikara...this, too, was customary.

Watch how the old boatman, Tai, makes good time through the misty water, standing stooped over at the back of his craft! How his oar, a wooden heart on a yellow stick, drives jerking through the weeds! In these parts he's considered very odd because he rows standing up...among other reasons. Tai, bringing an urgent summons to Doctor Aziz, is about to set history in motion...while Aadam, looking down into the water, recalls what Tai taught him years ago: 'The ice is always waiting, Aadam baba, just under the water's skin.' Aadam's eyes are a clear blue, the astonishing blue of mountain sky, which has a habit of dripping into the pupils of Kashmiri men; they have not forgotten how to look. They see—there! like the skeleton of a ghost, just beneath the surface of Lake Dal!—the delicate tracery, the intricate crisscross of colourless lines, the cold waiting veins of the future. His German years, which have blurred so much else, haven't deprived him of the gift of seeing. Tai's gift. He looks up, sees the approaching V of Tai's boat, waves a greeting. Tai's arm rises—but this is a command. 'Wait!' My grandfather waits; and during this hiatus, as he experiences the last peace of his life, a muddy, noisome sort of peace, I had better get round to describing him.

Keeping out of my voice the natural envy of the ugly man for the strikingly impressive, I record that Doctor Aziz was a tall man. Pressed flat against a wall of his family home, he measured twenty-five bricks (a brick for each year of his life), or just over six foot two. A strong man also. His beard was thick and red—and annoyed his mother, who said only Hajis, men who had made the pilgrimage to Mecca, should grow red beards. His hair, however, was rather darker. His sky-eyes you know about. Ingrid had said, 'They went mad with the colours when they made your face.' But the central feature of my grandfather's anatomy was neither colour nor height, neither strength of arm nor straightness of back. There it was, reflected in the water, undulating like a mad plantain in the centre of his face...Aadam Aziz, waiting for Tai, watches his rippling nose. It would have dominated less dramatic faces than his easily; even on him, it is what one sees first and remembers longest. 'A cyranose,' Ilse Lubin said, and Oskar added, 'A proboscissimus.' Ingrid announced, 'You could cross a river on that nose.' (Its bridge was wide.)

My grandfather's nose: nostrils flaring, curvaceous as dancers. Between them swells the nose's triumphal arch, first up and out, then down and under, sweeping it to his upper lip with a superb and at present red-tipped flick. An easy nose to hit a tussock with. I wish to place on record my gratitude to this mighty organ—if not for it, who would ever have believed me to be truly my mother's son, my grandfather's grandson?—this colossal apparatus which was to be my birthright, too. Doctor Aziz's nose—comparable only to the trunk of the elephant-headed god Ganesh—established incontrovertibly his right to be a patriarch. It was Tai who taught him that, too. When young Aadam was barely past puberty the dilapidated boatman said, 'That's a nose to start a family on, my princeling. There'd be no mistaking whose brood they were. Mughal Emperors would have given their right hands for noses like that one. There are dynasties waiting inside it,'—and here Tai lapsed into coarseness—'like snot.'

On Aadam Aziz, the nose assumed a patriarchal aspect. On my mother, it looked noble and a little long-suffering; on my aunt Emerald, snobbish; on my aunt Alia, intellectual; on my uncle Hanif it was the organ of an unsuccessful genius; my uncle Mustapha made it a second-rater's sniffer; the Brass Monkey escaped it completely; but on me—on me, it was something else again. But I mustn't reveal all my secrets at once.

(Tai is getting nearer. He, who revealed the power of the nose, and who is now bringing my grandfather the message which will catapult him into his future, is stroking his shikara through the early morning lake...)

Nobody could remember when Tai had been young. He had been plying this same boat, standing in the same hunched position, across the Dal and Nageen Lakes...forever. As far as anyone knew. He lived somewhere in the insanitary bowels of the old wooden-house quarter and his wife grew lotus roots and other curious vegetables on one of the many 'floating gardens' lilting on the surface of the spring and summer water. Tai himself cheerily admitted he had no idea of his age. Neither did his wife—he was, she said, already leathery when they married. His face was a sculpture of wind on water: ripples made of hide. He had two golden teeth and no others. In the town, he had few friends. Few boatmen or traders invited him to share a hookah when he floated past the shikara moorings or one of the lakes' many, ramshackle, waterside provision-stores and tea-shops.

   The general opinion of Tai had been voiced long ago by Aadam Aziz's father the gemstone merchant: 'His brain fell out with his teeth.' (But now old Aziz sahib sat lost in bird tweets while Tai simply, grandly, continued.) It was an impression the boatman fostered by his chatter, which was fantastic, grandiloquent and ceaseless, and as often as not addressed only to himself. Sound carries over water, and the lake people giggled at his monologues; but with undertones of awe, and even fear. Awe, because the old halfwit knew the lakes and hills better than any of his detractors; fear, because of his claim to an antiquity so immense it defied numbering, and moreover hung so lightly around his chicken's neck that it hadn't prevented him from winning a highly desirable wife and fathering four sons upon her...and a few more, the story went, on other lakeside wives. The young bucks at the shikara moorings were convinced he had a pile of money hidden away somewhere—a hoard, perhaps, of priceless golden teeth, rattling in a sack like walnuts. Years later, when Uncle Puffs tried to sell me his daughter by offering to have her teeth drawn and replaced in gold, I thought of Tai's forgotten treasure...and, as a child, **Aadam Aziz** had loved him.

   He made his living as a simple ferryman, despite all the rumours of wealth, taking hay and goats and vegetables and wood across the lakes for cash; people, too. When he was running his taxi-service he erected a pavilion in the centre of the shikara, a gay affair of flowered-patterned curtains and canopy, with cushions to match; and deodorised his boat with incense. The sight of Tai's shikara approaching, curtains flying, had always been for Doctor Aziz one of the defining images of the coming of spring. Soon the English sahibs would arrive and Tai would ferry them to the Shalimar Gardens and the King's Spring, chattering and pointy and stooped. He was the living antithesis of Oskar-Ilse-Ingrid's belief in the inevitability of change...a quirky, enduring familiar spirit of the valley. A water Caliban, rather too fond of cheap Kashmiri brandy.

   Memory of my blue bedroom wall: on which, next to the P.M.'s letter, the Boy Raleigh hung for many years, gazing rapturously at an old fisherman in what looked like a red dhoti, who sat on—what?—driftwood?—and pointed out to sea as he was told his fishy tales...and the Boy Aadam, my grandfather-to-be, fell in love with the boatman Tai precisely because of the endless verbiage which made others think him cracked. It was magical talk, words pouring from him like fools' money, past his two gold teeth, laced with hiccups and brandy, soaring up to the most remote Himalayas of the past, then swooping shrewdly on some present detail, Aadam's nose for instance, to vivisect its meaning like a mouse. This friendship had plunged Aadam into hot water with great regularity. (Boiling water. Literally. While his mother said, 'We'll kill that boatman's bugs if it kills you.') But still the old soliloquist would dawdle in his boat at the garden's lakeside toes and Aziz would sit at his feet until voices summoned him indoors to be lectured on Tai's filthiness and warned about the pillaging armies of germs his mother envisaged leaping from that hospitably ancient body on to her son's starched white loose-pyjamas. But always Aadam returned to the water's edge to scan the mists for the ragged reprobate's hunched-up frame steering its magical boat through the enchanted waters of the morning.

'But how old are you really, Taiji?' (Doctor Aziz, adult, redbearded, slanting towards the future, remembers the day he asked the unaskable question.) For an instant, silence, noisier than a waterfall. The monologue, interrupted. Slap of oar in water. He was riding in the shikara with Tai, squatting amongst goats, on a pile of straw, in full knowledge of the stick and bathtub waiting for him at home. He had come for stories—and with one question had silenced the storyteller.

'No, tell, Taiji, how old, *truly*?' And now a brandy bottle, materialising from nowhere: cheap liquor from the folds of the great warm chugha-coat. Then a shudder, a belch, a glare. Glint of gold. And—at last!—speech. 'How old? You ask how old, you little wethead, you nosey...' Tai, forecasting the fisherman on my wall, pointed at the mountains. 'So old, nakkoo!' Aadam, the nakkoo, the nosey one, followed his pointing finger. 'I have watched the mountains being born; I háve seen the Emperors die. Listen. Listen, nakkoo...'—the brandy bottle again, followed by brandy-voice, and words more intoxicating than booze—'...I saw that Isa, that Christ, when he came to Kashmire. Smile, smile, it is your history I am keeping in my head. Once it was set down in the old lost books. Once I knew where there. was a grave with pierced feet carved on the tombstone, which bled once a year. Even my memory is going now; but I know, although I can't read.' Illiteracy, dismissed with a flourish; literature crumbled beneath the rage of his sweeping hand. Which sweeps again to chugha-pocket, to brandy bottle, to lips chapped with cold. Tai always had woman's lips. 'Nakkoo, listen, listen. I have seen plenty. Yara, you should've seen that Isa when he came, beard down to his balls, bald as an egg on his head. He was old and fagged-out but he knew his manners. "You first, Taiji," he'd say, and "Please to sit"; always a respectful tongue, he never called me crackpot, never called me tu either. Always aap. Polite, see? And what an appetite! Such a hunger, I would catch my ears in fright. Saint or devil, I swear he could eat a whole kid in one go. And so what? I told him, eat, fill your hole, a man comes to Kashmir to enjoy life, or to end it, or both. His work was finished. He just came up here to live it up a little.' Mesmerized by this brandied portrait of a bald, gluttonous Christ, Aziz listened, later repeating every word to the consternation of his parents, who dealt in stones and had no time for 'gas'.

'Oh, you don't believe?'—licking his sore lips with a grin, knowing it to be the reverse of the truth; 'Your attention is wandering?'—again, he knew how furiously Aziz was hanging on his words. 'Maybe the straw is pricking your behind, hey? Oh, I'm so sorry, babjai, not to provide for you silk cushions with gold brocade-work—cushions such as the Emperor Jehangir sat upon! You think of the Emperor Jehangir as a gardener only, no doubt,' Tai accused my grandfather, 'because he built Shalimar. Stupid! What do you know? His name meant Encompasser of the Earth. Is that a gardener's name? God knows what they teach you boys these days. Whereas I'...puffing up a little here...'I knew his precise weight, to the tola! Ask me how many maunds, how many seers! When he was happy he got heavier and in Kashmir he was heaviest of all. I used to carry his litter...no, no, look, you don't believe again, that big cucumber in your face is waggling like the little one in your pyjamas! So, come on, come on, ask me questions! Give examination! Ask how many times the leather thongs wound round the handles of the litter—the answer is thirty-one. Ask me what was the Emperor's dying word—I tell you it was "Kashmir". He had bad breath and a good heart. Who do you think I am? Some common ignorant lying pie-dog? Go, get out of the boat now, your nose makes it too heavy to row; also your father is waiting to beat my gas out of you, and your mother to boil off your skin.'

In the brandy bottle of the boatman Tai I see, foretold, my own father's possession by djinns...and there will be another bald foreigner...and Tai's gas prophesies another kind, which was the consolation of my grandmother's old age, and taught her stories, too...and pie-dogs aren't far away...Enough. I'm frightening myself.

Despite beating and boiling, Aadam Aziz floated with Tai in his shikara, over and over again, amid goats hay flowers furniture, lotus-roots, though never with the English sahibs, and heard over and over again the miraculous answers to that single terrifying question: 'But Taiji, how old are you, *honestly*?'

From Tai, Aadam learned the secrets of the lake—where you could swim without being pulled down by weeds; the eleven varieties of water-snake; where the frogs spawned; how to cook a lotus-root; and where the three English women had drowned a few years back. 'There is a tribe of feringhee women who come to this water to drown,' Tai said. 'Sometimes they know it, sometimes they don't, but I know the minute I smell them. They hide under the water from God knows what or who—but they can't hide from me, baba!' Tai's laugh, emerging to infect Aadam—a huge, booming laugh that seemed macabre when it crashed out of that old, withered body, but which was so natural in my giant grandfather that nobody knew, in later times, that it wasn't really his (my uncle Hanif inherited this laugh; so until he died, a piece of Tai lived in Bombay). And, also from Tai, my grandfather heard about noses.

Tai tapped his left nostril. 'You know what this is, nakkoo? It's the place where the outside world meets the world inside you. If they don't get on, you feel it here. Then you rub your nose with embarrassment to make the itch go away. A nose like that, little idiot, is a great gift. I say: trust it. When it warns you, look out or you'll be finished. Follow your nose and you'll go far.' He cleared his throat; his eyes rolled away into the mountains of the past. Aziz settled back on the straw. 'I knew one officer once—in the army of that Iskandar the Great. Never mind his name. He had a vegetable just like yours hanging between his eyes. When the army halted near Gandhara, he fell in love with some local floozy. At once his nose itched like crazy. He scratched it, but that was useless. He inhaled vapours from crushed boiled eucalyptus leaves. Still no good, baba! The itching sent him wild; but the damn fool dug in his heels and stayed with his little witch when the army went home. He became—what?—a stupid thing, neither this nor that, a half-and-halfer with a nagging wife and an itch in the nose, and in the end he pushed his sword into his stomach. What do you think of that?'

...Doctor Aziz in 1915, whom rubies and diamonds have turned into a half-and-halfer, remembers this story as Tia enters hailing distance. His nose is itching still. He scratches, shrugs, tosses his head; and then Tai shouts.

'Ohé! Doctor Sahib! Ghani the landowner's daughter is sick.'

The message, delivered curtly, shouted unceremoniously across the surface of the lake although boatman and pupil have not met for half a decade, mouthed by woman's lips that are not smiling in long-time-no-see greeting, sends time into a speeding, whirligig, blurry fluster of excitement...

...'Just think, son,' Aadam's mother is saying as she sips fresh lime water, reclining on a takht in an attitude of resigned exhaustion, 'How life does turn out. For so many years even my ankles were a secret, and now I must be stared at by strange persons who are not even family members.'

...While Ghani the landowner stands beneath a large oil painting of Diana the Huntress, framed in squiggly gold. He wears thick dark glasses and his famous poisonous smile, and discusses art. 'I purchased it from an Englishman down on his luck, Doctor Sahib. Five hundred rupees only—and I did not trouble to beat him down. What are five hundred chips? You see, I am a lover of culture.'

...'See, my son,' Aadam's mother is saying as he begins to examine her, 'What a mother will not do for her child. Look how I suffer. You are a doctor...feel these rashes, these blotchy bits, understand that my head aches morning noon and night. Refill my glass, child.'

...But the young doctor has entered the throes of a most unhippocratic excitement at the boatman's cry, and shouts, 'I'm coming just now! Just let me bring my things!' The shikara's prow touches the garden's hem. Aadam is rushing indoors, prayer-mat rolled like cheroot under one arm, blue eyes blinking in the sudden interior gloom; he has placed the cheroot on a high shelf on top of stacked copies of *Vorwärts* and Lenin's *What Is To Be Done?* and other pamphlets, dusty echoes of his half-faded German life; he is pulling out, from under his bed, a second-hand leather case which his mother called his 'doctori-attaché', and as he swings it and himself upwards and runs from the room, the word HEIDELBERG is briefly visible, burned into the leather on the bottom of the bag. A landowner's daughter is good news indeed to a doctor with a career to make, even if she is ill. No: *because* she is ill.'

...While I sit like an empty pickle jar in a pool of Anglepoised light, visited by this vision of my grandfather sixty-three years ago, which demands to be recorded, filling my nostrils with the acrid stench of his mother's embarrassment which has brought her out in boils, with the vinegary force of Aadam Aziz's determination to establish a practice so successful that she'll never have to return to the gemstone-shop, with the blind mustiness of a big shadowy house in which the young Doctor stands, ill-at-ease, before a painting of a plain girl with lively eyes and a stag transfixed behind her on the horizon, speared by a dart from her bow. Most of what matters in our lives takes place in our absence: but I seem to have found from somewhere the trick of filling in the gaps in my knowledge, so that everything is in my head, down to the last detail, such as the way the mist seemed to slant across the early morning air...everything, and not just the few clues one stumbles across, for instance by opening an old tin trunk which should have remained cobwebby and closed.

...Aadam refills his mother's glass and continues, worriedly, to examine her. 'Put some cream on these rashes and blotches, Amma. For the headache, there are pills. The boils must be lanced. But maybe if you wore purdah when you sat in the store...so that no disrespectful eyes could...such complaints often begin in the mind...'

...Slap of oar in water. Plop of spittle in lake. Tai clears his throat and mutters angrily, 'A fine business. A wet-head nakkoo child goes away before he's learned one damn thing and he comes back a big doctor sahib with a big bag full of foreign machines, and he's still as silly as an owl. I swear: a too bad business.'

...Doctor Aziz is shifting uneasily, from foot to foot, under the influence of the landowner's smile, in whose presence it is not possible to feel relaxed; and is waiting for some tic of reaction to his own extraordinary appearance. He has grown accustomed to these involuntary twitches of surprise at his size, his face of many colours, his nose...but Ghani makes no sign, and the young Doctor resolves, in return, not to let his uneasiness show. He stops shifting his weight. They face each other, each suppressing (or so it seems) his view of the other, establishing the basis of their future relationship. And now Ghani alters, changing from art-lover to tough-guy. 'This is a big chance for you, young man,' he says. Aziz's eyes have strayed to

Diana. Wide expanses of her blemished pink skin are visible.
...His mother is moaning, shaking her head. 'No, what do you know, child, you have become a big-shot doctor but the gemstone business is different. Who would buy a turquoise from a woman hidden inside a black hood? It is a question of establishing trust. So they must look at me; and I must get pains and boils. Go, go, don't worry your head about your poor mother.'
...'Big shot,' Tai is spitting into the lake, 'big bag, big shot. Pah! We haven't got enough bags at home that you must bring back that thing made of a pig's skin that makes one unclean just by looking at it? And inside, God knows what all.' Doctor Aziz, seated amongst flowery curtains and the smell of incense, has his thoughts wrenched away from the patient waiting across the lake. Tai's bitter monologue breaks into his consciousness, creating a sense of dull shock, a smell like a casualty ward overpowering the incense...the old man is clearly furious about something, possessed by an incomprehensible rage that appears to be directed at his erstwhile acolyte, or, more precisely and oddly, at his bag. Doctor Aziz attempts to make small talk...'Your wife is well? Do they still talk about your bag of golden teeth?'...tries to remake an old friendship; but Tai is in full flight now, a stream of invective pouring out of him. The Heidelberg bag quakes under the torrent of abuse. 'Sistersleeping pigskin bag from Abroad full of foreigners' tricks. Big shot bag. Now if a man breaks an arm that bag will not let the bonesetter bind it in leaves. Now a man must let his wife lie beside that bag and watch knives come and cut her open. A fine business, what these foreigners put in our young men's heads. I swear: it is a too-bad thing. That bag should fry in Hell with the testicles of the ungodly.'
...Ghani the landowner snaps his braces with his thumbs. 'A big chance, yes indeed. They are saying good things about you in town. Good medical training. Good...good enough...family. And now our own lady doctor is sick so you get your opportunity. That woman, always sick these days, too old, I am thinking, and not up in the latest developments also, what-what? I say: physician heal thyself. And I tell you this: I am wholly objective in my business relations. Feelings, love, I keep for my family only. If a person is not doing a first-class job for me, out she goes! You understand me? So: my daughter Naseem is not well. You will treat her excellently. Remember I have friends; and ill-health strikes high and low alike.'

...'Do you still pickle water-snakes in brandy to give you virility, Taiji? Do you still like to eat lotus-root without any spices?' Hesitant questions, brushed aside by the torrent of Tai's fury. Doctor Aziz begins to diagnose. To the ferryman, the bag represents Abroad; it is the alien thing, the invader, progress. And yes, it has indeed taken possession of the young Doctor's mind; and yes, it contains knives, and cures for cholera and malaria and smallpox; and yes, it sits between doctor and boatman, and has made them antagonists. Doctor Aziz begins to fight, against sadness, and against Tai's anger, which is beginning to infect him, to become his own, which erupts only rarely, but comes, when it does come, unheralded in a roar from his deepest places, laying waste everything in sight; and then vanishes leaving him wondering why everyone is so upset...They are approaching Ghani's house. A bearer awaits the shikara, standing with clasped hands on a little wooden jetty. Aziz fixes his mind on the job in hand.

...'Has your usual doctor agreed to my visit, Ghani Sahib?'...Aadam's hesitant question is brushed lightly away. The landowner says, 'Oh, she will agree. Now follow me, please.'

...The bearer is waiting on the jetty. Holding the shikara steady as Aadam Aziz climbs out, bag in hand. And now, at last, Tai speaks directly to my grandfather. Scorn in his face, Tai asks, 'Tell me this, Doctor Sahib: have you got in that bag made of dead pigs one of those machines that foreign doctors use to smell with?' Aadam shakes his head, not understanding. Tai's voice gathers new layers of disgust. 'You know, sir, a thing like an elephant's trunk.' Aziz, seeing what he means, replies: 'A stethoscope? Naturally.' Tai pushes the shikara off from the jetty. Spits. Begins to row away. 'I knew it,' he says. 'You will use such a machine now, instead of your own big nose.'

My grandfather does not trouble to explain that a stethoscope is more like a pair of ears than a nose. He is stifling his own irritation, the resentful anger of a cast-off child; and besides, there is a patient waiting. Time settles down and concentrates on the importance of the moment.

The house was opulent but badly lit. Ghani was a widower and the servants clearly took advantage. There were cobwebs in corners and layers of dust on ledges. They walked down a long corridor; one of the doors was ajar and through it Aziz saw a room in a state of violent disorder. This glimpse, connected with a glint of light in Ghani's dark glasses, suddenly informed Aziz that the landowner was blind. This aggravated his sense of unease: a blind man who claimed to appreciate European paintings? He was, also, impressed, because Ghani hadn't bumped into anything...they halted outside a thick teak door. Ghani said, 'Wait here two moments,' and went into the room behind the door.

In later years, Doctor Aadam Aziz swore that during those two moments of solitude in the gloomy spidery corridors of the landowner's mansion he was gripped by an almost uncontrollable desire to turn and run away as fast as his legs would carry him. Unnerved by the enigma of the blind art-lover, his insides filled with tiny scrabbling insects as a result of the insidious venom of Tai's mutterings, his nostrils itching to the point of convincing him that he had somehow contracted venereal disease, he felt his feet begin slowly, as though encased in boots of lead, to turn; felt blood pounding in his temples; and was siezed by so powerful a sensation of standing upon a point of no return that he very nearly wet his German woollen trousers. He began, without knowing it, to blush furiously; and at this point his mother appeared before him, seated on the floor before a low desk, a rash spreading like a blush across her face as she held a turquoise up to the light. His mother's face had acquired all the scorn of the boatman Tai. 'Go, go, run', she told him in Tai's voice. 'Don't worry about your poor old mother.' Doctor Aziz found himself stammering, 'What a useless son you've got, Amma; can't you see there's a hole in the middle of me the size of a melon?' His mother smiled a pained smile. 'You always were a heartless boy,' she sighed, and then turned into a lizard on the wall of the corridor and stuck her tongue out at him. Doctor Aziz stopped feeling dizzy, became unsure if he had actually spoken aloud, wondered what he'd meant by that business about the hole, found that his feet were no longer trying to escape, and realized that he was being watched. A woman with the biceps of a wrestler was staring at him, beckoning him to follow her into the room. The state of her sari told him that she was a servant; but she was not servile. 'You look green as a fish,' she said. 'You young doctors. You come into a strange house and your liver turns to jelly. Come, Doctor Sahib, they are waiting for you.' Clutching his bag a fraction too tightly, he followed her through the dark teak door.

...Into a spacious bedchamber that was as ill-lit as the rest of the house; although here there were shafts of dusty sunlight seeping in through a fanlight high on one wall. These fusty rays illuminated a scene as remarkable as anything the Doctor had ever witnessed: a tableau of such surpassing strangeness that his feet began to twitch towards the door once again. Two more women, also built like professional wrestlers, stood stiffly in the light, each holding one corner of an enormous white bedsheet, their arms raised high above their heads so that the sheet hung between them like a curtain. Mr Ghani welled up out of the murk surrounding the sunlit sheet and permitted the nonplussed Aadam to stare stupidly at the peculiar tableau for perhaps half a minute, at the end of which, and before a word had been spoken, the Doctor made a discovery:

In the very centre of the sheet, a hole had been cut, a crude circle about seven inches in diameter.

'Close the door, ayah,' Ghani instructed the first of the lady wrestlers, and then, turning to Aziz, became confidential. 'This town contains many good-for-nothings who have on occasion tried to climb into my daughter's room. She needs,' he nodded at the three musclebound women, 'protectors.'

Aziz was still looking at the perforated sheet. Ghani said, 'All right, come on, you will examine my Naseem right now. *Pronto.*'

My grandfather peered around the room. 'But where is she, Ghani Sahib?' he blurted out finally. The lady wrestlers adopted supercilious expressions and, it seemed to him, tightened their musculatures, just in case he intended to try something fancy.

'Ah, I see your confusion,' Ghani said, his poisonous smile broadening, 'You Europe-returned chappies forget certain things. Doctor Sahib, my daughter is a decent girl, it goes without saying. She does not flaunt her body under the noses of strange men. You will understand that you cannot be permitted to see her, no, not in any circumstances; accordingly I have required her to be positioned behind that sheet. She stands there, like a good girl.'

A frantic note had crept into Doctor Aziz's voice. 'Ghani Sahib, tell me how I am to examine her without looking at her?' Ghani smiled on.

'You will kindly specify which portion of my daughter it is necessary to inspect. I will then issue her with my instructions to place the required segment against that hole which you see there. And so, in this fashion the thing may be achieved.'

'But what, in any event, does the lady complain of?'—my grandfather, despairingly. To which Mr Ghani, his eyes rising upwards in their sockets, his smile twisting into a grimace of grief, replied: 'The poor child! She has a terrible, a too dreadful stomach-ache.'

'In that case,' Doctor Aziz said with some restraint, 'will she show me her stomach, please.'

Mercurochrome

Padma—our plump Padma—is sulking magnificently. (She can't read and, like all fish-lovers, dislikes other people knowing anything she doesn't. Padma: strong, jolly, a consolation for my last days. But definitely a bitch-in-the-manger.) She attempts to cajole me from my desk: 'Eat, na, food is spoiling.' I remain stubbornly hunched over paper. 'But what is so precious,' Padma demands, her right hand slicing the air updownup in exasperation, 'to need all this writing-shiting?' I reply: now that I've let out the details of my birth, now that the perforated sheet stands between doctor and patient, there's no going back. Padma snorts. Wrist smacks against forehead. 'Okay, starve starve, who cares two pice?' Another louder, conclusive snort...but I take no exception to her attitude. She stirs a bubbling vat all day for a living; something hot and vinegary has steamed her up tonight. Thick of waist, somewhat hairy of forearm, she flounces, gesticulates, exits. Poor Padma. Things are always getting her goat. Perhaps even her name: understandably enough, since her mother told her, when she was only small, that she had been named after the lotus goddess, whose most common appellation amongst village folk is 'The One Who Possesses Dung'.

In the renewed silence, I return to sheets of paper which smell just a little of turmeric, ready and willing to put out of its misery a narrative which I left yesterday hanging in mid-air—just as Scheherazade, depending for her very survival on leaving Prince Shahryar eaten up by curiosity, used to do night after night! I'll begin at once: by revealing that my grandfather's premonitions in the corridor were not without foundation. In the succeeding months and years, he fell under what I can only describe as the sorcerer's spell of that enormous—and as yet unstained—perforated cloth.

'Again?' Aadam's mother said, rolling her eyes. 'I tell you, my child, that girl is so sickly from too much soft living only. Too much sweetmeats and spoiling, because of the absence of a mother's firm hand. But go, take care of your invisible patient, your mother is all right with her little nothing of a headache.'

In those years, you see, the landowner's daughter Naseem Ghani contracted a quite extraordinary number of minor illnesses, and each time a shikara-wallah was despatched to summon the tall young Doctor sahib with the big nose who was making such a reputation for himself in the valley. Aadam Aziz's visits to the bedroom with the shaft of sunlight and the three lady wrestlers became almost weekly events; and on each occasion he was vouchsafed a glimpse, through the mutilated sheet, of a different seven-inch circle of the young woman's body. Her initial stomach-ache was succeeded by a very slightly twisted right ankle, an ingrowing toenail on the big toe of the left foot, a tiny cut on the lower left calf. ('Tetanus is a killer, Doctor Sahib,' the landowner said. 'My Naseem must not die for a scratch.') There was the matter of her stiff right knee, which the Doctor was obliged to manipulate through the hole in the sheet...and after a time the illnesses leapt upwards, avoiding certain unmentionable zones, and began to proliferate around her upper half. She suffered from something mysterious which her father called Finger Rot, which made the skin flake off her hands; from weakness of the wrist-bones, for which Aadam prescribed calcium tablets; and from attacks of constipation, for which he gave her a course of kaolin, since there was no question of being permitted to administer an enema. She had fevers and she also had subnormal temperatures. At these times his thermometer would be placed under her armpit and he would hum and haw about the relative inefficiency of the method. In the opposite armpit she once developed a slight case of tineachloris and he dusted her with yellow powder; after this treatment—which required him to rub the powder in, gently but firmly, although the soft secret body began to shake and quiver and he heard helpless laughter coming through the sheet, because Naseem Ghani was very ticklish—the itching went away, but Naseem soon found a new set of complaints. She waxed anaemic in the summer and bronchial in the winter. ('Her tubes are most delicate,' Ghani explained, 'like little flutes.') Far away the Great War moved from crisis to crisis, while in the cobwebbed house Doctor Aziz was also engaged in a total war against his sectioned patient's inexhaustible complaints. And, in all those war years, Naseem never repeated an illness. 'Which only shows,' Ghani told him, 'that you are a good doctor. When you cure, she is cured for good. But alas!'—he struck his forehead—'She pines for her late mother, poor baby, and her body suffers. She is a too loving child.'

So gradually Doctor Aziz came to have a picture of Naseem in his mind, a badly fitting collage of her severally-inspected parts. This phantasm of a partitioned woman began to haunt him, and not only in his dreams. Glued together by his imagination, she accompanied him on all his rounds, she moved into the front room of his mind, so that waking and sleeping he could feel in his fingertips the softness of her ticklish skin or the perfect tiny wrists or the beauty of the ankles; he could smell her scent of lavender and chambeli; he could hear her voice and her helpless laughter of a little girl; but she was headless, because he had never seen her face.

His mother lay on her bed, spreadeagled on her stomach. 'Come, come and press me,' she said, 'my doctor son whose fingers can soothe his old mother's muscles. Press, press, my child with his expression of a constipated goose.' He kneaded her shoulders. She grunted, twitched, relaxed. 'Lower now,' she said, 'now higher. To the right. Good. My brilliant son who cannot see what that Ghani landowner is doing. So clever, my child, but he doesn't guess why that girl is forever ill with her piffling disorders. Listen, my boy: see the nose on your face for once: that Ghani thinks you are a good catch for her. Foreign-educated and all. I have worked in shops and been undressed by the eyes of strangers so that you should marry that Naseem! Of course I am right; otherwise why would he look twice at our family?' Aziz pressed his mother. 'O God, stop now, no need to kill me because I tell you the truth!'

By 1918, Aadam Aziz had come to live for his regular trips across the lake. And now his eagerness became even more intense, because it became clear that, after three years, the landowner and his daughter had become willing to lower certain barriers. Now, for the first time, Ghani said, 'A lump in the right chest. Is it worrying, Doctor? Look. Look well.' And there, framed in the hole, was a perfectly-formed and lyrically lovely...'I must touch it,' Aziz said, fighting with his voice. Ghani slapped him on the back. 'Touch, touch!' he cried, 'The hands of the healer...'Forgive me for asking; but is it the lady's time of month?'...Little secret smiles appearing on the faces of the lady wrestlers. Ghani, nodding affably: 'Yes. Don't be so embarrassed old chap. We are family and doctor now.' And Aziz, 'Then don't worry. The lumps will go when the time ends.'...And the next time, 'A pulled muscle in the back of her thigh, Doctor Sahib. Such pain!' And there, in the sheet, weakening the eyes of Aadam Aziz, hung a superbly rounded and impossible buttock...And now Aziz: 'Is it permitted that...' Whereupon a word from Ghani; an obedient reply from behind the sheet; a drawstring pulled; and pajamas fall from the celestial rump, which swells wondrously through the hole. Aadam Aziz forces himself into a medical frame of mind...reaches out...feels. And swears to himself, in amazement, that he sees the bottom reddening in a shy, but compliant blush.

That evening, Aadam contemplated the blush. Did the magic of the sheet work on both sides of the hole? Excitedly, he envisaged his headless Naseem tingling beneath the scrutiny of his eyes, his thermometer, his stethoscope, his fingers, and trying to build a picture in her mind of *him*. She was at a disadvantage, of course, having seen nothing but his hands...Aadam began to hope with an illicit desperation for Naseem Ghani to develop a migraine or graze her unseen chin, so they could look each other in the face. He knew how unprofessional his feelings were; but did nothing to stifle them. There was not much he could do. They had acquired a life of their own. In short: my grandfather had fallen in love, and had come to think of the perforated sheet as something sacred and magical, because through it he had seen the things which had filled up the hole inside him which had been created when he had been hit on the nose by a tussock and insulted by the boatman Tai.

On the day the World War ended, Naseem developed the longed-for headache. Such historical coincidences have littered, and perhaps befouled, my family's existence in the world.

He hardly dared to look at what was framed in the hole in the sheet. Maybe she was hideous; perhaps that explained all this performance...he looked. And saw a soft face that was not at all ugly, a cushioned setting for her glittering, gemstone eyes, which were brown with flecks of gold: tiger's eyes. Doctor Aziz's fall was complete. And Naseem burst out, 'But Doctor, my God, what a *nose*!' Ghani, angrily, 'Daughter, mind your...' But patient and doctor were laughing together, and Aziz was saying, 'Yes, yes, it is a remarkable specimen. They tell me there are dynasties waiting in it...' And he bit his tongue because he had been about to add, '...like snot.'

And Ghani, who had stood blindly beside the sheet for three long years, smiling and smiling and smiling, began once again to smile his secret smile, which was mirrored in the lips of the wrestlers.

Meanwhile, the boatman, Tai, had taken his unexplained decision to give up washing. In a valley drenched in freshwater lakes, where even the very poorest people could (and did) pride themselves on their cleanliness, Tai chose to stink. For three years now, he had neither bathed nor washed himself after answering calls of nature. He wore the same clothes, unwashed, year in, year out; his one concession to winter was to put his chugha-coat over his putrescent pajamas. The little basket of hot coals which he carried inside the chugha, in the Kashmiri fashion, to keep him warm in the bitter cold, only animated and accentuated his evil odours. He took to drifting slowly past the Aziz household, releasing the dreadful fumes of his body across the small garden and into the house. Flowers died; birds fled from the ledge outside old Father Aziz's window. Naturally, Tai lost work; the English in particular were reluctant to be ferried about by a human cesspit. The story went around the lake that Tai's wife, driven to distraction by the old man's sudden filthiness, pleaded for a reason. He had answered: 'Ask our foreign-returned doctor, ask that nakkoo, that German Aziz.' Was it, then, an attempt to offend the Doctor's hypersensitive nostrils (in which the itch of danger had subsided somewhat under the anaesthetizing ministrations of love)? Or a gesture of unchangingness in defiance of the invasion of the doctor-attaché from Heidelberg? Once Aziz asked the ancient, straight out, what it was all in aid of; but Tai only breathed on him and rowed away. The breath nearly felled Aziz; it was as sharp as an axe.

In 1918, Doctor Aziz's father, deprived of his birds, died in his sleep; and at once his mother, who had been able to sell the gemstone business thanks to the success of Aziz's practice, and who now saw her husband's death as a merciful release for her from a life filled with responsibilities, took to her own deathbed and followed her man before the end of his own forty-day mourning period. By the time the Indian regiments returned at the end of the war, Doctor Aziz was an orphan, and a free man—except that his heart had fallen through a hole some seven inches across.

Desolating effect of Tai's behaviour: it ruined Doctor Aziz's good relations with the lake's floating population. He, who as a child had chatted freely with fishwives and flower sellers, found himself looked at askance. 'Ask that nakkoo, that German Aziz.' Tai had branded him as an alien, and therefore a person not completely to be trusted. They didn't like the boatman, but they found the transformation which the Doctor had evidently worked upon him even more disturbing. Aziz found himself suspected, even ostracized, by the poor; and it hurt him badly. Now he understood what Tai was up to: the man was trying to chase him out of the valley.

The story of the perforated sheet got out, too. The lady wrestlers were evidently less discreet than they looked. Aziz began to notice people pointing at him. Women giggled behind their palms...'I've decided to give Tai his victory,' he said. The three lady wrestlers, two holding up the sheet, the third hovering near the door, strained to hear him through the cotton wool in their ears. ('I made my father do it,' Naseem told him, 'These chatterjees won't do any more of their tittling and tattling from now on.') Naseem's eyes, hole-framed, became wider than ever.

...Just like his own when, a few days earlier, he had been walking the city streets, had seen the last bus of the winter arrive, painted with its colourful inscriptions—on the front, GOD WILLING in green shadowed in red; on the back, blue-shadowed yellow crying THANK GOD!, and in cheeky maroon, SORRY-BYE-BYE!—and had recognized, through a web of new rings and lines on her face, Ilse Lubin as she descended...

Nowadays, Ghani the landowner left him alone with the earplugged guardians, 'To talk a little; the doctor-patient relationship can only deepen in strictest confidentiality. I see that now, Aziz Sahib—forgive my earlier intrusions.' Nowadays, Naseem's tongue was getting freer all the time. 'What kind of talk is this? What are you—a man or a mouse? To leave home because of a stinky shikara-man!...'

'Oskar died,' Ilse told him, sipping fresh lime water on his mother's takht. 'Like a comedian. He went to talk to the army and tell them not to be pawns. The fool really thought the troops would fling down their guns and walk away. We watched from a window and I prayed they wouldn't just trample all over him. The regiment had learned to march in step by then, you wouldn't recognize them. As he reached the streetcorner across from the parade ground he tripped over his own shoelace and fell into the street. A staff car hit him and he died. He could never keep his laces tied, that ninny'...here there were diamonds freezing in her lashes...'He was the type that gives anarchists a bad name.'

'All right,' Naseem conceded, 'So you've got a good chance of landing a good job. Agra University, it's a famous place, don't think I don't know. University doctor!...sounds good. Say you're going for that, and it's a different business.' Eyelashes drooped in the hole. 'I will miss you, naturally...'

'I'm in love,' Aadam Aziz said to Ilse Lubin. And later, '...So I've only seen her through a hole in a sheet, one part at a time; and I swear her bottom blushes.'

'They must be putting something in the air up here,' Ilse said.

'Naseem, I've got the job,' Aadam said excitedly. 'The letter came today. With effect from April 1919. Your father says he can find a buyer for my house and the gemstone shop also.'

'Wonderful,' Naseem pouted. 'So now I must find a new doctor. Or maybe I'll get that old hag again who didn't know two things about anything.'

Because I am an orphan,' Doctor Aziz said, 'I must come myself in place of my family members. But I have come nevertheless, Ghani Sahib, for the first time without being sent for. This is not a professional visit.'

'Dear boy!' Ghani, clapping Aadam on the back. 'Of course you must marry her. With an A-1 fine dowry! No expense spared! It will be the wedding of the year, oh most certainly, yes!'

'I cannot leave you behind when I go,' Aziz said to Naseem. Ghani said, 'Enough of this tamasha! No more need for this sheet tomfoolery! Drop it down, you women, these are young lovers now!'

'At last,' said Aadam Aziz, 'I see you whole at last. But I must go now. My rounds...and an old friend is staying with me, I must tell her, she will be very happy for us both. A dear friend from Germany.'

'No, Aadam baba,' his bearer said, 'since the morning I have not seen Ilse Begum. She hired that old Tai to go for a shikara ride.'

'What can be said sir?' Tai mumbled meekly. 'I am honoured indeed to be summoned into the home of a so-great personage as yourself. Sir, the lady hired me for a trip to the Mughal Gardens, to do it before the lake freezes. A quiet lady, Doctor Sahib, not one word out of her all the time. So I was thinking my own unworthy private thoughts as old fools will and suddenly when I look she is not in her seat. Sahib, on my wife's head I swear it, it is not possible to see over the back of the seat, how was I to tell? Believe a poor old boatman who was your friend when you were young...'

'Aadam baba,' the old bearer interrupted, 'excuse me but just now I have found this paper on her table.'

'I know where she is,' Doctor Aziz stared at Tai. 'I don't know how you keep getting mixed up in my life; but you showed me the place once. You said: certain foreign women come here to drown.'

'I, Sahib?' Tai shocked, malodorous, innocent. 'But grief is making your head play tricks! How can I know these things?'

And after the body, bloated, wrapped in weeds, had been dredged up by a group of blank-faced boatmen, Tai visited the shikara halt and told the men there, as they recoiled from his breath of a bullock with dysentry, 'He blames me, only imagine! Brings his loose Europeans here and tells me it is my fault when they jump into the lake!...I ask, how did he know just where to look? Yes, ask him that, ask that nakkoo Aziz!'

She had left a note. It read: 'I didn't mean it.'

I make no comment; these events, which have tumbled from my lips any old how, garbled by haste and emotions, are for others to judge. Let me be direct now, and say that during the long, hard winter of 1918-19, Tai fell ill, contracting a violent form of skin disease, akin to that European curse called the King's Evil; but he refused to see Doctor Aziz, and was treated by a local homeopath. And in March, when the lake thawed, a marriage took place in a large marquee in the grounds of Ghani the landowner's house. The wedding contract assured Aadam Aziz of a respectable sum of money, which would help buy a house in Agra, and the dowry included, at Doctor Aziz's especial request, a certain mutilated bedsheet. The young couple sat on a dais, garlanded and cold, while the guests filed past dropping rupees into their laps. That night my grandfather placed the perforated sheet beneath his bride and himself and in the morning it was adorned by three drops of blood, which formed a small triangle. In the morning, the sheet was displayed, and after the consummation ceremony a limousine hired by the landowner arrived to drive my grandparents to Amritsar, where they would catch the Frontier Mail. Mountains crowded round and stared as my grandfather left his home for the last time. (He would return, once, but not to leave.) Aziz thought he saw an ancient boatman standing on land to watch them pass—but it was probably a mistake, since Tai was ill. The blister of a temple atop Sankara Acharya, which Muslims had taken to calling the Takht-e-Sulaiman, or Seat of Solomon, paid them no attention. Winter-bare poplars and snow-covered fields of saffron undulated around them as the car drove south, with an old leather bag containing, amongst other things, a stethoscope and a bedsheet, packed in the boot. Doctor Aziz felt, in the pit of his stomach, a sensation akin to weightlessness.

Or falling.

(...And now I am cast as a ghost. I am nine years old and the whole family, my father, my mother, the Brass Monkey and myself, are staying at my grandparents' house in Agra, and the grandchildren—myself among them—are staging the customary New Year's play; and I have been cast as a ghost. Accordingly—and surreptitiously so as to preserve the secrets of the forthcoming theatricals—I am ransacking the house for a spectral disguise. My grandfather is out and about his rounds. I am in his room. And here on top of this cupboard is an old trunk, covered in dust and spiders, but unlocked. And here, inside it, is the answer to my prayers. Not just a sheet, but one with a hole already cut in it! Here it is, inside this leather bag inside this trunk, right beneath an old stethoscope and a tube of mildewed Vick's Inhaler...the sheet's appearance in our show was nothing less than a sensation. My grandfather took one look at it and rose roaring to his feet. He strode up on stage and unghosted me right in front of everyone. My grandmother's lips were so tightly pursed they seemed to disappear. Between them, the one booming at me in the voice of a forgotten boatman, the other conveying her fury through vanished lips, they reduced the awesome ghost to a weeping wreck. I fled, took to my heels and ran into the little cornfield, not knowing what had happened. I sat there—perhaps on the very spot on which Nadir Khan had sat!—for several hours, swearing over and over that I would never again open a forbidden trunk, and feeling vaguely resentful that it had not been locked in the first place. But I knew, from their rage, that the sheet was somehow very important indeed.)

I have been interrupted by Padma, who brought me my dinner and then withheld it, blackmailing me: 'So if you're going to spend all your time wrecking your eyes with that scribbling, at least you must read it to me.' I have been singing for my supper—but perhaps our Padma will be useful because it's impossible to stop her being a critic. She is particularly angry with my remarks about her name. 'What do you know, city boy?' she cried—hand slicing the air. 'In my village there is no shame in being named for the Dung Goddess. Write at once that you are wrong, completely.' In accordance with my lotus's wishes, I insert, forthwith, a brief paean to Dung.

Dung, that fertilizes and causes the crops to grow! Dung, which is patted into thin chapati-like cakes when still fresh and moist, and is sold to the village builders, who use it to secure and strengthen the walls of kachcka buildings made of mud! Dung, whose arrival from the nether end of cattle goes a long way towards explaining their divine and sacred status! Oh, yes, I was wrong, I admit I was prejudiced, no doubt because its unfortunate odours do have a way of offending my sensitive nose—how wonderful, how ineffably lovely it must be to be named for the Purveyor of Dung!

...April 6th, 1919, the holy city of Amritsar smelled (gloriously, Padma, celestially!) of excrement. And perhaps the (beauteous!) reek did not offend that ur-Nose on my grandfather's face—after all, Kashmiri peasants used it, as described above, as a kind of plaster. Even in Srinegar, hawkers with barrows of round dung-cakes were not an uncommon sight. But then the stuff was drying, muted, useful. Amritsar dung was fresh and (worse) redundant. Nor was it all bovine. It issued from the rumps of the horses between the shafts of the city's many tongas, ikkas and gharries; and mules and men and dogs attended nature's calls, mingling in a brotherhood of shit. But there were cows, too: sacred kine roaming the dusty streets, each patrolling its own territory, staking its claims in excrement. And flies! Public Enemy Number One, buzzing gaily from turd to steaming turd, celebrated and cross-pollinated these freely-given offerings. The city swarmed about, too, mirroring the motion of the flies. Doctor Aziz looked down from his hotel window on to this scene as a Jain in a face-mask walked past, brushing the pavement before him with a twig-broom, to avoid stepping on an ant, or even a fly. Spicy sweet fumes rose from a street-snack barrow. 'Hot pakoras, pakoras hot!' A white woman was buying silks from a shop across the street and men in turbans were ogling her. Naseem—now Naseem Aziz—had a sharp headache; it was the first time she'd ever repeated an illness, but life outside her quiet valley had come as something of a shock to her. There was a jug of fresh lime water by her bed, emptying rapidly. Aziz stood at the window, inhaling the city. The spire of the Golden Temple gleamed in the sun. But his nose itched: something was not right here.

Close-up of my grandfather's right hand: nails knuckles fingers all somehow bigger than you'd expect. Clumps of red hair on the outside edges. Thumb and forefinger pressed together, separated only by a thickness of paper. In short: my grandfather was holding a pamphlet. It had been inserted into his hand (we cut to a long-shot—nobody from Bombay should be without a basic film vocabulary) as he entered the hotel foyer. Scurrying of urchin through revolving door, leaflets falling in his wake, as the chaprassi gives chase. Mad revolutions in the doorway, roundandround; until chaprassi-hand demands a close-up, too, because it is pressing thumb to forefinger, the two separated only by the thickness of urchin-ear. Ejection of juvenile disseminator of gutter-tracts; but still my grandfather retained the message. Now, looking out of his window, he sees it echoed on a wall opposite; and there, on the minaret of a mosque; and in the large black type of newsprint under a hawker's arm. Leaflet newspaper mosque and wall are crying: *Hartal* Which is to say, literally speaking, a day of mourning, of stillness, of silence. But this is India in the heyday of the Mahatma, when even language obeys the instructions of Gandhiji, and the word has acquired, under his influence, new resonances. *Hartal—April 7*, agree mosque newspaper wall and pamphlet, because Gandhi has decreed that the whole of India shall, on that day, come to a halt. To mourn, in peace, the continuing presence of the British.

'I do not understand this hartal when nobody is dead,' Naseem is crying softly. 'Why will the train not run? How long are we stuck for?'

Doctor Aziz notices a soldierly young man in the street, and thinks—the Indians have fought for the British; so many of them have seen the world by now, and been tainted by Abroad. They will not easily go back to the old world. The British are wrong to try and turn back the clock. 'It was a mistake to pass the Rowlatt Act,' he murmurs.

'What rowlatt?' wails Naseem. 'This is nonsense where I'm concerned!'

'Against political agitation,' Aziz explains, and returns to his thoughts. Tai once said: 'Kashmiris are different. Cowards, for instance. Put a gun in a Kashmiri's hand and it will have to go off by itself—he'll never dare to pull the trigger. We are not like Indians, always making battles.' Aziz, with Tai in his head, does not feel Indian. Kashmir, after all, is not strictly speaking a part of the Empire, but an independent princely state. He is not sure if the hartal of pamphlet mosque wall newspaper is his fight, even though he is in occupied territory now. He turns from the window...

...To see Naseem weeping into a pillow. She has been weeping ever since he asked her, on their second night, to move a little. 'Move where?' she asked. 'Move how?' He became awkward and said, 'Only move, I mean, like a woman...'. She shrieked in horror. 'My God, what have I married? I know you Europe-returned men. You find terrible women and then you try to make us girls be like them! Listen Doctor Sahib, husband or no husband, I am not any...bad word woman.' This was a battle my grandfather never won; and it set the tone for their marriage, which rapidly developed into a place of frequent and devastating warfare, under whose depredations the young girl behind the sheet and the gauche young doctor turned rapidly into different, stranger beings... 'What now, wife?' Aziz asks. Naseem buries her face in the pillow. 'What else?' she says in muffled tones. 'You, or what? You want me to walk naked in front of strange men.' (He has told her to come out of purdah.)

He says, 'Your shirt covers you from neck to wrist to knee. Your loose-pajamas hide you down to and including your ankles. What we have left are your feet and face. Wife, are your face and feet obscene?' But now she wails, 'They will see more than that! They will see my deep-deep shame!'

And now an accident, which launches us into the world of Mercurochrome...Aziz, finding his temper slipping from him, drags all his wife's purdah-veils from her suitcase, flings them into a wastepaper basket made of tin with a painting of Guru Nanak on the side, and sets fire to them. Flames leap up, taking him by surprise, licking at curtains. Aadam rushes to the door and yells for help as the cheap curtains begin to blaze...and bearers guests washerwomen stream into the room and flap at the burning fabric with dusters towels and other people's laundry. Buckets are brought; the fire goes out; and Naseem cowers on the bed as about thirty-five Sikhs, Hindus and untouchables throng in the smoke-filled room. Finally they leave, and Naseem unleashes two sentences before clamping her lips obstinately shut.

'You are a mad man. I want more lime water.'

My grandfather opens the windows, turns to his bride. 'The smoke will take time to go; I will take a walk. Are you coming?'

Lips clamped; eyes squeezed; a single violent No from the head; and my grandfather goes into the streets alone. His parting shot:

'Forget about being a good Kashmiri girl. Start thinking about being a modern Indian woman.'
   ...While in the Cantonment area, at British Army H.Q., one Brigadier R.E. Dyer is waxing his moustache.

It is April 7th, 1919, and in Amritsar the Mahatma's grand design is being distorted. The shops have shut; the railway station is closed; but now rioting mobs are breaking them up. Doctor Aziz, leather bag in hand, is out in the streets, giving help wherever possible. Trampled bodies have been left where they fell. He is bandaging wounds, daubing them liberally with Mercurochrome, which makes them look bloodier than ever, but at least disinfects them. Finally he returns to his hotel room, his clothes soaked in red stains, and Naseem commences a panic. 'Let me help, let me help, Allah what a man I've married, who goes into gullies to fight with goondas!' She is all over him with water on wads of cotton wool. 'I don't know why can't you be a respectable doctor like ordinary people and just cure important illnesses and all? O God you've got blood everywhere! Sit, sit now, let me wash you at least!'
   'It isn't blood, wife.'
   'You think I can't see for myself with my own eyes? Why must you make a fool of me even when you're hurt? Must your wife not look after you, even?'
   'It's Mercurochrome, Naseem. Red medicine.'
   Naseem—who had become a whirlwind of activity, seizing clothes, running taps—freezes. 'You do it on purpose,' she says, 'to make me look stupid. I am not stupid. I have read several books.'

It is April 13th, and they are still in Amritsar. 'This affair isn't finished,' Aadam Aziz told Naseem. 'We can't go you see: they may need doctors again.'
   'So we must sit here and wait until the end of the world?'
   He rubbed his nose. 'No, not so long, I am afraid.'
   That afternoon, the streets are suddenly full of people, all moving in the same direction, defying Dyer's new Martial Law regulations. Aadam tells Naseem, 'There must be a meeting planned—there will be trouble from the military. They have banned meetings.'
   'Why do you have to go? Why not wait to be called?'
   ...A compound can be anything from a wasteland to a park. The

largest compound in Amritsar is called Jallianwala Bagh. It is not grassy. Stones cans glass and other things are everywhere. To get into it, you must walk down a very narrow alleyway between two buildings. On April 13th, many thousands of Indians are crowding through this alleyway. 'It is peaceful protest,' someone tells Doctor Aziz. Swept along by the crowds, he arrives at the mouth of the alley. A bag from Heidelberg is in his right hand. (No close-up is necessary.) He is, I know, feeling very scared, because his nose is itching worse than it ever has; but he is a trained doctor, he puts it out of his mind, he enters the compound. Somebody is making a passionate speech. Hawkers move through the crowd selling channa and sweetmeats. The air is filled with dust. There do not seem to be any goondas, any troublemakers, as far as my grandfather can see. A group of Sikhs has spread a cloth on the ground and is eating, seated around it. There is still a smell of ordure in the air. Aziz penetrates the heart of the crowd, as Brigadier R.E. Dyer a.rives at the entrance to the alleyway, followed by fifty white troops. He is the Martial Law Commander of Amritsar—an important man, after all; the waxed tips of his moustache are rigid with importance. As the fifty-one men march down the alleyway a tickle replaces the itch in my grandfather's nose. The fifty-one men enter the compound and take up positions, twenty-five to Dyer's right and twenty-five to his left; and Aadam Aziz ceases to concentrate on the events around him as the tickle mounts to unbearable intensities. As Brigadier Dyer issues a command the sneeze hits my grandfather full in the face. 'Yaaaakh-thooo!' he sneezes and falls forward, losing his balance, following his nose and thereby saving his life. His 'doctori-attaché' flies open; bottles, liniment and syringes scatter in the dust. He is scrabbling furiously at people's feet, trying to save his equipment before it is crushed. There is a noise like teeth chattering in winter and someone falls on him. Red stuff stains his shirt. There are screams now and sobs and the strange chattering continues. More and more people seem to have stumbled and fallen on top of my grandfather. He becomes afraid for his back. The clasp of his bag is digging into his chest, inflicting upon it a bruise so severe and mysterious that it did not efface until after his death, years later, on the hill of Sankara Acharya or Takht-e-Sulaiman. His nose is jammed against a bottle of red pills. The chattering stops and is replaced by the noises of people and birds. There seems to be no traffic noise whatsoever. Brigadier Dyer's fifty men put down their machine-guns and go away. They have fired a total of one thousand six hundred and fifty rounds into the unarmed crowd. Of these, one thousand five hundred and sixteen have found their mark, killing or wounding some person. 'Good shooting,' Dyer tells his men, 'We have done a jolly good thing.'

When my grandfather got home that night, my grandmother was trying hard to be a modern woman, to please him; and so she did not turn a hair at his appearance. 'I see you've been spilling the Mercurochrome again, clumsy,' she said, appeasingly.

'It's blood,' he replied, and she fainted. When he brought her round with the help of a little sal volatile, she said, 'Are you hurt?'

'No,' he said.

'But *where* have you *been*, my *God?*'

'Nowhere on earth,' he said, and began to shake in her arms.

My own hand, I confess, has begun to wobble; not entirely because of its theme, but because I have noticed a thin crack, like a hair, appearing in my wrist, beneath the skin...No matter. We all owe death a life. So let me conclude with the uncorroborated rumour that the boatman Tai, who recovered from his scrofulous infection soon after my grandfather left Kashmir, did not die until 1947, when (the story goes) he was infuriated by India and Pakistan's struggle over his valley, and walked to Chhamb with the express purpose of standing between the opposing forces and giving them a piece of his mind. Kashmiri for the Kashmiris: that was his line. Naturally, they shot him. Oskar Lubin would probably have approved of his rhetorical gesture; R.E. Dyer might have commended his murderers' rifle skills.

I must go to bed. Padma is waiting; and I need a little warmth.

Angela Carter
Cousins

The people who live in its shadow have no relation to the mountain itself other than one of use, though you could say that the mountain also uses them, uses them up, exhausts not only their energies, their work, but also their imaginations. The vastness of their world oppresses them; their servitude to the elements kills them.

A girl from a small village on the lower slope of the mountain married a man who lived by himself on the far side of a certain river. She was from a fairly well-off family, he was dirt poor, he had an acre or two of stones, that was his farm, lonely beyond belief. He got her in the family way and she went off with him one early summer. They thought, when her time was near, she'd go to her widowed mother in the village for her confinement but the equinoctial storms came, thunder, lightning, and she went into labour. Since she could not go to her mother, her man went to fetch her mother to her. If the river had not swollen twice its size, due to the rain, and been washing down earth and boulders, he'd have crossed it easily but he drowned, somebody hooked his corpse out miles down, weeks later, he'd travelled further in death than he'd ever done living.

The old woman knew her daughter couldn't cross the river in her condition, in such weather. When the storm was over, the river calmed down, the old woman and her son went over to the farm themselves. The young woman lay on the straw mattress, she had bled to death. The roof of the building had caved in during the storm. By the traces of wolf dung, they knew wolves had got in. There was no sign of the baby, except those that showed it had been born.

The old woman's son carried his sister home on his back. Absolute quiet followed the tempest; there is something mutilating about the silence of the mountain. Then the wolves began to howl. After that, it was winter. When the snow melted, it was spring. The old woman's son married the blacksmith's daughter, she moved in with them. By Christmas, there was a bouncing grandson but the old woman still crossed herself when she heard the wolves on the mountain. Time passed. Then came a granddaughter; then a stillbirth; compensated for by twins, a boy and a girl. And so on.

The summer the eldest grandson was seven, he went up with his father and their goats to the high pastures, as was the village custom, to lodge in a shelter up the mountainside while the goats gorged themselves on young grass. The boy was sitting in the sun, plaiting straws and watching the kids butt one another when he saw the shadow of what he had been told to fear most, a wolf, advancing silently along the lea of an outcrop of rock. Then another wolf, and another, while his charges frisked and nibbled on.

If they had not been the first wolves he ever saw, the boy would not have looked at them so closely; the russet-grey pelts, the lovely, plumey tails; the sharp, inquiring masks. Because he looked at them so intently, he saw, or thought he saw, a bald one, a naked one, going on all fours, as they did, but furless, though with a kind of brown mane.

He was so awe-struck and fascinated by this bald wolf that he would have lost his flock, maybe himself been eaten and certainly been beaten to the bone, had not the goats themselves sniffed danger, their hooves drumming off down the slope, their terrified whinnying, so the men came, firing off guns, making hullabaloo, scaring the wolves away.

The boy was cuffed round the head and sent home in disgrace. His mother was feeding the baby and his grandmother sat at the table shelling peas into a pot.

'Grandmother, there was a little girl with the wolves,' he said. He wasn't sure why he thought it was a little girl. He just had a feeling. His grandmother went on shelling peas.

'About my age,' he said. His grandmother threw away a flat pod. 'I saw her,' he said. His grandmother tipped water into the pot and put it on the fire. There wasn't time, that night, but, next morning, she herself took the boy up to the high pastures, again, and said:

'Tell your father what you told me.'

They went to examine the wolves' tracks. On a bit of dampish ground, they found a print, not like that of a dog's paw, but even less like that of a child's footprint—yet curiously like that one of the great cats. Only, here we are high in the cool North; all the cats, here, are small, sit by the fire, and purr. But *this* print was like that of the five-toed paw of a great cat; or, more, like the beautiful and mysterious prints on the suave pelts of certain great cats, that carry markings like the glyphs of a script we cannot read.

'She was running on all fours with her arse stuck up in the air,' said the boy. 'Therefore, she'd put all her weight on the ball of her foot, wouldn't she. And splay out her toes, see...just like that.'

He inserted the ball of his own foot in the print, to show his father and the others how it would go, if he, too, ran habitually on all fours. His foot fitted the print perfectly.

'And, see, no use for a heel, if you run that way.... Stands to reason. That's why there's no heel-print, see?'

They searched a long way before they found her asleep in a sandy hollow not far from the ruins of the house in which she had been born. Her head lay on the flank of a grey, grizzled, old bitch. The men banged cans and rattled sticks to keep the other wolves away; when the sleepers woke, the girl's uncle blasted the bitch to pieces with his gun. The grandmother tried to put her arms round the girl but she bit the old woman's hand. Then the other men caught hold of the girl.

She scratched, fought, and bit so much they tied her wrists and ankles together with twine, then slung her from a pole and carried her, like game, back to the village. She neither screamed nor cried out, she didn't seem able to. She made only a few dull, guttural, choking sounds. Her eyes watered all the time but not as though she were crying. She was skinny, all her ribs stuck out, there was no flesh on her, not like the plump, potato-fed boy. She was burned almost black, and filthy, and she was scored and scabbed all over with dozens of the scars of sharp abrasions of rock and thorn. Her matted hair was so long it hung down to the ground as they carried her. It was stuck with burrs. She was dreadfully verminous. She stank riotously.

Solemn with wonder, her little cousin trotted behind her. Granny kept her bitten hand wrapped up in her apron. When they dumped the girl on the earth floor of her grandmother's house, the boy secretly stretched out and touched her upper arm. Her flesh felt warm but hard as wood. She had given up struggling, now; she lay on the floor, trussed up, and pretended to be dead.

Granny's house had the one big room, half byre, half home, the beasts who lived with them in winter segregated by a wood partition from where the family lived. There was a ladder up to the hayloft. There was soup on the fire and the table laid, it was now about supper time but still light; night comes late on the summer mountain.

'Untie her,' said grandmother.

Her son wasn't willing but she would not be denied. He got the breadknife and cut the rope round the girl's ankles. All she did was kick out a bit. But when he cut the rope round her wrists, it was as if he had let a fiend loose. The onlookers ran out of the door, the family ran for the ladder to the hayloft and roosted there, out of her way, all of them but gran and the eldest boy, who both made for the door to pull it to and shoot the bolt, to keep her in.

The trapped one knocked round the room, bang, over went the table, crash, dishes shattering, bang, crash, the dresser fell on its face. Over went the meal barrel; she coughed, she sneezed just like a human being sneezes, she bounded around, bewildered, in a white cloud until the flour settled. She made little rushes here and there, all her movements were jagged, violent, illogical. She was mad with terror.

She never rose up on two legs; she crouched, all the time, on her hands and the tips of her feet, yet it was not quite like crouching, you could see how all fours, now, came naturally to her, as though she had made a different pact with gravity than we have. You could see how strong the muscles in her thighs had grown, how taut and twanging the arches of her feet were, how she used her heels only when she sat back on her haunches. She growled; now and then, she hiccuped out those thick grunts of distress. All you could see of her rolling eyes were the whites. Several times, her bowels opened, apparently involuntarily.

She careered into the hearth, yelped with burned pain, and knocked over the pan hanging on the hook. The spilled contents of the pan put out the fire; hot soup spilled over her forelegs. When the soup scalded her, she was shocked rigid. Then, squatting on her hindquarters, holding up her hurt paw before her dangling piteously from its wrist, she howled, she howled, she howled. It sounded like the birth of tragedy.

Even the old woman, who had contracted with herself to love the child of her dead, beloved daughter, was afraid when she heard that. But the grandson was not afraid; he hardly heard it, he could not take his eyes off the crevice of her child's sex, that was perfectly visible to him as she sat square on the base of her spine. Her purple inner lips opened up as she howled; she offered him a view of a set of Chinese boxes of whorled flesh that opened one upon the other into herself, perpetually receding, his first, devastating intimation of infinity.

You could see a white thread of moon in the blond sky through the chimney hole. It was neither dark nor light in the room but the boy could see her genitals clearly.

She howled. From the bald mountain, first singly, then in complex polyphony, answered at last voices in the same language. She howled for a long time. Soon it was impossible for the occupants of the house to deny to themselves that the answering howling was coming closer and closer to them.

When all the air outside was full of the sound of wolves, she seemed consoled, sank down, laid her head on her paws so that her hair trailed in the cooling soup, and waited. The household gun hung on a nail over the fireplace, where the man of the house had put it when he came in. When he put his foot on the top of the ladder in order to come down and retrieve it, the girl jumped up, yapping, snarling and showing long, yellow canines; he stayed where he was. Now the howling outside was mixed with the shrieks of terrified domestic beasts. All the other villagers had locked themselves up fast in these houses that could convert to fortresses. It was a siege, but their enemy was bolted inside with this family.

The girl began to howl, again, but in a different way. She squatted in the middle of the floor, pointed her nose to the roof and howled with a kind of wild triumph. An answering howling now came from directly outside the door. The stout door shuddered; a sharp snout poked underneath. Her son leant out of the hayloft and said to his mother: 'Come up.'

She took hold of her grandson's hand with the one of hers that had not been bitten, that was not throbbing. The howling girl allowed them to pass by. The boy pushed his grandmother up the ladder in front of him and drew it up behind them.

The door shook with the impact of many furry shoulders throwing themselves against it. It was secured on the inside by an iron bar that rocked in its socket. The ambiguous light, not night nor day, filled the room like transparent milk, but the boy could not see his cousin's cunt anymore, he was at the wrong angle. He looked, instead, at her nakedness, that was, unlike human nakedness, beyond innocence or display. He was filled with a terrified excitement.

Now she stopped howling, leapt at this side of the door, and began to worry and rattle the iron bar with her muzzle and forepaws. The carnivorous wind-band of the mountain encouraged her. It was only a matter of a few moments before she worried the bar out of its socket and the door flew open.

The family in the hayloft, staring as if tranced down through the trap, felt themselves to be on a precarious cloud floating above a sudden whirlpool. The whirlpool had eyes and teeth and red mouths and ululated like all the winds of winter caught in a bag. The fur and wild swirled round the house. A gaunt, brindled dog, four feet through his shoulders, reared on his haunches; in the loft, the baby started whimpering and its mother stuffed her nipple in its mouth to hush it. Below, the girl threw her leg over the dog's back and hugged his thick neck.

The last glimpse the grandson had of her was of her clotted hair shifting with speed as the tide of wolves swept outdoors.

Leaving behind wrecked furniture, smashed crocks, a stench of urine, irremediable silence.

The grandson thought the old woman would cry, now, but she seemed unmoved. When all was safe, they came down the ladder one by one. Although it was well past midnight, the old woman and her daughter-in-law went to the river for water to scrub the house out, they did not want to sleep in a place that smelled of wolves. They threw away the broken things; the man nailed the table and the dresser back together. While they worked, the neighbours came out into the frail moonlight and chattered about the strangeness of the night. The wolves had not taken so much as a single chicken from any village coup. No goat, nor oxe, nor cow, nor donkey was a mite harmed.

People brought out beer, and the schnapps they made from potatoes, and snacks, because the excitement made everybody hungry. Soon there was a grand, impromptu party going on but granny said nothing, although you could see her injured hand was hurting her.

Next day, she went to the graveyard and sat for a while by the wooden cross over the place where her daughter was buried, but she did not pray. Then she went home and started chopping cabbage for the evening meal but had to leave off because her right hand was festering.

That winter, when there was more leisure, her grandson went to the priest to learn to read and write because his parents decided it was high time somebody in the family could do so. It was as though the incident with the wolves had somehow precipitated them all forwards; as though they realized the key to its inexplicability lay elsewhere than on the mountain. The boy learned his letters so quickly and with such enthusiasm that he continued to visit the priest for lessons in mathematics, Latin, and then Greek as his duties with the herd permitted. The summer he was fourteen, the priest told his father and mother their eldest son had exhausted his own store of knowledge and now should go to the seminary in the town and, perhaps, one day become a priest, himself. Gran was dead, by then.

The boy's parents were now prosperous and had five strong young sons, altogether, besides three daughters. They could easily spare the eldest, indeed, perhaps had hopes of him. Although he did not want to be a priest, he knew the seminary was the only way off the mountain. It was decided the priest should take the boy the twenty mile walk to the seminary and make the arrangements for his schooling there after the goats came down from the high pasture for the winter.

The journey would take a day and a half; the priest was old. The nights were already chilly. The priest and the boy lit a fire, ate bread and cheese they brought with them, and talked for a while about some problems in Greek grammar the boy was encountering. The fire would keep wild beasts away. They slept, but the boy was agitated by nervous dreams. He wanted to leave the mountain but was afraid of doing so. In the first light that no more than clarifies the dark, they woke and went to the river for water.

On the other side, a wolf crouched, lapping water that contained mauve cloud; her mouth seemed to liquify the sky. Two cubs played on the bank near her, rolling and cuffing one another. All silent as a dream. At first, in the weird dawn, you did not see how her pelt was the wrong colour for a wolf; that she was tailless; and had no ears. Then she lifted her round head towards them.

Indeed, she had become abundantly hairy. Her forearms were thick with hair, so were her loins and legs, and the hair on her head hung over her face in such a way you could hardly make out her features and these had suffered a feral change, a girl who lived without mirrors, who did not acknowledge the reflection in the river as that of herself, a face the mirror of a different consciousness than ours. Her eyes, the fruit of night on the mountain, were extraordinarily luminous. The priest involuntarily mumbled something in Latin. She cocked her head at the vague, river-washed sound. The scared cubs left off playing and ran to her, to burrow their heads in her sides.

The boy started to tremble violently. She soon decided there was no danger and lowered her muzzle, again, to the surface of the water that took hold of her hair and spread it round her head in a wide circle. When she had finished her drink, she retreated a few paces, shaking her wet head; the boy saw how the little cubs now fastened their mouths on her dangling breasts.

He could not help it, he broke out crying. Tears rolled down his face and splashed on the grass. He took a few steps forward, into the river, with his arms held open, intending to cross over to her, perhaps to embrace her, perhaps to exorcize the vertiginous memory of the depths within depths he had once glimpsed within her.

But his cousin took fright at the sudden movement, wrenched the teats away from the cubs, and ran off. The cubs scampered, squeaking after. She ran on hands and feet as if it were the only way to run, towards the higher ground, into the pale maze of the unfinished dawn.

The boy scrubbed his face with his sleeve, sat down, took off his boots, and dried his feet and legs on the tail of his shirt. Then he and his companion ate something and continued on towards the seminary in silence. There was no language in which they could speak of what they had seen. The boy walked barefoot, carrying his soaked boots slung on his back by the laces. It was the last time he would ever walk barefoot.

The birds woke up and began singing. The sun came up and the mountain, which now lay behind them, began to aquire a two-dimensional look, to recede to manageable proportions, to seem more and more like a piece of mise-en-scene, a backdrop for the emblematic display of fabulous events.

The boy shot one glance over his shoulder, saw how the mountain shrank and thought: 'If I look back again, I shall turn into a pillar of salt.'

As if his life depended on it, he began to babble away about Greek irregular verbs.

Desmond Hogan
Southern Birds

Come this time of year there were huge aggravated cloud patterns in the sky, and a place usually just forlorn took on a harsh elemental quality as though it had not been built by modern estate planners but by prehistoric forces.

The tinkers camped nearby; boys lounged in the cemetery, smoking dope, drinking sherry. At night a whine often rose from the youth club where a record played for a while, couples jived hesitantly. The action took place at the cemetery—the young people of Ballyfermot integrating, getting drunk or stoned silly.

Dublin is a beautiful city, a Viking city. There are inspiring inlets but Ballyfermot is a devil's dream. Just before you come to the Midlands it lies, another city altogether, an embarrassment, a cage. Jeremy grew up in Ballyfermot; he was a child of the metropolis, a youth in blue denim. In Ballyfermot he had acquired a certain fame, having written a play about a pie-bald horse that toured community centres. His friend Leo had played the horse. Altogether there was comradeship between them, two boys just out of school.

Sometimes one detected an anti-British slogan, visiting relatives from the North daubing their trade mark 'Brits Out' on the garden walls; but the North was miles from here. There were different problems—little bread and what there was of bread stale and unwholesome. This was the product of a poets' revolution, the Bible of Irish politicians, the 1916 revolution.

A grim, dirty, seedy, unwanted estate, it spread, enlarging and growing a culture, the culture in Jeremy's and Leo's heads, the culture of search. All the young people here searched, whether through drugs or drink—they sought ways out. Some took them on a boat. One or two boys had gone North and joined the provos, but they were few and usually of wildly Republican backgrounds. Jeremy however wrote plays and if he did go with the others it was really as an outsider.

Physically he was tall, and it was his face one noticed most, full of changes of expression, a fullness and a kindness, a leniency that more than often got him into trouble. He was 'soft' his mother said, vulnerable and attractive to women. Nuns had a special liking for him, the black and grey nuns of Ballyfermot. Unlike the other boys he was shy, polite, and although he didn't dress too neatly he had a manner that one earnestly trusted.

Leo, smaller, had trusted his friend for a long time. They'd gone to vocational school together and now finished, harboured joints over Ballyfermot, pausing, looking down on a city they knew was not made of pearls and diamonds but of seedy night clubs, mannequins from colour advertisements, run down pubs, and modern buildings billowing like blankets on a line.

'Let's go somewhere,' Leo suggested one night, the suggestion hardly reaching Jeremy's ear, he staring down, pondering on the faraway Liffey, lifting its skeleton finger against the night. Young men and women sat around, smoking, drinking. They heard trains passing, a sound that penetrated the moon.

Jeremy registered Leo's words at last. No job, no money. Why not go away? But they did need money to leave. Leo got a job in a pub at night and fiddled greatly, taking money from the till. Jeremy got a job in the convent, cleaning floors. Sister Mary Martha was full of stories about her childhood in Mayo, stories about banshees and headless horsemen. Hovering over him like an overgrown leprechaun, she sprouted out of her black shoes like a bad cabbage.

Some money in early September. Indifferent to the weather Jeremy and Leo headed off towards Belfast, hitch-hiking past the airport.

Belfast was a city of searing blackness; they stayed with Leo's aunt off the Falls Road. Rain splashed. Lights bloomed, naked, white, saracens rushed by in the deluge.

Fish and chips were wrapped in Republican newspapers, prayers for dead soldiers, invocations of the many blessings of Our Lady Queen of Ireland for commandants who died in action and now filled the air of Milltown cemetery with their ghosts.

Leo's aunt was quiet; she avoided discussing years of tragedy. Resentment of the British army was everywhere, yet an odd fear of what would happen if they left. The provies were never referred to by name but Jeremy understood their lordship.

There were gulls in Belfast, rain. But in his gut Jeremy hated it, this war torn city, boys just out of school in England standing around in uniform.

There were words about King Billy and chiding remarks about the Pope. The young were endowed with the centuries as a gift, centuries of fear, of siege, of blind hatreds and winnowing Lagan breezes.

Jeremy saw them paralyzed, the young, Protestant and Catholic. He saw the British between them, teenagers, statues in the alley ways. He wondered if anything would ever come between Catholics and Protestants other than British soldiers. He imagined delayed festivity, coming for years, wondering what would speed it. Now there was silence, silence of streets, pattering rain, gutters gulping as street lamps reflected on the kind of black only Belfast knew.

They left Belfast hitchhiking around the coast, meeting a tinker in Ballymena who told them about the Ballinasloe horsefair, and they turned in its direction, leaving the North of Ireland, a quarter of privation and uncertainty, heading South, towards the most ancient fair in Europe.

Ballyfermot sometimes crossed their minds, but as it was autumn the strong whiff of leaves took their breath and senses away—leaves tidying themselves, little burdens of orange and gold outside rectories that looked as though they were about to blow away.

The tinkers were there, hundreds of them, brightly painted caravans, all kinds of deceits painted. Madame Lucy reads the cups, Ziza Mandala sees your future in your palm.

Smoke rose from caravans, always a little element of torture in it, the presence of autumn undefined but controlling things like smoke, bark with its odd mixture of scents.

The two boys wandered through the town and got lodging in a house where Wolf Tone was reputed to have stayed once while visiting the fair. They slept in one big bed under a quilt that had all colours in it. It could indeed have been the end of the eighteenth century when Tone was rallying Catholics and Irish Protestants to revolution.

Leo was smaller than Jeremy, and as ducks wandered on farms outside Ballinasloe they lay close; realizing there was male kinship at least.

They'd spent little but now had fun drinking in the amusement arcade, sharp shooting. Ballinasloe exploded, dynamite of stars and big wheel.

They met Catriona in a pub, black haired woman sitting over a pint of Guinness as though it imposed a threat. How conversation between them began they couldn't remember afterwards except that she kept smattering cigarette ashes on the floor and Jeremy asked her about it, his mother referring to people who did this kind of thing as 'low down Cork Street tripes.'

She philosophized about shaking ash on the floor, saying that the abandon of this gesture suited her personality. Her accent was Irish but she was quick to inform the boys that her mother had been an Irish tinker who had married into the English upper classes.

'We're here for the crack,' Leo told her, 'What are you here for?'

'I come because I'm one of the travelling people,' she said, 'instinct. The instinct that heralds the Indian to the elk.'

No elk could be sighted in Ballinasloe, but Catriona was correct about the instinct; there were many gipsies with coal black Romany eyes, dogs that had strayed from Famine times, those tinker women with hair like beaten copper and features that shot out like the bulbs of spring flowers.

Catriona had them buy her hot whiskey and then bought them Guinness.

She lived in a caravan in the fairgreen she said, having travelled from Kerry, drawn by horses. She lived usually by the ocean, selling her paintings of mares to American or British tourists. She had come to Ballinasloe because she believed it was what the past demanded of her. The urgency with which she told them of her past was remarkable, the husband who'd drowned himself, her solitude, her moments of creation, her life wedded now to the birds.

They returned to her caravan that evening. She gave them tea and whiskey, and then courtesy let them take leave of her.

When they returned to the green late the following day her caravan was gone and they in their inspiration decided to follow her.

Portumna, Nenagh, Limerick, Abbeyfeale.

Outside Tralee they came to the village she spoke of, and there they were directed towards her site. A caravan; a dog they hadn't seen before; a cage outside the caravan with two Mongolian mice. Catriona came to the door. Behind her were mountains, rough and wild, and the ocean.

She now looked like a rainbow of things, grief and abundant joy, abandon and mediocre uncertainty. She welcomed the boys; by now they were beginning to realize that her mind had somewhat flown.

Nearby was a cottage which was her studio, and after tea she led them there; it was a surprise, a revelation, horses of all kinds, mares like prehistoric mares, dots on white, tails like banners on them and manes like fork lightening. There were prizes she'd won around, trophies of one sort or another, certificates.

Catriona's accent moved between West of Ireland and upper class English with a bit of Lancashire; her husband's accent.

By the ocean she spoke of the legendary heroes of Ireland, the Tuatha de Danann. One wondered from her intensity if they would return. Night came over the sea, evening a ball rolled round and around.

They had tea again; Catriona spoke of life in an upper class English home, tomatoes forever verging on ripeness, foetal green merging into red. Her father was an aristocrat, wore green and purple jerseys. Her mother for that matter was an aristocrat too, Famine Irish, eyes that had gathered the horror of that time, horror of hunger. They'd loved one another but Catriona at sixteen had left the Benedictine nuns, a convent school, run away, taken up with gipsies who picked hops in Kent, married a Lancashireman, come to Ireland.

Her dad's name was O Fogarthy, a proper name for a valiant mongrel who had the airs of a woodhound.

They stayed in her studio; smell of paint in their dreams; Ballyfermot only in their nightmares, the cemetery, the river frozen with orange blooms.

Songs of summer rose and merged into a Kerry autumn, birds gathered, disciplined regiments of them. The beady eyes of starlings stared at the imminent grey. They would take bag and baggage to azure places.

Jeremy wrote messages on the beach. Leo climbed mountains, encountered old men who stared at far off peninsulas as though a new world.

Rain came. The boys painted the house. The painted the caravans and performed little chores.

Although there were few trees around tiny filaments of leaves arrived, haunting the light breezes.

Alone at night they laughed at Catriona, the stained glass window of her past.

She was a fine artist, and Kerry and Limerick men who owned stores came and bought her wares, paintings of Irish horses dancing against the moon.

At night lying on separate mattresses they heard the banshee, a howling orchestrated sound. The wind was rushing through a gap in a stone wall but to Jeremy it was the scream of a young soldier in Belfast, fragmented by an I.R.A. bullet, the wail of a siren over a Catholic domain, the hysteria of a thrush in some avenue in Belfast witnessing a door step killing. He got up, roused into an extravagant eroticism, walked into Catriona's caravan—lay by her and entered her, aware of a power in his body, the shedding of seed, the lonesomeness, the cry of sex.

She looked more like an Irish country girl after that. The following Saturday night both Jeremy and Leo got drunk in Tralee, cycled home on the same bicycle, both lying with her.

She was a strange woman, skin olive, a mixture of British reserve and Irish coarseness.

She was like a nun who wanted her body for herself but being generous gave it freely. She wore raincoats in the early November rain, a farmer's wife now.

The Atlantic thundered in. Jeremy discerned saracen tanks in it.

Catriona drank whiskey in a nearby pub. She had returned to the first posture they'd noticed in her, distance.

They made love to her but it was as though she was a passive thing, only giving, never demanding, an echo of pleasure for herself.

Jeremy backed away first, knowing he'd been liked by nuns. He stopped making love to her, and Leo, somewhat touched by all the things that made up Jeremy, retreated too. They lived together again, the two boys, in the studio, and Catriona talked to the dog.

Her husband's body was washed in Donegal, she said; on a May day more like autumn. They could never place an age on her; nor did they know if she told the truth.

She read the Ecclesiastes at night in a big King James bible. They read comics or paperbacks. The dog read nothing.

She talked about burying herself in the earth, as an artist should, merging with the clay, bringing forth a tree, a flower. She spoke of absolute abandon. She remarked on rainbows, on the southern flight of birds.

If only her caravan could go straight south.

She became less tinker, less gipsy, more young woman with purified features who was a painter and a seeker. She'd driven her husband mad she said, too much of the creative within her. Creativity destroys she said, the making, the healing of things. Man is made for the mundane. The inkling of beauty distracts and disturbs.

Whales peeled south.

A procession of gulls went by, a seal visited the strand, an emissary from the sea. He returned. He would come back with the apocalypse.

Leo spoke of the holiday being over. Jeremy thought of southern places, sand, sea that was blue.

The absence of promiscuity changed Catriona, refined her. Her features emerged as an apparition, forehead, eyes, nose. She cooked for them.

She read a Protestant bible.

Eventually she cracked up.

Her paintings were wild and uncontrollably joyous, but she, in her isolation, developed the cancer of retribution; it was guilt, guilt over always leaving everything for the sake of articulated beauty, family, friends, husband. The hands that touch a canvas are the hands of a diseased person. The disease Jeremy decided is love of beauty.

A simple woman, she began speaking of nuns and birds; congregations of birds became gatherings of nuns. The bleat of birds heralded a Georgian chant for her; English Catholicism, talk of redemption.

She took to wearing short skirts, plastic coats that made her look like any young woman. She walked the beach. She gathered bark. Where was her madness perceptible? In her silence. In the strain of anguish on her face, eyes that became so blue they twisted an hallucination with them, the blue of a summer's day, southern blue.

Her husband had drowned himself. Why they didn't know. Only that if he hadn't something else would have happened to him. All they knew about him was he mended tin and always got the King of Hearts in cards despite his imminent death.

A priest visited one night, had tea, spoke about the Holy Father, told dirty jokes, informed them about a production by the amateur drama group in Tralee, eventually tried to convert them, was pushed into the night by Catriona.

That night she seduced them both, gave something to them, anger, pain, took something from them, momentarily their souls, souls made up of Ballyfermot nights, an endless longing for that which wasn't there.

They felt bereaved and shaken afterwards. In his nakedness Jeremy took a bottle of sour Guinness and began drinking it on the floor.

Leo lay in bed with the woman. Jeremy wanted to destroy something in himself. He had been deceived by this woman. She had mutilated the order in him.

Leo lived with the woman in the caravan while Jeremy made a house for himself in the studio. Winter was coming, anger, torment of wind and spray.

And then they knew she wanted them to go, their moment over with her, her need for solitude again intact.

She stopped speaking to them, made toast for herself, piled tinned peas on it.

At gay moments in the night she conjured soup but drank it herself.

The boys felt mouse-like, rejected, scared.

The birds were gone.

They left Tralee one November morning, hitching to Dublin. Leo had slept with Catriona the previous night but it was as though he'd picked up a woman in a dancehall and she'd got that kind of salacious pleasure from him.

Jeremy's seed had leaked on a blanket that night. Nearby was the sea, angry remains of trees.

Catriona had been up painting when they left. She said goodbye but her heart wasn't in the farewell; they were tourists who'd come and were going now.

Back in Dublin they found the city had shrunken, all the jobs grabbed up; Grafton Street was thronged with record sleeves. The green had a lament rising from it, a visible lament, trees lowered into grey, ducks paddling, letting out little cries that got lost in the willow trees.

Leo and Jeremy left Dublin on the mailboat, pocket money in their jackets, enough to get another boat to France. They'd go south; it was too late to pick grapes now but perhaps they'd get to Crete and get jobs in a cork factory or on an industrial plant on the island.

A busker played with string and Dublin sat up against the evening light, chimneys, domes; the curtain call of a country where men murdered children, where British army vehicles weighed purposelessly against the night, where prosperity wrestled with poverty, where in one part a woman judged her canvas a terrible peace in her eyes.

Alan Sillitoe
A Scream of Toys

*E*die looked a long time at blue sky in a pool of water after rain before dipping her finger down for a taste. It got wet. The edge of a cloud was bitter with soil and mouldy brick, telling her that the old backyard was in the sky as well. It was everywhere, even when she walked out and onto the street, and to the road at the of the street, for wherever she was she knew she had to go back to Albion Yard because that was where she lived.

She liked the water best when it settled into a mirror and showed her face. It wasn't nice to taste the sky, but just to look at the big white cloud creeping back across her frock to cover both knees so that she couldn't see them. You got seven years bad luck if you broke a mirror, so it was best only to look at it.

She stood up and waved the cloud goodbye, but still saw her mouth and hair saying hello to the sky. It couldn't talk to her so what was the use. And if it did she'd cheek it back, her mother would say. She would jump in it except that she didn't want bad luck. If she got any of that her mam would smack her in the chops, and dad would thump her like he did mam when she broke the sugar basin last week.

A horse and cart went along the street loaded with bottles of lemonade that rattled against each other. If one fell she would catch it and run off to drink it dry in the lavatory—but it didn't. The big horse was black and white, and the man on the dray shouted and shot a whip at its neck. If a lemonade bottle did fall it would smash before she could reach out and hold it. It'd be empty, anyway.

She'd like to ride on the horse through the pools of water. It went by in no time, leaving big tods steaming on the cobbles. Mr Jones who worked on the railway opened his door and came out with a dustpan. He scooped 'em up and carried 'em back inside as if they was puddings straight out of the saucepan. She'd like lemonade better, but none fell off. He'd give the puddings to his plant pots for their tea. A woman came out with a broken shovel but she was too late. She would have to wait till she heard another horse and cart, and until Mr Jones was at work, because he always got there first.

When she came back to the puddle it was still there. Nobody had dug it out and taken it away. They didn't like water because there was plenty in the tap, and besides, it was wet. It wasn't so big now though, because the sun had come out.

'You'll come to no good,' she said to herself, playing at her mother, staring at the fire and gazing at the sky. It was wrong to pull your knickers down and pee in water. There'd be no mirror left, but the pool would get bigger, though only for a minute. Johnny Towle put his finger there yesterday and she kicked him on the leg so hard that the buttons flew off her shoe. 'I'll tell yer mam I fucked yer,' he shouted right round the yard. She didn't know what it meant, but it wasn't good, so now she did know.

It was better to look down at the sky when she couldn't see her face.

Next day Johnny Towle came running into the yard, arms wide-out, and a big round scream at his mouth, and his eyes shining like the black buttons she had kicked off her shoe.

'There's TOYS,' he shouted to everybody. 'A man's just left a big box of lovely toys at the end o't street. Quick, run, or they'll all be gone.'

'You're daft' Edie didn't want to run, but her heart shook at his absolute certainty of this abandoned box of real yellow and red treasure-toys waiting for them to dip and snatch, then take home and play with forever. Not only his mouth had said it, but his whole body and legs as well, so it must be true, and she ran after the others to get her share.

All it was was a pile of cardboard boxes, and in their disappointment they kicked them to pieces. Johnny Towle booted them harder than anyone, as if he had been tricked as well, but they hated him ever after for his rotten scream of toys when there hadn't been anything but boxes.

When she mentioned it to her mother her mother said she should have had more bleddy sense because nobody leaves a box of toys at the end of the street. Edie wanted to cry about this, but didn't, because maybe one day they would.

When your bones ached you could see a long way off, the toolsetter had once said for a joke, fixing the belt on her machine so that it would go for another half an hour at least. Some women were getting new lend-lease machines from America but her turn wouldn't come for at least six months, the gaffer said.

All dressed up and nowhere to go, she stood on Trent Bridge and looked into the water. It was a windy summer so her coat was fastened, causing half the month's toffee ration to bulge from her pocket. The water was like oil-cloth. Her bones always ached by Friday night, but she had five bob in her purse, and no work tomorrow or Sunday, so the bit of a back-ache made her feel better.

When she turned round three army lorries went by and a swaddie whistled at her from the back of the last one. She waved back. Cheeky bleeder. But why not? Amy had asked her to go into a pub but she didn't because you had to be eighteen, though Amy didn't care, for she said: 'We have a sing-song, and it's a lot o' laughs. The Yanks'll always buy you a drink.'

The wind brought a whiff from the glue factory, and the water smelled cold. A barge made an arrow, and a man at the front who steered it wore only a shirt and smoked a pipe, and stared at the bridge he had to go under. She wondered if it would ever come out the other side. If it vanished in the middle and wasn't seen again it would be reported in the *Evening Post*. She wanted to run across the wide road and look over the parapet to make sure. You're not a kid anymore, so don't, she told herself, watching smoke come up from its chimney.

She looked at aeroplanes flying over, small black shapes scattered across the sky. Maybe she would go to the Plaza picture-house and see Spencer Tracy or Leslie Howard or Robert Taylor. There might be ice cream on sale. Or she'd call at the beer-off for some lemonade and go home to drink it. If she went in the pub with Amy her mam and dad might be there. Or somebody would see her and tell them. After fifteen planes had gone over she lost count.

A man walked along, and stopped near her. They're going to bomb somebody, but they're brave blokes all the same. Oh dear. He leaned with his back to the bridge, looking at the wide road. He tilted his head at the noise of the aeroplanes, and spoke to himself. She laughed. He didn't like aeroplanes, she thought. His big moustache came over his lips like a bush. If it hadn't been for that he would have reminded her of Robert Donat, who had a thin tash.

She didn't want to look at him in case he thought she was looking at him, and then he would look at her, and she might have to look back, and if you looked at somebody they might not like it. They'd have to lump it, though, so she looked at him anyway. He had dark eyes, and laughed so that his teeth shone. He'll bite me if I don't go away, but it's my bridge as much as his.

The chill wind reminded her that there were ten Park Drives in her pocket. It was so cold she wanted to smoke. Her mam didn't like it so she could never have a puff at home. Her dad smoked, though. His pipe smoked all the time. You'll smoke yourself into a kipper, her mam told him every week when she got his tobacco from the Co-op. So she had to do her smoking at work, one day in her dinner hour, a packet a week, which left three to spare. At Christmas a woman had given her some rum, and when they got back from the pub she was sick. Then she dropped asleep on a heap of uniforms. The gaffer came by, but didn't say anything. She didn't like boozing after that. The gaffer had had a few, as well.

He was like a soldier, but not quite a soldier, in his greeny sort of uniform. She wanted to walk away, and knew she should, but then he might follow her, so she stayed where she was. The water pushed and shoved itself under the bridge, but she couldn't look at it anymore, in case it sucked her in. There was a bit of red and orange in the sky by the War Memorial and paddling pool. A woman walked along the embankment with a pram. The kid in it kicked a shoe off, and Edie heard a smack. Another army lorry came by, but the back was covered up.

The kid cried. She took her fags out, and the man stared so hard she put them back again. Then he smiled: 'You walk with me?'

Her grandad had lived with them, and she wondered why he got smaller and smaller. When he first came he was bigger than she was, but then he shrank till he was only a titch, and trembled when he got up from his chair at night to close the curtains. When he spilled his tea dad shouted at him. Fancy shouting like that at your own dad. He used to give her pennies but then he'd got no money left, so she gave him one of her fags when nobody was in, but it made him cough and he threw it on the fire, which was a waste. When he died he got buried, but mam and dad didn't wear black clothes at the funeral because they didn't have any, or couldn't be bothered, more like. They hadn't been to his grave since, but she'd gone twice and put wild flowers on, because you had to visit peoples' graves after they died. If you didn't they wouldn't remember you when you met them again.

It was a daft idea because where would you walk to when you met each other, but she took out her cigarette packet and held it towards him. You couldn't say what he was, because there were no badges on his battledress that told her anything. He was funny. He saluted her, then came and took a fag, looking carefully to choose one, though they were all the same.

'Thank you,' he said. 'Now, we walk?'

She felt a touch at her elbow, by a hand on its way to put the fag in his mouth. He puffed while it was still unlit, waved it about in his lips as she searched for a box of matches. Her dad bought a lighter at work which went nearly every time.

'I ain't got any.' She wanted a lighter for herself. Maybe she would buy one when the war was over, after she had got a bike and a handbag.

His face was misery, and she was tempted to laugh, till she thought he might not be acting. But he was. His eyes almost closed, and his eyebrows went down to his nose. She had a photo of Robert Donat from Picturegoer under her mattress that she took out and looked at with her flashlight before going to sleep. He stretched his arms out wide, smacked his head—even louder than the woman who'd slapped her grizzling kid—undid his top pocket, searched half a minute as if expecting to find a leg of beef there, and fetched a single match out in his fingers. Then his smile was as big as the bridge.

She shivered when he looked at her, and at the lit match between his eyes. 'I'm Italian,' he said, 'prisoner of war—collaborator now.'

He's come a long way, she supposed—watching the lantern made with cupped hands, and then smoke as he put his head almost inside as if he was going to cook it. The dead match somersaulted over the parapet, and she thought she heard a sizzle as it hit the water and was carried away. It'll be in the sea by morning, she didn't wonder.

A man who'd lived next door chucked himself over into the water last year, and drowned. They found the body near Colwick Weir. He'd gone to the doctor's with a sore throat thinking it was cancer, and when the doctor said it was nothing to worry about he thought he was only trying to hide it from him, so did himself in because he'd seen his mother die of it two years ago. There'd been nothing wrong with him at all, except that he'd gone off his head.

He held his cigarette close to hers. 'Now we walk?'

'You'll have to follow me.' She didn't mind at all when he bowed and took her arm. They said at work that foreigners were well brought up, though she supposed everybody was when they wanted something. But when you didn't think you had much to give it was nice to be bowed to like on the pictures, and smiled at, and walked with arm in arm. You didn't care whether it rained or not. And even without being told, he walked on the side the wind was coming from.

Two ATS girls looked at her gone-out. Seen enough, you nosey bleeders? she'd have said if they had stared a second longer. Officers' comforts was what they called them at work, where the two years spent there seemed as long as since she'd been born, a place where she thought she'd learned enough to last the rest of her life.

People couldn't see who you were with when it got dark, so she was glad when it did. Even when walking with Johnny Towle whom she had once gone out with she hadn't wanted to be seen because it hadn't got anything to do with anybody who she was with, and whether she was happy or not, or what they thought she was doing walking out at night.

He'd hardly said a word since leaving the bridge, and now squeezed her arm and walked in step and, as if realizing that such silence was no way to behave in face of his good luck at having found someone to talk to him, stopped abruptly and faced her. She was glad when he broke into her thoughts:

'My name is Mario. Your name, please?'

'Edie.'

'Edie,' he said, as if that settled something.

'That's right.'

Mario sounded like a woman's name to her.

'Twenty eight years,' he said.

'What?'

'Age.'

She'd thought he was at least thirty.

'I'm sixteen,' she told him.

He said he was learning English and asked would she teach him. She said she couldn't teach anybody anything and that if he listened to her his English wouldn't be much good—though because she had sometimes come top of the class at school, she might try.

He said yes please when she stopped at the smell and mentioned buying fish and chips. At the shop you had to get in and shut the door before an air raid warden spotted the light, and Mario had never seen anyone vanish from his sight so quickly.

He leaned against a wall to wait. He almost went to sleep. How to wait was one of the fine arts of a soldier, and he still found it difficult not to regard himself as one. He also knew after eight years in the army that to receive and to have something done for you bound the person to you who gave or did it. There was no surer way. He had money in his wallet which he couldn't share with this pale dark-haired girl.

He had worked in South Africa, and saved it from his meagre pay, yet it was no use to him here. They had been fetched out of camp and put on a train to take ship for England at such short notice that he hadn't had time to change the two big notes for English money. It was true that the camp sergeants had offered to change them, but their rate was so low that he decided to wait and do it later. When they said you couldn't cash them in England he thought they were lying, but after he got here he found it was so.

The fact that he had been robbed never ceased to bite and hurt. It was only one of many such times that something had been taken from him. All through life you were robbed. At the beginning the greatest act of robbery was when you were taken from the safety of your mother's womb and fobbed off with air that barely allowed you to breathe. Nobody had any choice about that, but the various robberies of life multiplied thereafter, each occasion leaving you more at the world's mercy.

Everything contrived to separate you from that middle area of happiness and dignity. You could never escape the robbery that went on all the time. While you expected to lose watch, shirt, money, or boots (having in any case done your share of robbery whenever you'd had the chance, for it was only the poorest of the poor who never got such opportunities) you didn't expect to be parted from your spirit.

He had been brought up to believe that his spirit was of little value, though he'd never accepted the fact. Even so your beliefs were continually waylaid and overwhelmed, but year by year they had become strong again, till such strength was the only thing of importance. As soon as this was realized your spirit got stronger until nothing could break it at last. It had survived the attacks of church and school, and then worst of all the God-almighty State in the shape of

Mussolini standing on a shield and held aloft by his gang, the man and the Party you were expected to die for as you had once stood in church and been told to adore somebody who was supposed to have died for you—when nobody had a right to die for you except yourself, and what fool would want to do that? He had had enough for the rest of his life, and smiled at the truth that he would never be able to do anything about such assaults while he continued to blame nobody but himself. Being taken as a prisoner of war was the final indignity, but it was also the point from which he had begun to hope.

The fat in the vat was smooth and smokey. The end of your finger would skate if it didn't get scorched. With three people in front she stared at the dark ice starting to split and bubble, and sending up shrouds of lovely mouth-smelling steam when the man poured a wire basked of raw chips in. His scrawny wife who wore glasses and a turban was pulling a handle on spuds that had been peeled white and then fell as neat chips into an enamel bowl.

'Two pennorth o' chips and a couple o' fish, please,' Edie said. She didn't know why she had left Mario outside in the dark, but it wasn't raining so she didn't worry. To be seen with a lad or a man would have made her feel daft, and being with an Italian was as bad as going out with a Yank, she felt, in that people said all sorts of rotten things, and if they didn't say so you could tell what they were thinking, though at work they might have had a bit of a laugh over it. One of the older women could pull a meagrim if you as much as mentioned having a good time before peace was declared, in which case somebody was bound to call out: 'Well, Mrs Smith, it's a bleddy free country, ain't it?'

She hoped he'd be gone, but was glad he wasn't.

'Long time.' He hadn't expected to see her again.

She opened the bundle. 'I had to wait till they was done.'

'Done?'

'Cooked.' It was black but the stars were out, and the smell of vinegar and chips drew her face back to the batter-steam and fish clinging to her fingers. 'You'd better get some, or they'll be gone.'

He picked into the paper, and ate more as if to please her than feed any hunger. 'Good.' His approval seemed like a question. 'Thank you.'

Her smile could not be seen in the dark. 'Lovely, aren't they? They don't fry every night, so we was lucky.'

'You are a good girl.' He spoke solemnly, then laughed at her and at himself. The wall held him up. He leaned as if nobody lived inside the house.

He *is* funny, she told herself, though I don't suppose he'll murder me. 'Let's walk for a bit.'

He held her arm in such a way that it seemed to her as if he was blind or badly and wanted to be led somewhere. 'I was in...', he began.

'In where?' she asked, after a while.

'In where?' she asked, after a while.

Their feet clattered the pavement. A soldier passed. Another man in the dark nearly bumped into them, and stood for a moment as if to say something. He smelled drunk. If it was daylight he might have spoken but if so she'd tell him to get dive-bombed, or to mind his own effing business—whichever was more convenient to his style of life—as they said at work, with more laughs than she could muster at the moment. Mario snorted, as if thinking something similar. 'You're in Nottingham now,' she whispered.

Their feet clattered the pavement. A soldier passed. Another man in the dark nearly bumped into them, and stood for a moment as if to say something. He smelled drunk. If it was daylight he might have spoken but if so she'd tell him to get dive-bombed, or to mind his own effing business—whichever was more convenient to his style of life—as they said at work, with more laughs than she could muster at the moment. Mario snorted, as if thinking something similar. 'You're in Nottingham now,' she whispered.

'Nottingham, I know.' His normal voice made the name sound like the end of the world, and maybe it was, in the blackout, in the Meadows. 'I was in Addis Ababa. You know where that is?'

'I'm not daft. It's Abyssinia, ain't it?'

He laughed, and pressed her arm. She was glad at getting it right, saw a wild land full of black people and high mountains. Or was it jungle? As they turned into Arkwright Street the crumpled chip paper slipped from her other hand. There was always a smell of soot when it got dark, and a stink of parafin from factories. A late trolley bus with lights hardly visible was like a tall thin house rumbling along the cobbles. The Methodist Hall was silent, all doors barred against tramps and ghosts.

'It in't a church,' she said. 'It's a British restaurant. I sometimes eat my dinner there, because it only costs a shilling.'

He seemed to belong to her, even more so when he released her arm and held her hand. At the Midland Station he stopped. 'Not possible to go to centre of city. Not allowed for us.'

She was glad. In Slab Square people would look at them, and talk, and maybe call out. They turned back. She was also angry, because he no longer belonged to her when he couldn't go where he liked. There were different laws for him, so they weren't alone even while walking together in the dark. 'It's daft that we can't go downtown,' she said. 'It's not right.'

He held her hand again, as if to say that he was not blaming her, a warm mauler closing over her fingers. 'Not public houses, either, but cinema we can go.'

Nobody would take any notice if they went and sat on the back row, but it cost more than at the front. Youths would shout out, and there'd be a fight perhaps. 'We can go to the Plaza. That's a nice one.'

He pulled her close into a doorway. He smelt of hair and cloth, and stubbed-out fags—and scent. 'Tomorrow?'

'Don't kiss me, then.'

She couldn't fathom the scent. It wasn't even haircream. His hair was dry. He didn't, and as they walked along wide Queen's Drive towards Wilford Bridge she shared a bar of chocolate and the bag of caramels from her toffee ration. You had to pay a ha'penny if you wanted to cross the Trent there, so they called it Ha'penny Bridge. To her it always seemed the only real way to get out of Nottingham, to leave home and vanish forever into a land and life which could never be as bad as the one she'd felt trapped in since birth. But she had only been taken over to play as a child—or she'd gone across for a walk by herself and come back in half an hour because there didn't seem anywhere to go.

They passed the police station, and three years ago she had stood outside reading lists of dead after the air raid, long white sheets of paper covered in typewritten names. Spots of rain had fallen on them, and people queued to see if anybody was on that they didn't already know about.

Houses were heaps of slates, laths, and bricks. If anybody was dead a Union Jack was sometimes put over. Johnny Towle's name was on the list. She'd only seen him the Sunday before, when they went to

Lenton for a walk. He said he loved her, and sometimes she dreamed about him. A man stopped her when she walked by one smashed house and said: 'Would you believe it? My mother was killed in that house, and I put a flag over it. It ain't there anymore. Somebody's stolen it.' He was wild. He was crying, and she told him before hurrying away: 'They'd nick owt, wouldn't they?'

She wanted Mario to talk because she didn't know what else to say after telling everything that had been in her mind, but he wouldn't. He didn't understand when she said: 'A penny for your thoughts!' Everybody must have something in their heads, but he only wanted to walk, and listen to her, asking her now and again to explain a word he didn't know.

Before reaching the bridge she said: 'Let's turn round.' The thought of water frightened her, and she had no intention of crossing to the other side. Their footsteps echoed, and she was glad when she heard others.

'After Abyssinia'—his voice startled her—'go to South Africa. A long way. Then to England. Soon, Italy, when war is finished. I go to work. War is no good.'

'What will you do?'

'I do business.' He rubbed his fingers so hard that she heard chafing skin before actually looking towards it. '*Affari!*' he said, and she could tell it made him cheerful to say it, the first Italian word she had learned.

'*Affari!*' she echoed him. 'Business!'—so that she also laughed. 'I like that word—*affari*.' She would remember it because it sounded *real*. It was good to do business. Two years ago pennies were short for putting in gas and electric meters, so she and Amy did business by standing on street corners selling five pennies for a sixpenny bit. Some people told them to bogger off, but others were glad to buy. Then a copper sent them away, and she daren't do it again, though Amy did it with somebody else. She used to collect milk money at school so she could always get the pennies. Mario laughed when she told him about it.

'*Affari?*' she said.

'Yes, *affari!*'

She knew nothing about him, but liked him because even English wasn't his language, and he had been all over the world. Unlike the lads at work, he was interesting. She took out another cigarette and, embarrassed for him at having to accept it said, hoping he wouldn't be offended: 'Ain't you got any?'

'No. We are paid sixpence a day. Italian collaborators work. Pay tomorrow, so we go to cinema, both, eh?'

They stood close so as to coax the cigarettes alight. 'You've got a one-track mind,' she said.

'You teach me English!'

On Arkwright Street they turned back towards Trent Bridge. She still wondered whether he was having her on. 'You know it already.'

'I learn. But speech makes practice. Good for *affari!*'

She laughed. He was funny. 'If you like. Pictures, then, tomorrow night?'

'Pictures? Museum?'

She knew it couldn't be hard for him to understand what was said because she'd never been able to talk as if she had swallowed the dictionary. 'No. Pictures means cinema. Same thing.'

She didn't want to lose him, but felt a bit sick after she had agreed. They said at work she never talked, not deep dark Edie Clipston at her sewing and seaming machine earning fifty bob a week. But she did—when nothing else seemed possible. The lad who humped work to and from the machine tried to kiss her, and she threatened him with the scissors, but she let him last Christmas when somebody held mistletoe over them.

'It didn't mean anything, though,' she told Mario as they stood on the bridge. He had a watch, and said it was half past nine. He had to be in by ten, so pressed her hands hard, and kissed one quickly.

He walked away and she forgot all about him. She didn't know what he looked like, and wondered if she would recognize his face on meeting him again. But she felt as if the cobbles had fur on them as she walked back to Muskham Street.

Hearing no noise through the door she tried the knob and was able to go in, glad the house was empty. She filled the kettle and lit the gas. The cat rubbed against her ankle.

'Gerroff, you've had yer supper already.' It followed her around the room, mewing, so she gave it a saucer of bread and milk. Then she put coal on the fire. When they got back from the boozer they might wonder why she'd done so, but she didn't care what they thought.

Her father was tall and thin, and worked on a machine at the gun factory. He took his cap and jacket off and threw them across to the sofa. 'Pour me some tea, duck.'

Her mother came in a few minutes afterwards, pale like Edie but her face thinner and more worn. She took off her brown coat with its fur collar and put it on a hanger behind the stairfoot door. 'What did you bank the fire up for?'

'It's cold.'

'It is when you stand in a queue to buy the coal.'

She sat by the glow to warm her hands. Her legs were mottled already from sitting too close too often. She had never queued for coal, anyway, because a delivery man emptied a hundredweight bag outside the back door every week.

'Kids don't understand,' her father nodded at the teapot. 'Let's have some, then.'

Joel Clipston had once spent four months in quad for 'causing grievous bodily harm' to a man who, wilting under opinionated hammerblows of logic during an argument on politics had called Joel's wife a foul name as the only way—so he thought—of stopping his gallop and getting back at him. Joel had kept silent in court, ashamed to say out loud what the man had called Ellen, and so he had no defence against having half-killed somebody while waiting for opening time outside a pub one Sunday morning. He said nothing to the magistrate, and got sent down for 'such a vicious attack.' There are worse places than Lincoln, he said when he came out, though he was more or less cured of ever doing anything to get sent there again. For a while he roamed the streets looking for the man who had called Ellen a prostitute, but then heard he had gone into the army. If he don't get killed I'll wait for him when he comes out, soldier or not.

He lost his job over the court case, but now that the war had started it was easy to get another. He was set to digging trenches on open ground for people to run into from nearby houses when aeroplanes came over from Germany. If he worked twelve hours a day he made more money than he'd ever had in his pocket before. Then he got work as a mechanic, and found he was good at it. There was either no work at all, or there was too much, but never exactly as much as you needed. He preferred to read newspapers, play draughts, sit listening to the wireless with a mug of tea in his hand, or spend a few hours in the boozer, rather than work more time than he thought necessary—war or not.

They sometimes went over the river at Ha'penny Bridge and into the fields beyond Wilford. In spring Ellen baked lemon curd tarts and made sandwiches, and Joel filled two quart bottles with tea for a picnic by Fairham Brook. The air seemed fresher beyond Wilford village, where the smell of water lingered from the river which rounded it on three sides.

Even though her brother Henry was younger he chased Edie with a stick, till the end of it flicked her, so she turned round and threw it into the river and both of them watched it float away like a boat. Joel was glad they got on so well. Henry was squat-faced and fair, while Edie was dark-haired and had olive skin like her mother.

Edie poured tea into his own big white mug, and put in a whole spoon of sugar. 'When the war's over,' he said, 'I'll get half a ton of sugar from the shop. Then I can put three spoons in. You can't even taste one.'

'Pour me a cup as well, duck,' her mother said. 'Where did you go tonight?'

Edie took the tea-cosey off. 'A walk.'

Her legs ached as well as her back. It seemed a long way that she had gone, though she remembered every place as close enough—but far off all the same when somebody talked to you who had seen so much of the world, and then kissed your hand. The pot was poised over the cup and saucer.

'Where to?' Ellen asked.

'I just went out.' She wondered what else there was to say, for it didn't concern anyone where she had been, and tonight she felt no connection to her mother or father, nor would she to Henry when he came in.

'Sly little bleeder!'

Joel tapped at the bars with a poker. 'You'll never get a straight answer from her.'

It had been the same ever since she was born, that if one of them started to get on at her, the other would always join in. She had the feeling that they knew where she had been, and wanted to drag her out of it and back to what she had always hated. She didn't know how they could tell, but was sure they'd twigged something.

'You ought to stay in at least one night of the week.' Her mother stood up to cut bread for Joel's lunch next day. 'And clean the house up a bit. I have enough to do as it is when I get home from work.'

She had also noticed, as soon as they came in, that both of them smelled of beer. 'I go to work as well,' she reminded her mother, knowing that as soon as she spoke they would have succeeded in pulling her out of her dreams. But she'd never say who she had been with. She brought more than two pounds into the house every week, which seemed enough for them to get out of her. 'I scrubbed the parlour floor last Sunday, didn't I?'

Hot tea sprayed over the saucer and the cloth, and the pot rolled itself onto the floor before she could stop it. The cup broke with the weight of the big brown teapot. She didn't know how. Dropped onto it. The noise shocked every bone, and she stood with fingers curled as if the pot were still gripped—or as if, should she keep them held like that, the teapot bits would reassemble and jump back into place.

In spite of her mother saying that she was always in a dream, that she was as daft as they come, that she had never known anybody to be so clumsy—and several other remarks that she wouldn't listen to but that would come back to her later when, she knew, she would have even less use for them—she felt that if there had been a hammer close enough she would have lifted it and smashed the remains of the teapot and cup to smithereens.

But she didn't care as she looked at the bits of pot mixed among the tealeaves and stains. She remembered Mario's face by the bridge, when he had taken the cigarette and put a hand over while lighting it, as close as if the whole meeting was happening bit by bit again. She saw both herself and him as real and plain as ever, the pair of them right by her side. The picture hypnotized her, and held her rigid with surprise and a feeling that gave some protection for what was sure to come now that she had smashed the teapot.

'She allus was clumsy,' her father put in, a mild response which told her to be on her guard. The jollier they were on coming home from the pub only meant that they would be nastier and more hateful later. It was best to be out of their way at such times, but unless you went to bed there was nowhere to take refuge, and she didn't want to go to sleep so early after talking to Mario.

'I couldn't help it.' She heard the tone of fear, apology, and shame, which made her more angry with herself than at dropping the teapot. The accident didn't seem important, anyway. She wasn't a bit clumsy at work. 'My fingers slipped.'

Her father put his half drunk mug of tea on the mantle shelf, as if it would be safe from her there. 'What am I going to do in the morning, then? There's nowt to make the tea in.'

If she looked up he would hit her, but in turning away she saw his grey eyes lifeless with anger, and his lips tight. Ellen picked a few bits of the saucer from the cloth.

'Let *her* do it,' Joel said quietly. 'She dropped the bleddy thing.'

He sometimes chased her and Henry around the room in fun. All three laughed, but Ellen looked on as if thinking they should act their age and have more sense. But the last time Joel had been playful they suddenly felt too old for it. The time had passed when they could play together.

Edie sometimes said things without thinking, and when she did she was frightened. If she had known beforehand that she was going to be frightened she would still have spoken because she was never able to stop herself even when she thought about it. The words seemed to jump from outside of her: 'I'm not going to clear it up.'

He sat down with his tea, and she felt sorry she had cheeked him, so picked some brown sharp pieces of the teapot to put in a little heap on the corner of the table. This methodical enjoyment of her task caused a flash of rage to blot out Joel's brain. Edie knew it was only right that she should try to clear the mess up, though her mother had already done most of it, and had come back from the coal place with a dustpan to start clattering bits onto it.

It couldn't have been worse if a ten-ton bomb had dropped on the place and killed them. All because of a teapot, Edie told herself, about to cry, as if she alone in her might and viciousness had broken the spirit of the house. There was such gloom that, after a few moments, the only thing possible was to laugh. She wanted to be walking again with Mario—while doubting that she ever would—crossing a bright green field with him, under a pale sky full of sunshine instead of bombers.

It was as if her father had picked up the wall and hit the side of her face with it. She wondered how he knew what she had been thinking. The blow threw her across the room, and coconut matting scraped her skin as she slid with eyes closed and banged her head at the skirting board. In darkness she saw nothing, but it was followed by a dazzle of blue lights as his boot came at her.

When her father lashed out like this her mother always got on at him to have more sense, and now she tried to pull him off, telling him not to be stupid or he'd get in trouble knocking her about like that, thinking of the times he'd pasted her, Edie supposed, but then wondering if she interfered out of spite, because he only answered by giving her another kick that was worse than the rest.

As she lay half stunned Edie knew she would go to the bridge again and meet him as often as she liked because he had been so gentle and interesting. They didn't know, but even if they did they couldn't stop her seeing somebody who made her feel she need never be anybody except herself.

After a parting half-hearted kick at her back which she hardly felt, her father sat down to light his pipe and finish his tea, ignoring her agonized and shouted out wish that it would choke him.

The drawn curtains in her room made the black out complete, but when she put off the light it was so dark she couldn't go to sleep. She ached from the last big kick but cried no more, not even when she hoped a German plane would drop a single bomb on them and make the black out so final that they would never be able to switch a light on again.

She'd die of shame if daylight ever came, but if it did, she would never let anybody hit her again. If her father lost his temper and tried to, she would blind him with whatever she could grab. That sort of thing was finished from now on. She didn't know how, yet knew it was, because she had made up her mind, hoping that when it looked like happening she would be able to remember what she had made up her mind to do, and blind him no matter what.

She heard them arguing downstairs, though not what was said. Their speech sounded like the flood of a river hitting a bridge before going underneath. Now that she wasn't there they could start on each other. They could kill each other for all she cared. They had been cat-and-dogging it for as long as she could remember, but no wonder when she thought about what her mother used to get up to.

When dad was out of work—she would tell Mario (whether he could understand or not, because if you didn't tell your thoughts to somebody there was no point in living) which went on for years and years—mam kept going down town at night saying she was off to Aunt Joan's, but one day after she'd bought some new shoes and a coat, and things for the house as well, and wouldn't say where she had got the money, dad followed and saw her on Long Row talking to somebody in a car.

He felt so rotten at the idea of her picking up men that he hadn't got the guts to put a stop to it. He didn't even let on he knew, though she must have known he did. But one night, after it had gone on for a long time, he decided he'd had enough, and caught her sitting in Yates's Wine Lodge as large as life with a man who'd had his nose blown off in the last war. Where the nose should have been there was wrinkled skin and two small holes that dripped if he didn't press a hanky to it.

When dad saw this he let his fists fall, but swore at them both and told mam never to come home again or he would murder her and the kids and then cut his own throat. Me and Henry liked what happened, because dad didn't even shout at us now she wasn't there. He pawned her clothes one day, and took us on a trackless into town and treated us to the pictures and an ice-cream each with the money. The woman who lived next door often gave us toffees when we came home from school because she was sorry for us having no mother. It made us feel like orphans, and we liked that.

We were drinking tea and eating toast one night when somebody knocked at the door. The tap on wood was soft, as if a beggar was hoping we'd ask him in and give him some of our supper, and when dad opened it we were surprised to see old No-nose come in from the cold. Dad was mad at being disturbed from his newspaper and his peace, but No-nose asked: 'I want to know if you'll be kind and take your Ellen back.'

'Take bloody *who* back?'

'Your Ellen,' No-nose said.

Dad stood by the mantelpiece, as if ready to crank his arm up for a real good punch. No-nose stayed just in the door. He wore a nicky-hat and was wrapped up in a good topcoat and scarf—as well as gloves—because he had an office job and was better off than us. He would have been good looking if he'd still had a nose.

Me and Henry was too frightened to say anything, and when dad, after a bit of an argument in which nobody said much, said that mam could come back if she liked, No-nose looked as happy as if his nose had come back onto his face, which made us want to laugh—though we daren't in case dad turned on us.

He went out to get mam. She'd been standing at the end of the street waiting for him to come and tell her whether it was all right or not. No-nose gave us some chocolates and sixpence each, then went away after shaking dad's hand but saying not a word to mam. He only nodded at her, as if he'd had enough of the trouble she'd caused—though he was to blame as well.

When he'd gone mam sat on the other side of the fireplace to dad. They scowled at each other for half an hour. Then mam laughed, and dad said a string of foul words. He's going to get the chopper and kill her, I thought, but suddenly he was laughing and so was she. Me and Henry was even more frightened at that, and said nothing, because we weren't able to make things out at all.

Mam and dad kissed, and sent us to buy a parcel of fish and chips out of the few quid that No-nose had given her. Afterwards we had a good supper, and everybody was supposed to be happy, though I wondered how long it would last.

When Edie started to feel more sorry for them than for herself she fell asleep.

With her coat tight-wrapped around her, and holding Mario's two South African banknotes folded into her pocket, Edie went downtown into Gamston's Travel Agency to try and change them for him. She was glad that only one other person was being served as she opened the notes out and showed them over the counter, feeling daft because she had not been in the place before.

'Can't change 'em,' the bloke said, an old man with a moustache who first looked over his glasses at them and then at her.

'Why can't you?' Money was money, she'd always thought, and Mario had earned every penny of whatever it was called.

He held a pen, as if about to write all over her face. 'Because we can't. We're not allowed to, that's why.'

She stood, hoping he'd alter his mind, whether they were supposed to or not. 'Oh.'

'We can't, anyway. It's regulations.'

He went to get a railway ticket for somebody but, not wanting to leave without doing what she had come for, she didn't move. Last night Mario had showed her some photographs of his mother and sister, and his two brothers, and they all looked as nice as Mario himself, and she felt that if she couldn't get his cash changed she'd be letting them down as well as him. So she held up the large gaudy-coloured banknotes again.

The man came back. 'There's nothing I can do for you. It's foreign money, and there's a war on, and that's why we can't change it. Come in after the war, then it might be all right!'

'It'll be too late, then. I need it now.'

A woman behind the counter put a cup of tea by his elbow, and maybe he didn't want to let it get cold because he said, as if ready to fetch the police to her: 'Where did you get 'em from?'

She saw by his face, and knew from his tone, that he thought she had nicked them or—she screwed the words painfully into her mind—earned them like *that*. Her mouth filled with swearing, but she couldn't spit it at him as he deserved, so walked out and then went quickly along Parliament Street towards a cafe where she could get a cup of tea.

The sun was in her eyes so she turned her back to it. When Mario walked onto the bridge she gave him the banknotes: 'Sorry.'

'No *affari*?'

'The bleeders wouldn't do it.'

He scowled. 'Bleeders?'

She explained.

'Never mind.'

Neither spoke for half an hour. They walked by rowing boats tied to wooden landing stages, and she wondered when and at what place they would reach the sea if she and Mario got into one of them. Maybe they'd land on a beach in Italy, and have no more trouble from anybody.

He held her hand tightly, so she knew he was brooding about something which it was no use asking him to explain. But he didn't seem angry. He was miles away, living in sounds and colours she had no hope of understanding, though she liked the warm and dreamy feeling when she tried to picture them. With an English bloke she wouldn't have had such dreams. They'd have joshed and teased like kids—whereas with Mario she saw mountains and yellow trees, and a sky so blue it would blind you if you looked straight at it. But she didn't want to because her dream was too far beyond her normal mind. You had to be grateful for small mercies, and this was bigger than most.

Grey water slopped at the concrete steps. There was a noise of children playing from the other side of the river. She felt easy with him because, though he had suffered and was far from home, he had a light heart and could make her laugh. But she took his larger hand in order to share his bitterness, and let whatever he felt was too much to bear pass into her. She had always known that there were some things you could only keep quiet about, though realized now that the one way of filling such silence was by touch.

The streak of green and blue turned into the last flush of the day. Children stopped playing suddenly. They were alone on the embankment with no one to see them. Not that she cared. She'd hold his hand whoever was looking on. They could take a running jump at themselves for all she'd bother. Once upon a time she had clutched her father's hand, but she hadn't spoken to that bully for days.

'Never mind,' she said to Mario. 'They're dirty robbers, that's what they are.'

Her whole body shook when he kissed her, and she could never remember feeling so protected.

'I love you,' he said.

She didn't know how to say anything. To speak like that seemed a funny way of putting it, though. They walked on, and she couldn't find words to answer, even when he said it again. It was time to say goodnight, and promise to meet another day, but she couldn't stop walking and say anything while still so close to that total change already made between leaving home and meeting him. To walk away from the comfort of holding hands seemed neither right nor possible.

She still felt stupid at not having got some English money for his foreign bank-notes, but it was a failure that brought them closer, and made her want to stay longer with him, so that she was almost glad they'd been so rotten to her at the travel agents'.

A policeman stood talking to the woman toll keeper who leaned by a tiny brick house to collect money from any carts or motors that went over Ha'penny Bridge.

'Not go there,' Mario said.

There was plenty of dusk to hide in, so she wondered what he meant. They were on the lowest step by the water which, had it come up another inch, would have flowed over her shoes. 'It don't matter, does it?'

'In camp at ten. No Italian out after ten o'clock.'

It was too late, anyway. The world was full of trouble when you did things that caused no harm. She wondered who started it, but didn't know. If Mario walked about after ten at night it wouldn't stop the day beginning tomorrow. 'Will you get shouted at?'

He smiled. 'I have given sergeant money. But the police don't know, and they ask for papers, maybe, then send me back, and tell Captain. Then Mario will not walk with Edie for three weeks.'

If they crossed Ha'penny Bridge to the fields they'd be safe from prying eyes—and from having to make up their minds to go anywhere. He pressed his face to her hair, and said things she didn't understand but that she was happy to hear. She was also glad she had washed her hair last night.

He led her up the steps and back to the roadway. 'Police gone now,' he whispered.

She took two ha'pennies from her pocket. The old woman at the gate wore a thick coat and scarf to keep out the damp. The river pushed itself forcefully along, and the other side seemed far off from where they stood. The noise of a cow sounded from the fields.

The tollkeeper took her ha'pennies. 'You'd better be back before twelve.'

'Are you going to wind up the bridge, then?' Edie asked, thinking that coming back was too far in the future to worry about.

'Cheeky young devil!' the old woman called.

A sliver of sharp moon showed as if about to come down and cut the river to ribbons. But there were streaks of night mist towards Beeston, and white stars glittered above. Halfway over, Mario said: 'You give her money?'

'Only a penny. It's a *toll* bridge.'

'Toll?'

'Money to pay,' she said. 'Somebody private owns it.'

He walked more quickly. 'Not good.'

'It's always been like that.'

Her arm was folded with his so she had to keep pace. A plane flew over. 'One crashed last year. An American plane. The pilot knew a woman in a house at Wilford. He went over ever so low to wave at her. But he crashed, and everybody in the plane was killed.'

She didn't know whether he understood. It didn't seem to matter, but she went on: 'Five men died, and all for nothing. The pilot had wanted to say hello to his girl. And now she would wear black for evermore because he was dead. And she had a baby afterwards and they couldn't get married. She'd seen his plane blow up when it hit a tree with no leaves on in the middle of a field.'

'Bad story,' he said.

At the end of the bridge they walked down the lane, no lights showing from any house. They were used to the dark. She didn't know on which field the plane had crashed, but perhaps it was near Fairham Brook where she used to play with Henry when they went on picnics from Albion Yard. At work they'd said what a shame it was, and wondered whether the poor girl would ever get over it, and what would happen to her baby if she didn't, because she was packed off to live with her grandmother in Huntingdonshire. Others heard she'd killed herself, but all sorts of rumours flew about, and you couldn't believe anything, though she wouldn't be surprised.

When he stopped singing it was only to kiss her hand. She heard the grating cry of a crow from the river that looped on three sides of them. She liked his tune, and would have sung a bit herself if she had known it, though she was happy enough to listen as they went through the village that seemed dead to the world and into a field where they would stay till the bombers came home.

Emma Tennant
Alice fell

Mr Paxton went down to the river. It was late on a spring evening. He went without looking back—at the house, where the Old Man held like a clam to the greater proportion of corridors and half-furnished rooms—at the bright window above the back-door that was frame to the midwife's busyings. He walked with purpose, and nervously. Tall irises, machete-shaped, fell under his feet.

At that hour, the Old Man saw his friends. Something in the acid blue of the air, the yellow irises like lights on the river, the smell of blossom, intoxicated the Old Man and made him think of his youth. His arms rose and fell, as if he were conducting. He bowed to his friends Molly and Pam and rushed them to the window, so they could see the stars stiched above the vague apartment blocks, blocks of darker colour round the house as deep as the trunks of trees.

In the spring that Mr Paxton went down to the river, and the midwife made ready above the back-door, the Old Man showed no sign that anything new was happening in the house. He moved around in his part of it carelessly, like a troll in a great bed. He called for Mrs Paxton, and showed no surprise when only her husband came.

On this night, while Anthony Eden pronounced on the Suez crisis and the Old Man spoke to Molly and Pam, and there was a bear market which would have no effect on Mr Paxton because he owned no shares, and rockets were being constructed that would one day go to the moon, Mr Paxton arrived at his destination of the river and the moon came up behind him. The moon also shone in the window where the midwife stood black against the light. Over the Old Man's part of the house the stars vanished in dust as he pointed them out to the visitors. A mist came up over the river. Now the Old Man wanted ice for the drinks, and he went to the kitchen, not knowing what he would find.

Mrs Grogan the midwife laughed when she was asked to produce ice. She was doing different things with water: drawing hot clouds from the kettle which turned to tears on the walls, pressing towels damped with the precious hot water, folding newspapers that took a sudden boldness at the water's touch. She was about to carry the whole lot up the stairs behind the kitchen. Mrs Paxton lay in the room there, between the shadow of the ash tree on the wall, and the window, and the moon. Mrs Grogan flung open the kitchen door before leaving.

'Go and get it for yourself,' she said.

Mrs Grogan had no need to show politeness to the Old Man. She was here as a favour for Mrs Paxton. She had known Mr and Mrs Paxton in the old days, when Mr Paxton had been in the chemist's in the small town, before he got nervous and came to work for the Old Man. Mrs Grogan had watched Mr Paxton pouring red and yellow streams into bottles, and then when it was all tablets and capsules she had talked to Mr Paxton as he slid them into perspex containers. She had no respect at all for the Old Man. He lingered in the house of his birth when long ago he should have been out in the world, or been at sea or war. If the Old Man came to the kitchen, in his folly assuming there would be eggs in a brown basket on the table, and that by some process they would leap to the pan and make a supper for him, she snorted in contempt.

In the room where Mrs Paxton waited for Mrs Grogan, the lamp had been turned off. Agony belonged to night and would take advantage of the union, increase the whirligig of pain. In the dark, from where Mrs Paxton could see, the room was nevertheless invaded in three ways by light. The moon floated in the open upper window and too close. Mrs Paxton saw it on a steel tripod, examining with a critical eye the humps of her mountain body; then the moon on the ash tree made a white, ghostly rectangle on the wall opposite the bed; and once again the moon, reflected in the Old Man's bedroom window opposite, came in on the rebound and cut her down the middle carelessly, as she lay waiting for the hot water and towels.

Mrs Grogan climbed the stairs. As the Old Man went on with his conversation, his arabesque with the past, the house turned in darkness to the tops of the trees and the downs. The tops of the trees and the downs moved towards the house in the darkness. They rose above Mr Paxton as he walked to the river. The moon, too, passed over Mr Paxton. The downs above the house and the water-meadows to the south of the river, as they pulled the house and trees with them into night, had as little sense of the impending birth of the Paxtons' child as the Old Man. Only Mr Paxton knew something was going to happen. But he couldn't see exactly what.

The Old Man took the ice and went to sit with Molly and Pam in the room furthest away from the stables, and the Paxtons' part of the house. In wresting the ice from its tray, his fingers had wrinkled and the nails were water frozen to the bone. A tapestry woven with blue wools, and showing the pained eyes and long tresses of the women loved by the Symbolists, hung on the wall behind him.

Mrs Grogan arrived in Mrs Paxton's room. The three lines of light came out to her, and, swaying with her kettle, she nearly lost her step and fell into the web. She went with care to Mrs Paxton. She wanted to draw the child, smocked in white cream from the womb, into the world. Mrs Grogan turned on the light and knelt down by the bed. When she looked up she saw only the moon, and the ash tree upright outside the window, in a silver forceps over the bed.

Now the light was on in Mrs Paxton's room, a bowl went down and water from the kettle was poured in.

'Up she comes' and 'Push!' Mrs Grogan was saying. 'What a farmyard! Move the farmyard, Mrs Paxton!'

Mrs Paxton saw a fairy feast, tightly enclosed behind her red throbbing eyes. There was dancing, and every so often a shower of red balloons sprang out over the dancers and exploded in the air. In the clasp of her body, she felt feet tramp through halls where the roof was pulled down and down. Soon the roof would come right down on the tables, and crush the metal spoons, and then she would be shot out, like a woman from a cannon, into the void. Her body heaved and shuddered. It was a fight to the death between the woman and the child.

Mrs Grogan had bowls of water all round the bed. She sponged the new mother's face, which looked garish and unreal, a painted face of the dead at the entrance to the tomb. She laid newspapers under the vaults of Mrs Paxton. Despite the drama, Mrs Grogan thought of her own daughter who was coming over from the other side of the world, and how that girl should never have married Bob and fallen down there, and how she would be in time for the daffodils. It was unlikely to Mrs Grogan that there were such things as daffodils on the other side of the world. Only white flowers could grow there, very probably, as it was so dark.

Mrs Paxton groaned, and water came from her. Newspapers were flooded and Mrs Grogan rushed to change them: Suez Crisis and *Woman's Own* and in a last rush an old *Picture Post*. Winston Churchill was pushed under Mrs Paxton's monumental legs and lay in the water. His face frowned, and dissolved. 'Push down!' shouted Mrs Grogan.

Mr Paxton arrived at the edge of the river. The moon had completely deserted him and without light his hearing had grown foggy so he didn't hear the moans from his wife as her waters broke. He stared out anxiously instead across the river. He might have been expecting a visitor from the other shore. Mr Paxton tried to see the opposite bank, but mist obscured his view. He lit a match once, and saw his feet helpless in mud. In his sudden aura he stood in a dome of glass. Mr Paxton felt his absolute lack of necessity. He stood still in his crumpled suit until the match went out. The mist had taken perspective from his sight, but he was still waiting for something. Reeds flanked him, like an army of porcupines. The black river flowed invisibly under his feet.

Mist rose in furrows in the ground. In the cold spring night the earth breathed white steam, from the great flat mouth of the earth that was buried under grass and poplars. Mist took away the borders of the river and changed it to sea.

Mr Paxton looked out in expectation. He was the last man of the old world. He saw sails of a ship in the mist. Then he thought he saw the swan that lived in the bend in the river, coming towards him over the sea with mist-furled wings. He was the last man who could read the writing of the old world. Mud under his feet changed to sand, and the reeds, dipped in the ink-black sea, wrote for him on the white sand. The floating strands of mist took the messages out over the water again, and still Mr Paxton peered, hand over his eyes, a man lost at sea in a mist.

What was in the chest?

The chest lay at Mr Paxton's feet. It had come out of the sea. Mr Paxton thought of all the diseases that might be in it, or sea-serpents that would wriggle over his feet.

Mr Paxton opened the chest. It was small, bound with rope, and dry inside. He lifted out the infant. There was a letter pinned to the infant's dress. Mr Paxton could read the writing. The note said the infant had been abandoned. Mr Paxton couldn't read the signature. He set off for the house, holding the infant. As he got near to the house he heard Mrs Grogan's voice, leaping from Mrs Paxton's window to the ash tree and hanging in a string of vowels in the line between the ash tree and the moon.

That was how it was known the child had been born. Mr Paxton had a piece of paper, which told him he had custody of this daughter. She was not his, how could she be his, and although there was no paper to inform him of the day he would have to part with her, he saw the day quite clearly, as he stood in Mrs Paxton's room, and he even saw the man who would come to claim her.

Mrs Paxton was alone and free, beside the burst bubble of water where her daughter had lived. She was bled out, and Mrs Grogan had cut the cord and tied the remains of it in the shape of a piglet's tail. Mrs Paxton lay on her side, as if expecting the infant to climb up to a row of nipples. Mrs Grogan, packing a bag, said she would accept a lift from Mr Paxton and would collect the bicycle tomorrow. Mr Paxton went after her, walking on the tips of his toes. Mrs Paxton was supposed to be sleeping, and so was the infant, in its chest in the corner.

The Old Man's house grew silent with the going of Mr Paxton and Mrs Grogan, and it absorbed the existence of the child. There was silence, and the Old Man went to bed in absolute silence, as if taking the punishment for his earlier flippancy. For all the millions already in the world, something had happened. Mrs Paxton lay still, as if it were she who had had her lifeline severed. And the moon turned a fuller face down on her, spoon-feeding Mrs Paxton as she lay breathing softly on the bed.

*A*t this time, when England was trying to hold on, to keep what remained to it of the imperial dignity of the past, the first beat of a new sound came over the downs and the Old Man stood aghast at the window. He heard wailing, and a totemic beat, as the first sound of men brought up not to fight came in its loud lamentation from the woods, and the Old Stones danced on the radio. And he turned to speak to Mrs Grogan, who had come into the room to clean: he spoke of the collapse of belief in civilisation between the wars, and the wreck of all the sacred spaces, from industrialisation and this search for equality, and the people everywhere, in caravans and each moment losing the desire to fight for king and country. Now he wanted to know where this din came from. But Mrs Grogan wasn't sure. She didn't like the new race of young men, in black leather jackets and badgers' faces. She disliked the way they hung around Ella, and said they'd take her off to the pier at Brighton, where they would stomp, and menace, and hold her up against the palisade.

The Old Man watched Mrs Grogan intently as she continued her dusting of the room with the blue tapestry. He felt the spring relayed to him in an unacceptable manner. He wanted slow buds unfolding and a harmless appearance of green leaf, a ragged bunting in the trees, fairy lights set up crooked in the chestnuts. He was sent instead this raw pulse of young men stretching and shooting into idleness.

Mr Paxton was an anxious father in the spring of the birth of the child. He thought the child needed a ball at the end of the crib, and that without it, the endless minutes in her days would go unremarked, pile up, until after an avalanche of unrecorded time she would emerge suddenly old. He had no way of trusting Mrs Paxton's knowledge of time, which was measured off with knitting needles and the thud of the arrival on the kitchen table of a cup of tea. He said, if the ball could be got, everything would be at normal again, like before.

Ella, as she went about repairing an old pram found in one of the disused lower rooms, was hardly inclined to agree with this. She had long ago set her clock to be with Bob at the other side of the world, and his minutes marched against hers. There, leaves were falling and settling into the earth. She had no interest in the pushing up of shoots, because even the deepest of them could in no way come out the other side and tie a tendril about the neck of her Bob. Buds were the same: Ella looked at them as if they were warheads. She pushed the pram with the child lying folded inside shawls, over the wrong side of the earth. In the thicket down by the river she searched for a hole in the mulch of old leaves. There had been an air-raid shelter in that spot once, Mr Paxton said. It was deep, so if the Germans had come they would have seen nothing and flown away again. Ella was rash in wanting to jump into that roofless house, with walls of leaves, as if she hoped to dive into a cellar where Bob lay waiting. She was bound to upset the child one day. Mr Paxton swore he would keep a strict eye on Ella, and that he would find a ball.

With the reluctance and artificiality of the spring Molly and Pam came more and more often; and this the Old Man hated, for now he wanted to be alone. The plastics that had sprouted after the war in his new quarters at the top of the house where the Paxtons placed units with imitation wood handles and linos in triangles of black and white made the Old Man gaze at his surroundings in misery. There was nothing he could feel for here. He listened with a dull expression while Molly and Pam prattled of the new luxuries that had come at last to this country where they had been obliged for so long to wear grey flannel and eat inferior food. He listened gravely, with his arms around his knees, to talk of rhinestones, and planes that worked by jet, and dresses that were 'strapless', held up by a whale under the dress that propelled these new dancers over an ocean of parquet, under marquees of the most exquisite nylon net. The Old Man nodded, hearing of the return of extravagance and waste. 'But you must come up to London with us,' Molly said. 'These are an example,' said Pam, as she took off an ear-ring. 'Wouldn't you think they were real?'

In the shower of over-bright stones that Pam was waving, one broke free and flew out of the window that gave on the garden. But there was a whole spray of stones there, and it went unmissed: 'People put their real jewellery in the bank nowadays,' said Pam, 'and wear rhinestones like this. Don't you think it's wonderful?'

The child may have seen the glass ball as it went over her. The sun had come out, and Mr Paxton was pushing her in the pram, over the grass and white daffodils and primroses. The blue in the sky filled the glass ball, and the child may have looked up and caught its eye, as muddled and blue as hers. But Mr Paxton saw only his child's missing ball: as he raised his head in time to see the sun vanish behind clouds and the clouds come down to enfold the ball, he turned sharply and went after it, as it bounced now in the long grass on the way down the river.

Pam put her ear-ring back in, as Ella ran to the reeds and the boggy land down by the river. She knew where the ball might have led Mr Paxton and his child. Mrs Paxton looked out in surprise, from the kitchen, as she rolled pastry and scrumpled it up again.

Mr Paxton had put flowers in the pram. Ella saw the flowers, the white flowers of that spring, on the water near the swan's nest. The child and her father were nowhere to be seen. The pram was overturned and empty, like an old piece of scrap-metal on that river bank. Behind her, the Old Man strolled with Molly and Pam, out to take some air of the cold, late spring. The Old Man nodded in pleasure, at seeing the transmutation of the ball, the ball which had led Mr Paxton into danger and therefore the infant too, perhaps killing it, so he would no longer have to put up with its unacceptable, unnameable existence. The Old Man imagined the infant under the water, where it had sunk in the ooze, dropped by its father as he tried to swim over to retrieve the ball. He hoped Mr Paxton would rise soon, shaking himself and cold with the black water, on the far bank, and would care for him as he had in earlier days, bringing magazines and a silver pot of coffee out to a hammock under lilac in the garden. So the Old Man looked intently at the egg in the swan's nest in the middle of the river. He looked at the white ball of shell that had hung at Molly's ear as a false diamond, and had measured the days at the end of the infant's cot in an orb of white wool. And he pointed it out to Molly and Pam, but they looked away in scorn. A swan's egg had no place in their new world—of square blocks going up in the mess left by the war, and chemicals that grew into diamonds without even having to enter the crust of the earth.

Mr Paxton's cries could be heard from the wood. Molly and Pam went fussily after the Old Man, and with their heels speared dockets of dead leaves. They wanted the sun, which would turn the white flowers gold, and not the clumps of bamboo rising to damp beech and alder. By the lair in which the Old Man and Mr Paxton would have crouched if the bombers had come over, they paused and looked in through gloom the colour of leaf rotted to web. They heard the child wailing in there. And Mr Paxton thrashing about uselessly in the part that was to have been the larder, with cans of soup and an opener in case Mrs Paxton got bombed on the way from the house with a hot meal on a tray. Neither Molly nor Pam nor the Old Man had the slightest desire to scramble in the leaves, pulling the victims out.

After Ella had gone down, unblocked the entrance to the larder, and Mr Paxton had come out holding the child, and had had to look Ella in the eye and thank her for rescuing him from her own stupid accident, Mr Paxton was never so certain again of his rightness in handling matters concerning his family. He left the ball alone, and gave no advice to Mrs Paxton. But the fall provided the Old Man with some amusement. For, as the child was lifted from the hole, and the dying white flowers clenched in her fist turned yellow in the sun that poked down through the trees for the first time, the Old Man named her, and accepted the reality of her being in the world. He turned first to Molly and Pam—but they had gone, the sudden coming of the spring was too real for them—and he said: to himself, to the woods: 'Persephone!'

When Alice fell, and the Old Man walked back to the house alone, he went at a slow pace and with stooped shoulders. He was suddenly old since acknowledging the existence of the child and witnessing her first fall; made thoughtful by the great confusion of things around him all happening at the same time: the caterwauling on the downs that was birth-shriek to the new age, the end of him and the end of the line ushered in by a child that was female and, despite the changes he could see coming so clearly, unlikely to have any choice other than that of falling. The Old Man went to the furthest room, and looked at the Blue Women and then out of the window at the downs. The sudden arrival of Alice in this house filled him with unease and misgivings. He no longer knew if the women in the tapestry, his tormented idols, had also fallen, from lack of fulfilment, lack of love or ambitions realized, into their attitudes of woven despair. He saw, for a moment as the clouds danced like buffoons before being blown away altogether to the valleys beyond the downs, that Molly and Pam had fallen too in their effort to be independent, to be new. Their faces were hollow with children refused. Under the bright shingle, their mothers' minds raced, and tossed them against the cliffs of insecurity, domestic catastrophe, divorce. And on their slim legs, as they danced, and fell, and drank and smoked, the tides of the years' fashions went up and down, in hemlines that had more meaning than their lives.

In her sleep, as the child fell and spring came down suddenly from the trees to scoop the child, to fill the scoop where it had fallen with violets and crocuses, and to rock the child, safe now in its pram, in winds from south and west, a cat's cradle of winds that lifted ribbons from the bonnet of the child and wove them in invisible patterns in the air—in her sleep, into which she had fallen down the hole, Mrs Paxton dreamed. She was bound to a post out at sea. She cried, against the birds, and the terrible noise of the sea, which ran past her with always somewhere further to go. The cold sea, cold as the spring, might take heat on the surface, from the sun, but underneath it was all black hair, greasy and cold and black, under the tinted strand. Mrs Paxton cried to be heard. But the men and women on the shore could no more hear her than they could the birds, nor could they hear the ponderous message the waves laid down on the stones, before going out again. Mrs Paxton was her own daughter, strapped and tied, and crying in a language not even her mother could understand. She was powerless, swaddled by the iron bands of the sea.

Mrs Paxton woke, to the burnt-out kettle and the shamed face of Ella, on the scene of damage as usual, but too late. 'Now what'll we do?' said Mrs Paxton, but in spite of her anger she could only remember the sea—and Ella's thick legs, which were like posts sticking up out of the sea, as she mopped water from the exploded kettle on the floor. 'See if you can't nip into Boot's and get us one,' Mrs Paxton added. 'If only we could have an electric kettle, what a difference that would make!'

Alice was brought into the house, with dread on the part of Mr Paxton. And Ella screamed, at the accident following her own desire to jump (unless they were all destined to fall to the other side of the world); and Mr Paxton frowned, and went to put on a pan of water. He had been custodian, of this child who had come to him washed up from nowhere, with a message that he must care for her. Instead of which, he had fallen with her on to leaves that had been brushed aside to reveal stubby crocus shoots, pointing up like missiles and bruised purple at the top. Now, of all things, there was no kettle. Mr Paxton put the pan on gingerly, as if the world had been declared at an end and they were all adapting to the savage life, with a muddy child on the floor at their feet.

Mrs Paxton went over every inch of the child when Ella had finished with it, then, sighing in relief once she knew there was no harm done, said—and again and again—'Aren't you a clever little girl?' And: 'Wasn't she a clever girl, to find her way home then?'

Water boiled. Mr Paxton went over to the wireless in the corner and twiddled a knob, to hear news from Sir Anthony Eden. He would be reassured, to hear voices of men who spoke in a language neither his wife nor Ella nor the child on the floor could understand. He thought sternly of the loss of power in Suez. And he remembered, for Mr Paxton knew his nervousness when he saw Ella standing there, with the sun coming in under the door behind her in yellow stalks, and Ella seeing only her daffodils, and the face of Bob, that he had nearly lost his daughter and that he must once again return everything to normal as quickly as possible. He suggested a treat. 'After tea,' Ella was told, 'we'll go and visit the menagerie.'

The Old Man's menagerie lived in parts of the garden; but sometimes, when the time of the year was blank before spring, or the leaves fell too heavily, burying animals and reptiles and birds, fitting them out in newly stitched coats from which their eyes gleamed like diamond pins, they moved indoors and could be found in the five rooms of the house, that led off the main landing. Then, Mr Paxton went into the garden in vain. He stood in the emptiness of the stone-walled garden, where the old parrot had been, and on the grass by the river, stripped of colour now the green lizards had gone to the house to multiply, to make scaly green mountains in the room at the far end of the corridor, with so many blue eyes there was a sky flickering behind them. Mr Paxton shook his head in a mixture of rage and tolerance. He knew the presence in the house of these moving possessions of the Old Man's annoyed and upset Mrs Paxton. But he was glad to walk alone in the garden, especially with his daughter, rather than risk the sun covered by the wings of the parrot, and the lizards talking to the stones, with the child listening intently. He wanted to provide the child with his own face, and her mother's—but, unknown to him, it was already too late, for the menagerie had sought out this new addition to their ranks and for the few months she was theirs, completely owned her: Mr Paxton's face, looming above the child on afternoon walks, folded into wings of purple and red, and as Mrs Paxton and Ella spoke in the kitchen, green snakes fell from their mouths. If the Old Man's butterflies hatched in the rooms, the child was wrapped in their spotted skins until she was lifted, and put to the breast.

At this time of year, when spring was reluctant to come and the Old Man had to stay in his rooms, among the hills and glittering plains made by the lizards—the old parrot high on a cupboard, like a bunch of red blossoms in the unnatural spring—he would sit over his boxes of photographs and pull out the people he hoped to project on the walls of his shadowy rooms. He saw his father's father, summoned in his photograph from the eternal room upstairs and standing with an expression of impatience in the low hills of his land in the north. His beard was white, and after him, in the sliding palms of the Old Man's hands came the white beard of Freud, and then there was a group of aunts of Molly and Pam, with buttercup hats and pinched waists that looked ready to be threaded with a needle and joined together for life. The Old Man sighed, and remembered those hats, with ribbons that stuck out behind in the wind, then the aunts when they had become ill, and the hats forever on pegs in the hall. What had been wrong with these aunts would never be known, but the frames they had been placed in finally exploded, and they stopped dancing and fell into a swoon.

Sometimes, in the long days before the Old Man moved to the garden and took the menagerie with him, the photographs filled the house entirely. In the film of shadows in corners, and the sudden expanses of white on a wall, where a sitter had chosen a studio portrait, or where a white sky, firm as wax, was cut out around head and shoulders, there appeared the extreme anonymity of the Old Man's family, long-dead; and then the immortals, who rose from a scrapbook he had kept as a child, and transformed the house, just as they had formed the new age into which they had been born. Freud, and Alexander Fleming, and Rutherford—and Lenin and Jung and Joyce and Proust—and Stravinsky and Picasso and Yeats—walked in the house, and the shadows from the ash tree outside came in in the first rays of sun of the new spring and made libraries and laboratories, and orchestras in the creaking of the old house and the tossing of leaves on the ash tree outside, as they grew and unfurled in the sun. The immortals ignored the Old Man's family completely, as they walked in rooms that expanded or shrank as they entered, to suit their purpose. They looked at the aunts, and at Molly and Pam, and at the Blue Women, who had wandered by mistake into this black and white photographic world, as if they were no more than specks of dust, case-histories long pushed away in the archives, specimens on slides, millions on millions of them, in a discarded science of the past. They picked their way with expressions of scorn through the Old Man's rooms, and made for the kitchen wing. And they lingered there, after everyone had gone to bed, bringing black shadows, and a sudden exposure of white, as the moon came in at the doors and lit up a famous ear, or made a white turnip of a nose, or removed altogether the top of a distinguished hat. These great men had come to see Mrs Paxton, and Ella, and the child. They came in threes, these Wise Men, and stood loftily in the bright green room where Mrs Paxton liked to have her last cup of tea before feeding the child. They stared in great perplexity into the crib. When the Old Man threw down the scrap-book, they vanished again. They might never have been heard of by the Paxtons, and certainly there was no mention of them in the paper Mr Paxton brought his wife on the way back from a quick evening pint. They might have been a figment of the Old Man's imagination—but the house was nervous with them when they walked in it—and it seemed they had a fear that the child would destroy the world they had made around them.

The Old Man was certainly not pleased to find his ancestors despised in this way by the Immortals. He arranged again and again the flowers in great blue and white urns, rugs were thrown over banisters and draped from ceilings as if he were trying to show his house as a tent, to prove to these condescending men the transitoriness of things; he went more and more frequently to the upper room, where his statesmen forebears conferred on the problem of the Suez crisis and sent orders, from behind the green baize door, into the outside world. Perhaps, as apprehensive as the Great Men and, unlike them unable to divine the probable cause of unrest to come, he was simply more sensitive than usual on the subject of his surroundings, of the world which enclosed him. He knew, too, that the world the child would inherit would be empty both of the Great Men and of him.

As all this went on, and the days became slowly longer, Mrs Paxton took to carrying Alice about the house and then back to the kitchen again. 'Where've you been?' Mr Paxton said; for he had a dread of Mrs Paxton meeting Freud or some such on those landings which were so uncertain at this time of year, with the odd light and the shadows. 'If I can't clean without leaving her strapped down somewhere, I'd like to know what I can do,' said Mrs Paxton. And at this point, always, Ella would come in and say: 'I dreamt of Bob again last night!' and 'What do you think it can mean?'

Mr Paxton invariably stood by the stove when these exchanges took place. Ella's coming from Australia, and the long cord of dreams that held her to Bob at the other side of the world, made him fear for his own daughter, and her place on the spinning ball, where she might lose her footing and slip into space. In the years before Alice was born, he wished only for his solitary talks with the parrot, and a chat with the chemist in the afternoon, and a listening to the news in the evening with his eyes trained on the face of Mrs Paxton, as if the information were issuing from her lips; but in the year the child was born he knew the wrong child had come to him and that he must remedy this.

'Lalla...Lalla...Lalla...' sang Mrs Paxton at the cot.
'Lalla,' the child seemed to say, from a mouth festooned with spit.
'She said Ella,' Ella said.
'Lalla...Lalla...' went on Mrs Paxton. 'Do you know, we haven't even got a rattle for her yet and that's because Mrs Grogan said the rattles at Sturgis were unhygienic and the Morton child had thrush from one. Don't you think it's a shame?'

Mr Paxton still kept very close to the stove, as if the kettle might jump at him if he didn't guard it. 'Nothing is unhygienic at Sturgis,' he said finally, for that was the chemist's where he had worked, and where he went still, to savour the pleasure of not being there at all hours, nervous in a white coat behind the little window that said Prescriptions.
'I'll make her a rattle, though. I'll make her one.'
'Make her one,' said Mrs Paxton. 'That's a funny idea.'
'I dreamt of Bob standing with his back to a bank of daffodils,' Ella said. 'Don't you think that must mean he's coming soon?'

Mr Paxton went from stove to old wireless, cautiously. Sometimes, in mid-movement, he was caught and hurled off on some errand, or told sharply there were the chairs to mend in the junk room over the stable. This time he was lucky. As the child gurgled, and Mrs Paxton improvised this lullaby as she scraped carrots for the Old Man's supper, he heard the news and nodded his head to the time of the announcer's Oxford tones. As the new ball of white wool, bought at the chemist by Mrs Grogan and tied firmly to the end of the cot, swung to and fro, and the child's eyes followed it and then trembled shut, the father heard the tramp of marchers in the room.

The marchers were marching against the bomb, as they went from Aldermaston into Trafalgar Square, and the tramping of boots made him think of the war. To the side of Mr Paxton his wife hummed and grated, like a song whistled through a comb. The kitchen was dark, on the evening Mr Paxton understood that he would never be able to control or understand the events in the Old Man's house or in the world beyond. For, as the boots marched in his radio against a new ball of destruction he could never have dreamed as a boy, and Mrs Paxton hummed in a language only the child could hear, the white woollen ball flew off again—unnoticed by any of them. Later, when Mr Paxton questioned Ella and Mrs Paxton, he did so without any of the certainty of retrieval he had shown on earlier occasions. Like the Old Man, he found the spectre of the bomb and the presence of the child too unnerving. All Ella said was she could have sworn, when Mr Paxton asked her later, that she had seen a dumpling fly through the air, in the cauldron of steam that was the kitchen, with Mrs Paxton standing over the boiling water and only portions of Mr Paxton and Ella visible in the mist.

At about this time, the Old Man took to going frequently to the fifth room, at the end ot the landing at the top of the stairs, where he kept his treasures. There was a sea horse he kept on velvet in the bottom of the box, and sea grapes, and labyrinths of coral where flies hatched their eggs in winter. The Old Man put bracelets of elephants' hair on his wrists. Then, the room that was long and low and looked out under thatch at grass, and water-meadows that were all the time half under water, felt the rustle in the thatch of unseen animals; and far out over the meadows antelopes grazed, with legs as long and stiff as bulrushes. The Old Man liked this room better than any of the others in the house. Nothing had been brought into it that had died a violent death: he had made sure the skins of tigers and bears stayed on the upper floor, by the room where the statesmen gambled; and he liked to think that the yellowing seaweed fans, chipped shells and general flotsam had somehow drifted in of their own accord. From the days when the water had been higher in the meadows, and only the tops of the downs had crested the waves, these harmless fauna of the sea had wandered into the house, to become enclosed in walls of brown water, with a roof of yellow sea thatch as covering. For the Old Man liked to think, on days indifferent to dark or light, and marked off only by the baker's van or the postman coming red or white up to the back-door, that he was just as happy to live under the sea. He was as much in water as air, and the bright buttercups just opening in the meadows scattered in shoals when the wind blew, and lay tail side up. Then, when there was no African night to come down round him, no wide sky and stars, the Old Man twisted the ring of elephants' hair on his arm and he walked on the ancient seabed. At his feet, conch shells were crumbling, and sometimes, from the roof of sodden weed, a water-snake arched, and fell.

Mr Paxton went to the fifth room, on the night his wife had shown impatience with him. Mr Paxton's feet were the first part of him visible, in the mirror. This was propped on the floor and was in a gilt frame water-logged with Victorian fruit and now encrusted with dust. He bent down, and wiped at the surface of the mirror. His black shoes came back at him, and he walked away into the centre of the room, with his feet going down in the dusty room like a man walking for the first time on the surface of the moon. He saw the Old Man—and he stopped still, facing him as he stood by the window, under the straw beard of the dilapidated roof, while the Old Man stared at him, and then turned to look out at the water-meadows, or the African plains, where dark had hidden the animals and it was hard to see as far as the river-bank.

Mr Paxton said he had come to find something for the baby.

'Something like a toy,' said Mr Paxton, He was uneasy, catering for this child whose fingers could as yet only open and close, like the most primitive forms of life. He would go soon and get himself the child he deserved and had expected, a twelve-year-old son. But for now, he held in his mind this room at the end of the landing, filled with debris from the sea. Flotsam would be recognisable to the baby, baffled as it was by the strange shapes of the new world of the earth. As the child had floated in the sea of Mrs Paxton, or bobbed in its chest on the waves as it came up the river, seeking an old king for a father, it would have known the frayed sea wool, and coral white and malignant as an inner growth. Mr Paxton bent to examine a shawl of seaweed lace, and dismissed it for not being a toy. For a certain time he even stood stupidly, with a cuttlefish in his hand. He replaced it and stood staring at his hands, which were white and bony, as if the flesh had been nibbled away.

The Old Man said there was nothing here a child could possibly want. At the same time he pointed to a basket in the corner, where he had put things he was not quite able to throw away. The Old Man indicated to Mr Paxton that he should act as proxy for the child, and put his hand in the basket. And this Mr Paxton did, drawing out a comets tail of silk ties and a gourd and pomegranates tied up in a yellow handkerchief.

At first the Old Man, excited by the appearance of this forgotten fruit—which he had picked up, he thought, in Alexandria or in the courtyards of Granada, where the sun was red at three in the afternoon and the fruit withered instantly, shrinking, sucking itself in, and was hollow finally, with pips rattling about inside—at first, the Old Man held on to the yellow handkerchief and stood with eyes shining, back turned to the window and the watery world where he lived. He thought of the hot earth, and sun coming down through women's parasols, dotted red and white as the insides of figs. In his dream, as he held the pomegranate, he saw the red sun come down on white pillars and shoot out in black columns on the earth, as if the white temple, the crucible, had burnt up the fire from the sun and thrown it down into black pillars of shade. The Old Man wished he could get away from the watermeadows, and the caterwauling of the boys on the downs. He wished he could sit under a pine tree, with pine needles so hot and dry that one flash of his glass ring would set the forest alight.

Mr Paxton had taken back the bundle of fruit and now he was sorting which he would take, and the Old Man opened the pomegranate for him, so those were the seeds he sewed, in the end, into a cloth bag on the end of a wooden spoon handle. The seeds had a musty smell, and the Old Man sneezed as they rattled in his palm before handing them over.

The room was dark—all this had taken place as the last light went from the fields and the river—and it was lower, as if it had gone down, under the weight of thatch, into the ground. The Old Man and Mr Paxton hurried from it. The Old Man went to the upper landings, to see the Blue Women; and Mr Paxton went to the kitchen, to the hiss of the kettle, and sighs from Ella that were just out of time with it; and Mr Paxton sewed the seeds into a little pouch, so Alice could hear them rattle together at the lifting of a hand.

In the last days of the cold weather, when Mrs Grogan said summer was just around the corner and her daughter Ella thought immediately of the Australian winter and Bob covered in snow, the Old Man's house was scoured and cleaned. Doors opened from one side of the house to the next. Until the hot days came, scattering in the Old Man's rooms dead blossom and a film of pollen, there was a wholeness to the house which made it possible to go from one part of it to another with ease—from the rooms of the Paxtons, that were green and shining—to the newly cleaned rooms of the Old Man. The Blue Women, in the sudden respectability of the spring-cleaning, walked down from the tapestry and paid Sunday calls on the Paxtons. Their eyes were bright and indignant at Mrs Paxton's thrift. A smell of soap and water hung about them after her scrubbing. The Old Man coughed irritably when he sat with the Blue Women, and he cursed the patting and shaping that was bringing his house—long ago sprawled and dispersed into separate encampments over fields and garden, into one home. He could hardly see the necessity for it. He shuffled on the landing, ashamed when he saw his collection of famous men in corners where the cobwebs had been dusted away, or walking uncertainly in too harsh a light, curtains all removed for washing and starching, and the mystery of corridors gone at the stroke of a brush.

Mrs Paxton was happy to remove the traces of the Great Men as she made the house into a round ball, suffocating as a ball of wool. She drew thick veils of white paste over the glass, so there was no way of looking out and seeing the world. Freud's pinstripe trousers were quickly dismissed, no more than a wasp-shadow lying by the door to the third room off the landing. Picasso was more difficult, leaving as he did a mass of angles for Mrs Paxton to walk through, with Mrs Grogan trailing a mop behind: old newspapers reared up, at the slightest gust of wind when a door was opened, and flattened themselves messily on walls, and on the sheets of the Old Man's bed were little round black curls, the curly head of a Minotaur nestling in the sheets. Mrs Paxton scrubbled on, and put down poison for rats. The Blue Women went back to the tapestry and lay still. And Molly and Pam came to visit again, reassured by the odour of cleanliness. But the Old Man hardly bothered to hear their chatter, He missed the shadowy sounds that had once been in his rooms. The Great Men, sprayed out of existence, had been his only real companions. Mrs Paxton had kneaded the house to a ball, and it was intolerable to him. Ella, as she went about the gardens still waiting for the first burst of spring, saw him sometimes at a glistening window, where it seemed the glass has come away with the dirt: he stood there exposed, raw as the new buds that were hanging from the trees.

Mrs Paxton in her usual rounds 'did' the upper landing first, and flung open the window of the eternal smoking-room. A great coughing sound went out, like pigeons from the roof at the firing of a gun. The dead lungs of the elder statesmen wheezed and clapped, and baize card tables were scoured of ash, and a thousand cigar butts, each a political deliberation of ten minutes long, were emptied in Ella's pail. Without a second's hesitaiton, Mrs Paxton swept red pins from the military maps on the wall. And the house closed round a world that was no longer demarcated, that lay helpless before Mrs Paxton, ruled by her sceptre of feather, ensconced in a knitted ball. Ella raced the Hoover over ash-scattered carpet. Out by the river, where Mr Paxton stood at one stretch, in his perplexity gazing at the water and the Old Man stood at another, the hum of the Hoover came like a swarm of bees from the highest reaches of the house.

Mr Paxton thought of fighting bees, of smoking them out of an attic where in his mind they had already stung Ella on the legs and buttocks. He went sharply to the house. Mr Paxton saw the fiery kisses on Ella's skin, and clouds of smoke in the attic. But there was no war that could be fought against Mrs Paxton's Hoover—for now he was there he knew the sound—and Mr Paxton went back to his stretch, this time taking a rod with him for the look of it. The Old Man still stood in utter desolation, in the rushes and green swamp by the river's edge.

Mrs Paxton, now she had a child to take with her, was quick on the upper floor. She cleaned more cursorily in the abandoned rooms off the main landing, once she and Ella had gone backwards down the stairs, scrubbing and washing as they went, in a waterfall over the wood. Her hope was, now she had most of the house under her control, that she wouldn't have to go deep in the springs and mattresses of unused four-poster beds, as for some years she had found herself doing—and that, once she had banished the great artists and thinkers, and stilled the Blue Women, she would be able to return to the kitchen and feed the child. Alice was moved, along with buckets and mops, from floor to floor and from room to room. Her round eyes stared up at ceilings, which curved down to meet her gaze. Her mouth was a ring, in the great round nest of the house. And Mrs Paxton made the nest by pressing herself against walls as she scrubbed, by standing on her toes and spreading her arms as she dusted, and with her breasts pushing and battering the obdurate corners into shape.

Russell Hoban
Riddley Walker

On my naming day when I come 12 I gone front spear and kilt a wyld boar he parbly ben the las wyld pig on the Bundel Downs any how there hadnt ben none for a long time befor him nor I aint looking to see none agen. He dint make the groun shake nor nothing like that when he come on to my spear he wernt all that big plus he lookit poorly. He done the reqwyrt he ternt and stood and clattert his teef and made his rush and there we wer then. Him on 1 end of the spear kicking his life out and me on the other end watching him dy. I said, 'Your tern now my tern later.' The other spears gone in then and he wer dead and the steam coming up off him in the rain and we all yelt, 'Offert!'

The woal thing felt jus that littl bit stupid. Us running that boar thru that las littl scrump of woodling with the forms all roun. Cows mooing sheap baaing cocks crowing and us foraging our las boar in a thin grey girzel on the day I come a man.

The Bernt Arse pack ben follering just out of bow shot. When the shout gone up ther ears all prickt up. Ther leader he wer a big black and red spottit dog he come forit a littl like he ben going to make a speach or some thing til 1 or 2 bloaks uppit bow then he slumpt back agen and kep his farness follering us back. I took noatis of that leader tho. He wernt close a nuff for me to see his eyes but I thot his eye ben on me.

Coming back with the boar on a poal we come a long by the rivver it wer hevvyer woodit in there. Thru the girzel you cud see blue smoak hanging in be tween the black trees and the stumps pink and red where they ben loppt off. Aulder trees in there and chard coal berners in amongst them working ther harts. You cud see 1 of them in there with his red jumper what they all ways wear. Making chard coal for the iron reddy at Widders Dump. Every 1 made the Bad Luck go a way syn when we past him. Theres a story callit *Hart of the Wood* this is it:

Hart of the Wood

There is the Hart of the Wud in the *Eusa Story* that wer a stag every 1 knows that. There is the hart of the wood meaning the veryes deap of it thats a nother thing. There is the hart of the wood where they bern the chard coal thats a nother thing agen innit. Thats a nother thing. Berning the chard coal in the hart of the wood. Thats what they call the stack of wood you see. The stack of wood in the shape they do it for chard coal berning. Why do they call it the hart tho? Thats what this here story tels of.

Every 1 knows about Bad Time and what come after. Bad Time 1st and bad times after. Not many come thru it a live.

There come a man and a woman and a chyld out of a berning town they sheltert in the woodlings and foraging the bes they cud. Starveling wer what they wer doing. Dint have no weapons nor dint know how to make a snare nor nothing. Snow on the groun and a grey sky overing and the black trees rubbing ther branches in the wind. Crows calling 1 to a nother waiting for the 3 of them to drop. The man the woman and the chyld digging thru the snow they wer eating maws and dead leaves which they vomitit them up agen. Freazing col they wer nor dint have nothing to make a fire with to get warm. Starveling they wer and near come to the end of ther strenth.

The chyld said, 'O Im so col Im afeart Im going to dy. If only we had a littl fire to get warm at.'

The man dint have no way of making a fire he dint have no flint and steal nor nothing. Wood all roun them only there wernt no way he knowit of getting warm from it.

The 3 of them ready for Aunty they wer ready to total and done when there come thru the woodlings a *clevver* looking bloak and singing a littl song to his self:

> My roadings ben so hungry
> Ive groan so very thin
> Ive got a littl cook pot
> But nothing to put in

The man and the woman said to the clevver looking bloak, 'Do you know how to make fire?'

The clevver looking bloak said, 'O yes if I know any thing I know that right a nuff. Fires my middl name you myt say.'

The man and the woman said, 'Wud you make a littl fire then weare freazing of the col.'

The clevver looking bloak said, 'That for you and what for me?'

The man and the woman said, 'What do we have for whatfers?' They lookit 1 to the other and boath at the child.

The clevver looking bloak said, 'Iwl tel you what Iwl do Iwl share you my fire and my cook pot if youwl share me what to put in the pot.' He wer looking at the chyld.

The man the the woman thot: 2 out of 3 a live is bettern 3 dead. They said, 'Done.'

They kilt the chyld and drunk its blood and cut up the meat for cooking.

The clevver looking bloak said, 'Iwl show you how to make fire plus Iwl give you flint and steal and makings nor you dont have to share me nothing of the meat only the hart.'

Which he made the fire then and give them flint and steal and makings then he cookt the hart of the chyld and et it.

The clevver looking bloak said, 'Clevverness is gone now but littl by littl itwl come back. The iron wil come back agen 1 day and when the iron comes back they wil bern chard coal in the hart of the wood. And when they bern the chard coal ther stack wil be the shape of the hart of the chyld.' Off he gone then singing:

> Seed of the littl
> Seed of the wyld
> Seed of the berning is
> Hart of the child

The man and the woman then eating ther chyld it wer black nite all roun them they made ther fire bigger and bigger thrying to keap the black from moving in on them. They fel a sleap by ther fire and the fire biggering on it et them up they bernt to death. They ben the old 1s or you myt say the *auld* 1s and be come chard coal. Thats why theywl tel you the aulder tree is bes for charring coal. Some times youwl hear of a aulder kincher he carrys off childer.

> Out goes the candl
> Out goes the lite
> Out goes my story
> And so Good Nite

Coming pas that aulder wood that girzly morning I fealt my stummick go col. Like the aulder kincher ben putting eye on me. No 1 never had nothing much to do with the chard coal berners only the dyers on the forms. Ice a year the chard coal berners they come in to the forms for ther new red clof but in be twean they kep to the woodlings.

It wer Ful of the Moon that nite. The rain littlt off the sky cleart and the moon come out. We put the boars head on the poal up on top of the gate house. His tusks glimmert and you cud see a dryd up trickl from the corners of his eyes like 1 las tear from each. Old Lorna Elswint our tel woman up there getting the tel of the head. Littl kids down be low playing Fools Circel 9wys. Singing:

> Horny Boy rung Widders Bel
> Stoal his Fathers Ham as wel
> Bernt his Arse and Forkt a Stoan
> Done It Over broak a boan
> Out of Good Shoar vackt his wayt
> Scratcht Sams Itch for No. 8
> Gone to senter nex to see
> Cambry coming 3 times 3
> Sharna pax and get the poal
> When the Ardship of Cambry comes out of the hoal

Littl 2way Digman being the Ardship going roun the circel til it come chopping time. He bustit out after the 3rd chop. I use to be good at that I all ways rathert be the Ardship nor 1 of the circel I liket the busting out part.

I gone up to the platform I took Lorna a nice tender line of the boar. She wer sitting up there in her doss bag she ben smoaking she wer hy. I give her the meat and I said, 'Lorna wil you tel for me?'

She said, 'Riddley Riddley theres mor to life nor asking and telling. Whynt you be the Big Boar and Iwl be the Moon Sow.'

> When the Moon Sow
> When the Moon Sow comes to season
> Ay! She wants a big 1
> Wants the Big Boar hevvy on her
> Ay yee! Big Boar what makes the groun shake
> Wyld of the Woodling with the wite tusk
> Ay yee! That wyld big 1 for the Moon Sow

She sung that in my ear then we freshent the Luck up there on top of the gate house. She wer the oldes in our crowd but her voyce wernt old. It made the res of her seam yung for a littl. It wer a col nite but we wer warm in that doss bag. Lissening to the dogs howling aftrwds and the wind wuthering and wearying and nattering in the oak leaves. Looking at the moon all col and wite and oansome. Lorna said to me, 'You know Riddley theres some thing in us it dont have no name.'

I said, 'What thing is that?'

She said, 'Its some kynd of thing it aint us but yet its in us. Its looking out thru our eye hoals. May be you dont take no noatis of it only some times. Say you get woak up suddn in the middl of the nite. I minim youre a sleap and the nex youre on your feet with a spear in your han. Wel it wernt you put that spear in your han it wer that other thing whats looking out thru your eye hoals. It aint you nor it dont even know your name. Its in us lorn and loan and sheltering how it can.'

'I said, 'If its in every 1 of us theres moren 1 of it theres got to be a manying theres got to be a millying and mor.'

Lorna said, 'Wel there is a millying and mor.'

I said, 'Wel if theres such a manying of it whys it lorn then whys it loan?'

She said, 'Becaws the manying and the millying its all 1 thing it dont have nothing to gether with. You look at lykens on a stoan its all them tiny manyings of it and may be each part of it myt think its sepert only we can see its all 1 thing. Thats how it is with what we are its all 1 girt big thing and divvyt up amongst the many. Its all 1 girt thing bigger nor the worl and lorn and loan and oansome. Tremmering it is and feart. It puts us on like we put on our cloes. Some times we dont fit. Some times it cant fynd the arm hoals and it tears us a part. I dont think I took all that much noatis of it when I ben yung. Now Im old I noatis it mor. It dont realy like to put me on no mor. Every morning I can feal how its tiret of me and readying to throw me a way. Iwl tel you some thing Riddley and keap this in memberment. What ever it is we dont come naturel to it.'

I said, 'Lorna I dont know what you mean.'

She said, 'We aint a naturel part of it. We dint begin when it begun we dint begin *where* it begun. It ben here befor us nor I dont know what we are to it. May be wear jus only sickness and a feaver to it or boyls on the arse of it I dont know. Now lissen what Im going to tel you Riddley. It thinks us but it dont think *like* us. It dont think the way we think.

Plus like I said befor its afeart.'

I said, 'Whats it afeart of?'

She said, 'Its afeart of being beartht.'

I said, 'How can that be? You said it ben here befor us. If it ben here all this time it musve ben beartht some time.'

She said, 'No it aint ben beartht it never does get beartht its all ways in the woom of things its all ways on the road.'

'I said, 'All this what you jus ben telling be that a tel for me?'

She larft then she said, 'Riddley there aint nothing what *aint* a tel for you. The wind in the nite the dus on the road even the leases stoan you kick a long in front of you. Even the shadder of that leases stoan roaling on or stanning stil its all telling.'

Wel I cant say for cern no mor if I had any of them things in my mynd befor she tol me but ever since then it seams like they all ways ben there. Seams like I ben all ways thinking on that thing in us what thinks us but it dont think like us. Our woal life is a idear we dint think of nor we dont know what it is. What a way to live.

Thats why I finely come to writing all this down. Thinking on what the idear of us myt be. Thinking on that thing whats in us lorn and loan and oansome.

*W*alker is my name and I am the same. Riddley Walker. Walking my riddels where ever theyve took me and walking them now on this paper the same.

I dont think it makes no diffrents where you start the telling of a thing. You never know where it begun realy. No moren you know where you begun your oan self. You myt know the place and day and time of day when you ben beartht. You myt even know the place and day and time when you ben got. That dont mean nothing tho. You stil dont know where you begun.

Ive all ready wrote down about my naming day. It wernt no moren 3 days after that my dad got kilt in the digging at Widders Dump and I wer the loan of my name.

Dad and me we jus come off forage rota and back on jobbing that day. The hoal we ben working we ben on it 24 days. Which Ive never liket 12 its a judgd men number innit and this ben 2 of them. Wed pernear cleart out down to the chalk and hevvy mucking it ben. Nothing lef in the hoal only sortit thru muck and the smel of it and some girt big rottin iron thing some kynd of machine it wer you cudnt tel what it wer.

    Til then any thing big we all ways bustit up in the hoal. Winch a girt big buster rock up on the crane and drop it down on what ever we wer busting. Finish up with han hammers then theywd drag the peaces to the reddy for the melting. This time tho the 1stman tol us word come down they dint want this thing bustit up we wer to get it out in tack. So we ben sturgling with the girt big thing nor the woal 20 of us cudnt shif it we cudnt even lif it just that littl bit to get the sling unner neath of it. Up to our knees in muck we wer. Even with the drain wed dug the hoal wer mucky from the rains. And col. It wer only just the 2nd mooning of the year and winter long in going.

    We got hevvy poals and leavering it up just a nuff to get a roap roun 1 end of it we had in mynd to shif that girt thing jus a littl with the crane so we cud get it parper slung then winch it out of there. It wer a 16 man treadl crane with 2 weals 4 men inside 4 men outside each weal. Userly I wuntve ben on the crane we all ways put our hevvyes on them weals. All we had tho wer 20 in all and we neadit some mussl on the leaver poals so I wer up there on the lef han weal with our hardes hevvy Fister Crunchman we wer the front 2 on that weal. Durster Potter and Jobber Easting behynt us. Straiter Empy our Big Man he wer down in the hoal with Dad and 2 others. Us on the out side of the weals looking tords the hoal and them on the in side looking a way from it.

    We took up the slack then Straiter Empy gave the syn and Chalker Marchman the Widders Dump 1stman chanting us on:

> Gone ter morrer here to day
> Pick it up and walk away
> Dont you know greaf and woe
> Pick it up its time to go
> Greaf and woe dont you know
> Pick it up its time to go

    Roun we gone with the roap winching in and the A frame taking the strain. Straiter Empy and Skyway Moaters leavering the girt thing wylst we wincht and Dad and Leaster Digman working the sling unner.

London Town is drownt this day
Hear me say walk a way
Sling your bundel tern and go
Parments in the mud you know
  Greaf and woe dont you know
  Pick it up its time to go

Weals creaking stoppers knocking 32 legs going. The roap gone iron hard and the girt big thing coming up out of the muck all black and rottin under the grey sky. A crow going over and it had the right of us.

Dad and me looking up at the crow. I knowit that crow wer going to say something unner that grey sky. I knowit that crow wer going to tel.

The crow yelt, 'Fall! Fall! Fall!' I dont know if I wer falling befor he said that or not. The treadls wer wet and slippy but I had a good grip on the railing any how I thot I did. But ther I wer with my feet gone out from unner me and nothing in my han. Falling I wer knockt Durster Potter and Jobber Easting luce and they grabbit me they dint have nothing else to hol on to. Fister Crunchman cawt my arm only the railing he had holt of with his other han come a way in his han and off he gone with the res of us. I cud see in my mynd how funny it musve lookit I wer near larfing with it only I seen that weal going backards and I heard some thing tear luce it wer the stoppers 2 on each weal all 4 gone whanging off. Boath weals screachit and the 4 bloaks on the out side of the other weal shot off tords the hoal like stoans out of a sling. Wel it wer the load took charge and SPLOOSH! Down it come that girt big thing it made a jynt splosh and black muck going up slow and hy in the air. That girt old black machine fel back in to the muck with my dad unner neath of it. It all happent so fas the crow wer stil in site he larft then. 'Haw! Haw! Haw!' and off he flappit.

We pickt our selfs up then all but 1 of us. The roap wer stil fas to the girt big thing. We all got on that roap then we dint use the weal winch only the A frame and the pullys. Chalker Marchman chanting us on the strait pul:

Heard it and the news of 10
Sling your bundel haul agen
Haul agen and hump your load
Every bodys on the road

We shiffit the thing and got Dad out from unner. Parbly it kilt him soons it come down on him he dint have no time to drown in the muck. He wer all smasht up you cudnt tel whose face it ben it mytve ben any bodys.

I begun to clym all over that thing then. That girt big black thing. I wer looking to see if it had a name stampt in or raisd up in the iron of it like them things do some times. It had a shel of old muck stoan hard unner the new muck tho nor I cudnt fynd no name.

Every 1 wer saying, 'What is it Riddley whatre you doing?'

I said, 'My dad ben kilt by some thing I dont even know the name of aint that a larf.' I begun larfing then I cudnt stop.

They let me have my larfing out but I wer stil wanting some thing some kynd of las word some kynd of onwith. If I wernt going to get it from Dad at leas I wantit some thing for onwith even if it wernt nothing only the name of that girt black thing what smasht him flat so you cudnt even tel whose face it ben. I said that to Fister Crunchman.

He said, 'You look at your dads face Riddley thats what Widders Dump done to him theres your onwith.'

I said, 'It wernt Widders Dump done it to him it wer me I los my footing and I pult you with me. It wer me made the woal of us lose our perchis.'

Fister said, 'That load wer too much for that weal. It wernt us falling kilt your dad it wer the stoppers coming luce and the weal took charge.'

Straiter Empy said, 'Fisters right it wer too much of a load for that weal.'

Chalker Marchman said to Straiter, 'It wer you lot put it on the weal. All I tol you wer to get that thing out of the hoal. You cudve draggit cudnt you I never give you the do it for the weal. Any how the weal wudve ben all right if youd had a nuff hevvyness on it and kep your hevvyness where it ben meant to be.'

Straiter said, 'Widders Dumpwl give comping station for Brooder Walker tho youwl do that much wont you.'

Chalker Marchman said, 'O yes wewl sen Reckman Bessup with it hewl road back to fents with you.'

We borrert a drag to take Dad hoam. Going back to fents then all of us. They give us ful days meat at Widders Dump and Reckman Bessup he wer ther connexion man he brung the comping station. What we callit dead mans iron and he carrit on his back.

We wer going out thru the gate when there gone up behynt us the death wail loud and strong it musve ben 40 peopl at leas. All them voyces going up black and sharp and falling a way in a groan: AIYEEEEE.

I said to Reckman Bessup, 'That cant be for my dad he wernt nothing to them.'

He said, 'Its a babby dead beartht. That babby come into the worl dead same time as you dad gone with Aunty.'

I said, 'Is there a connexion?'

He said, 'Not I as Iwl make.'

Going back slow then there come dogs follering on our track we hadn't seen none that day til then. Shapit black is how I think of them tho mos of them are patchy colourt. Its the hy leggitness of them. Ther thick necks and littl heads and littl ears. It wer the Bernt Arse pack with ther black and red spottit leader. All of them head down and slumping on behynt us jus out of bow shot. I wer looking at the leader and waiting for some thing I cud feal it in my froat. He dint have his head down he had it up and looking tords us.

There begun to be some rowling and yipping and yapping from the other dogs then crowding the leader and him terning. Grooling and smarling he wer but the others crowdit on him then the leader he come running tords us. The other dogs dint foller they hung back and he come oansome.

All of us stoppt then and looking at the dog. Not 1 of us put arrer to string we all knowit wernt that kynd of thing. I steppt out a littl way from the others and they all movit a way from me it were like some thing you do in a dream. Straiter Empy said, 'Riddley hes offering and hes favering you.'

I stood there and holding ready with my spear. Nothing like it never happent befor but it wer like it all ways ben there happening. The dog getting bigger bigger unner the grey sky and me waiting with the spear. It dint seam like the running brung him on tho he were moving fas. It were mor like he ben running for ever in 1 place not moving on just getting bigger bigger til he wer big a nuff to be in front of me with his face all rinkelt back from his teef. Jus in that fraction of a minim the dogs face and the boars face from my naming day they flickert to gether with my dads face all smasht. I helt the spear and he run on to it. Lying there and kicking with his yeller eyes on me and I finish him with my knife.

Straiter Empy said, 'Look how his teefs woar down and hes all girzelt. A old leader come to his time and crowdit out come back to us to dy. Ive heard of it but I never seen it befor. Its Luck for you Riddley.'

We laid the dog acrost Dads legs. Reckman Bessup said to me, 'This dogs offert his self to your dad. Made his Plomercy and now theywl boath look at the nite to gether.'

I said to Reckman Bessup, 'Heres my dad dead and this dog and that babby at Widders Dump all on the same day. Be there a connexion?'

He said, 'Whynt you stop asking me that. What I connect is shows I aint no tel woman nor I dont know nothing about blips nor syns.'

I said, 'That's as may be but youre stanning here and seen what happent plus you ben at Widders Dump this morning.'

He thot on it a littl then. A sour man but cudnt help getting a little interstit. He said, 'I wunt try to nel but you can tel your oan self. Every 1 knows if you get blipful things to gether you take the farthes out 1 for the nindicater. Whats the farthes out 1 of the 3 youve namit?'

I said, 'The dog.'

He said, 'What's a dog? Its some thing you cant get close to. They keap ther farness nor you cant trap them nyther theyre too clevver. Plus theyre a danger theywl eat you if they catch you oansome and they go mad at Ful of the Moon. So here youve got a far thing come close and a danger thing as cudnt be trappt offers its self. How old myt you be?'

I said, 'I just come 12 at Ful of the Moon.'

He said, 'Heres a old woar out leader took by a boy what aint a boy no more hes come 12 and a man. You hearing any tel?'

I said, 'The far come close took by the littl come big.'

He said, 'You said it I dint. I dont say no farther you bes tel your oan self on from there. No use asking other peopl they dont know no moren you do. Now you dads gone youwl be connexion man at How Fents peopl wil be asking you in stead of you you asking them. You bes start putting things to gether for your self you aint a kid no mor.'

When we movit on the dogs they slumpt off back to Bernt Arse Dead Town it wer like they only come out that day for that 1 thing. Smoak coming up in Bernt Arse from the out poast there were all ways hevvys there on rota from the Ram. Every day we gone the same way to and from and every day we seen that smoak nor I never give it no thot. This day tho every thing begun to look diffrent. Like I never seen it befor. You know that kynd of playsy kids have some times. Its a funny face paintit on a flat peace of wood and theres 2 hoals to roal the eyes in to. Clay ball eyes and you slant the face 1 way and the other til they roal in to the hoals. Wel this day it seamt like the worl begun to roal. The worl begun to seam like 1 big crazy eye and roaling. I wer afeart it myt roal right off the face and dispear.

Looking at that smoak coming up in the dead town and my mynd stil running on the dogs. There ben the dead town all them years. Ram out poasts in 1 part of them and dogs hoalt up in other parts. And all them years you heard storys of dog peopl. Peopl with dogs heads and dogs with peopls heads. Some said come Ful of the Moon they all run to gether in the Black Pack. Dogs and dog peopl to gether. The Ram didnt allow no 1 in the dead towns but when I ben littl we use to sly in when ever we got the chance and kids a nuff for crowd. Trying if we cud see dog peopl. Fork Stoan it ben befor we livet near Bernt Arse. We never seen nothing only the hevvys and they all ways seen us off qwick. We heard things tho some times. Singing or howling or crying or larfing you cudn't qwite say what it wer or what it wernt.

My dad use to say all that about the dog peopl wer jus so much cow shit. He said hewd give odds it wer plittical and no dogs heads to it at all. Wel this aint the place to say no mor about it Iwl tel that part when I come to it. Ive only wrote this down here becaws my mynd ben running on it that day and if itd run farther I mytve knowit mor. There aint that many sir prizes in life if you take noatis of every thing. Every time wil have its happenings out and every place the same. What ever eats mus shit.

We got back to fents and then the death wail gone for Brooder Walker. We done comping station then. Reckman Bessup he said, '1 of yours is dead with us. I have it on me wil you take it off me?'

I said, 'Yes Iwl take it off.' I took the iron of his back then. That wer the onlyes iron I ever seen out of all them years jobbing at Widders Dump. 5 10wts of iron for Brooder Walker.

My dad he were 33 when he dyd. My mum she dyd of the coffing sickness when I wer 5. This what Ive ben writing down here it happent when I ben with How Fents. On the Bundel Downs near the Rivver Sour about 4 faggers Norf and Eas of Bernt Arse Dead Town and about 15 faggers Souf and Wes of Cambry.

This is stil that same day Im writing down here. The day my dad got kilt. We put the dogs head on the poal on top of the gate house. Lorna Elswint up there with it. Littl kids zanting down be low. Playing Black Pack and singing:

> Ful of the Moon Ful of the Moon
> Ful of the Moon nor dont look back
> Folleree Folleroo on your track
> Oo hoo hoo Yoop yaroo
> Folleree Folleroo follering you
> If they catch you in the darga
> Arga wargA.

Lorna she lookit over the side she said to the kids, 'There aint no Ful Moon this nite there aint no Plack Pack running. Its 2 days pas the Ful.'

Lttle Nimbel Potter he said, '3rd of the Ful and stil shewl pul. My dad he seen Riddley Walker kil that dog and my dad he said that dog wil fetch.'

Lorna said, 'Fetch what?'

Nimbel said, 'Fetch some 1 over to the dog peopl.' He laid his head over on 1 side to show his neck and he showit his teef like he wer a dog and going to bite.

Lorna said, 'Nimbel you ever seen any dog peopl?'

Nimbel said, 'O yes Ive seen them times a nuff.'

Lorna said, 'Whatd they look like then?'

Nimbel said, 'They throw a wite shadder dont they. Every body knows that.' He ternt his self roun then and gone back to playing with the others. Singing:

> Gennl men will do it front to back
> When they do it with the ladys of the Ful Moon pack
> All the ladys do it back to front
> When they drop ther nickers and they show ther
> Moony in the holler moony on the hil
> If you wont do it then your sister wil

I gone up on the gate house and looking at the head. The day gone colder. The muddling from the rains froze hard and the calling of the crows col on the air. Looking at that old leaders woar down teef.

Lorna said to me, 'You heard the story of why the dog wont show its eyes?'

I said, 'No I never.'

She said, 'Thats what happens with peopl on the way down from what they ben. The storys go.' She tol me the story then. This is it wrote down the same.

Why The Dog Wont Show Its Eyes

Time back way way back befor peopl got clevver they had the 1st knowing. They los it when they got the clevverness and now the clevverness is gone as wel.

Every thing has a shape and so does the nite only you cant see the shape of nite nor you cant think it. If you put your self right you can know it. Not with knowing in your head but with the 1st knowing. Where the number creeper grows on the dead stoans and the groun is sour for 3 days digging the nite stil knows the shape of its self tho we dont. Some times the nite is the shape of a ear only it aint a ear we know the shape of. Lissening back for all the souns whatre gone from us. The hummering of the dead towns and the voyces befor the towns ben there. Befor the iron ben and fire ben only littl. Lissening for whats coming as wel.

Time back way way back 1 time it wer Ful of the Moon and a man and woman sqwatting by ther littl fire. Sqwatting by ther littl fire and afeart of the nite. The dog wer in the nite and looking tords the fire. It wernt howling it wer jus looking at the fire. The man and woman seen the fire shyning in the dogs eyes. The man throwit meat to the dog and the dog come in to them by the fire. Brung its eyes in out of the nite then they all lookit at the nite to gether. The man and the woman seen the nite in the dogs eyes and thats when they got the 1st knowing of it. They knowit the nite the same as the dog knowit.

You know what they got 1st knowing of. She has diffrent ways she shows her self. Shes that same 1 shows her moon self or she jus shows her old old nite and no moon. Shes that same 1 every thing and all of us come out of. Shes what she is. Shes a woman when shes Nite and shes a woman when shes Death. The nite bearths the day. Every day has the shape of the nite what it come out of. The man as knows that shape can go in to the nite in the nite and the nite in the day time. The woman as knows that shape can be the nite and take the day in her and bearth the new day.

Wel they got that 1st knowing they got it looking in the dogs eyes in the Ful of the Moon. When the man and woman got that 1st knowing from the dog they made a contrack with the dog in the Ful of the Moon. The roadit on to gether with the dog and foraging to gether. Dint have no mor fear in the nite they put ther self right day and nite that wer the good time. Then they begun to think on it a littl. They said, 'If the 1st knowing is this good what myt the 2nd knowing and the 3rd be and so on?'

They cawt a goat and lookit in its eye. You know what eye the goat has its the clevver eye. The man and woman looking in that clevver eye and they thot: Why shud we be foraging the woal time? They cawt other goats they made a fents and pent them up. They gethert weat and barly they had bread and beer then they wernt moving on the lan no mor they startit in to form it. Stoppit in 1 place then with sheds and stock and growings. They wernt outside in the nite no more they were inside looking out. The nite jus lookit dark to them they dint see nothing else to it no mor. They los out of memberment the shapes of nite and worrit for ther parperty they myt get snuck and raidit. They made the dog keap look out for ther parpety.

Every morning they were counting every thing to see if any thing ben took off in the nite. How many goats how many cows how many measurs weat and barly. Cudnt stop ther counting which wer clevverness and making more the same. They said, 'Them as counts counts moren them as dont count.'

Counting counting they wer all the time. They had iron then and big fire they had towns of parpety. They had machines et numbers up. They fed them numbers and they fractiont out the Power of things. They had the Nos. of the rainbow and the Power of the air all workit out with counting which is how they got boats in the air and picters on the wind. Counting clevverness is what it wer.

When they had all them things and marvelsome they cudnt sleap realy they dint have no res. They were stressing ther self and straining all the time with counting. They said, 'What good is nite its only dark time it aint no good for nothing only them as want to sly and sneak and take our parpety a way.' They los out of memberment who nite wer. They jus wantit day time all the time and they wer going to do it with the Master Chaynjis.

They had the Nos. of the sun and moon all fractiont out and fed to the machines. They said, 'Wewl put all the Nos. in to 1 Big 1 and that wil be the No. of the Master Chaynjis.' They bilt the Power Ring thats where you see the Ring Ditch now. They put in the 1 Big 1 and woosht it roun there come a flash of lite then bigger nor the woal worl and it ternt the nite to day. Then everything gone black. Nothing only nite for years on end. Playgs kilt peopl off and naminals nor there wernt nothing growit in the groun. Man and women starveling in the blackness looking for the dog to eat it and the dog out looking to eat them the same. Finely there come day agen then nite and day regler but never like it ben befor. Day beartht crookit out of crookit nite and sickness in them boath.

Now man and woman go afeart by nite afeart by day. The dog all lorn and wishful it keaps howling for the nites whatre gone for ever. It wont show its eyes no more it wont show the man and woman no 1st knowing. Come Ful of the Moon the sadness gets too much the dog goes mad. It follers on the man and womans track and arga warga if it catches them.

 The fires col
 My storys tol

I said to Lorna, 'I thot it ben Eusa made the 1 Big 1.'

Lorna said, 'I never said he dint.'

I waid, 'Wel you jus tol in this story it ben that man and woman done it plus they bilt the Power Ring and all.'

She said, 'You hear diffrent things in all them way back storys but it dont make no diffrents. Mosly they aint strait storys any how. What they are is diffrent ways of telling what happent.'

I said, 'Ben there is a strait story past down amongst the tel women?'

She said, 'There bint no tel women time back way back. Nor there aint never ben no strait story I ever heard. Bint no writing for 100s and 100s of years til it begun agen nor you wunt never get a strait story past down by mouf over that long. All them storys tol by mouf they ben put to and took from and changit so much thru the years theyre all bits and blips and all mixt up.'

I said, 'That about the 1st knowing in the story. How they got it looking in the dogs eyes. Be that blip or jus a way of waying or what?'

She said, 'Why you asking?'

I said, 'Wel that old dog I kilt I lookit in its eyes dint I. Nor I never got no 1st knowing out of it did I.'

She said, 'May be you got it only you dont know it yet.'

I said, 'Have you got it?'

She said, 'Every body got it its in every 1 of us only we cant get to it til it comes to us 1 way or a nother.'

I said 'Its come to you aint it.'

She said, 'Yes its come to me nor there aint no use asking what it is becaws its what there aint no words for.'

Wel any way thats the story of why the dog wont show its eyes.

Back then in this time I ben writing of I never knowit any 1 ben dog kilt only a kid it wer Follery Digman he got dog et years back. It wer Ful of the Moon and he staggelt behynt a trade crowd coming back. Some times other times of mooning it lookit to me like the dogs ben near ready to come frendy only it never happent. Nor I never heard of no 1 tame a pup. Heard of some 1 got 1 1ce I dont know how they done it. They never tamit tho. Soons it got big a nuff it dug unner the fents and gone.

Weare off to Widders Dump when heres the Bernt Arse pack come out of the woodlings like it ben ther rota to show us the way.

And heres that black leader with his ears prickt up and waiting for a staytmen.

I cud feal my self getting humpyer by the minim I cud see why they callit getting the hump I fealt like I wer growing 1. All my bother hevvy on my back and tingling and like coming to a point. That dog wer looking at me that cern way I uppit bow but the clevver sod wunt even move he knowit he wer out of bow shot.

Straiter Empy wer out with the forage rota it wer Fister Crunchman the 1stman of us that day. He said to me, 'That dogs looking this way like hes got some thing on his mynd.'

I said, 'There's no knowing what a dog myt have on his mind.'

Durster Potter said, 'Not without youre dog clevver.'

Fister said, 'Not that Ive numbert off that pack by colour but I never noatist that black dog til he come leader.'

I said, 'I never seen that dog til after Brooder Walker dyd.'

I said, 'Whatre you getting at Durster?'

He said, 'Wel you know theres some wil tel you of peopl dying in the Ful of the Moon and then theres 1 mor in the Black Pack. May be you shud ask that dog to show you hows your father.' He begun to larf he wer killing his self with it.

I ben carrying 2 throwing spears and a fighting spear like all ways. I ternt them roun and shovit the foot of them in Dursters belly. The wind gone out of him: Hoo! Then I swung them 3 spears and clubbit him on the head with the shafs of them. Down he gone. He come up with blood running down his face and come for me with his fighting spear poynt 1st. Fister grabbit the spear and back handit him 1 acrost the meat hoal and he gone flying.

Dursters all of a heap in the mud but he aint interstit in moving til hes sure its all clear with Fister.

Fister says to him, 'Durster Trubba not but wud you mynd if I call Plomercy right there? Im afeart if you and Riddley settl some I myt get bad hert. All right?'

Durster hes got 1 or 2 teef less in his mouf but he says, 'All right Fister no Trubba.'

On we gone then and I tryd to let my self go easy but I wernt easy. Becaws Id noatist the same as Fister and Durster and it ben working on me. Id never seen that black dog til after I kilt the old leader. I dint think my dad gone in to no black dog but it did seam to me that dog musve come special from some where or ben sent to tel me some thing some how. I never heard of no such thing but thats the fealing I had. Plus I pernear did think it myt tern into some 1 in front of my eyes. Not my dad nor I dint know who but it wuntve snuck me at all to see that dog tern in to a man. Lorna Elswint tol me some thing Ice the others mus neverve heard it or some 1 wudve brung it in sure:

3 black dogs and 1 says, 'The Pry Mincers dead I jus come from the berning.'

Up jumps the bigges of the 3 then on his hynt legs he says,
'I bes walk tall Im No. 1 now.'

Coming a long the hy groun sholder where it wer hevvy woodit on the hy side the dogs run on a head of us and gone out of site amongst the trees.

I wer walking fastern I ben you know how youwl do some times youwl put a space be twean your self and some 1 as ben giving you bother. Walking with my head down not looking a roun. You perwel all ways know what youre doing is my beleaf. I wuntve livet to be 12 years old walking that way but that day I musve wantit to give some thing a chance to happen.

Littl by littl getting farther a head of the others I come roun a ben oansome and all on a sudden theres the black leader stanning oansome in front of me. He aint no moren 2 spear lenths a way from me and his yeller eyes ful on me.

I said, 'What?' and going tords him. Not liffing spear nor making no move with my hans.

We wer stood there looking at each other then I heard the others coming. I throwt my self to 1 side and a arrer hisselt pas me. I ternt and I seen Durster Potter with a emty bow in his han and 2 dogs on him. Theyre in and out like a flash and theres Durster on the groun with his froat and his pryvits toar out and blood sperting all over and the dogs dispeart. They done it quickern it takes to tel of. I ternt roun agen and where the black dog ben it wernt nothing only emty space. No dogs in site at all. There hadnt even ben no noys nor not 1 scream from Durster hed never had no time for that. Nor I hadnt had no time to help him.

Durster ben about as far in front of the others as I ben in front of him. They come roun the ben then the other 17 of them. Wel you know there wer a big hulla bulla every 1 talking at 1ce nor no body never seen nor heard nothing like it. Broad in the day time and 5 days pas Ful of the Moon.

Coarse the upper asking mos in every 1s mynd were: Why Durster? Why not me? I ben the oansome 1 coming roun that ben 1st and the others not in site. Whynt they jump me whyd they wait for Durster? Peopl wer looking at me funny and Iwdve lookit at me the same ben I them. Becaws it lookit like them dogs ben watching when Durster and me had that littl rumpa and they contrackt my nemminy ther nemminy.

I bes put the red cord strait here becaws looking back over what I ben writing it looks like may be Durster ben shooting that arrer at me not at the black dog. I wont never know for cern but I dont think he ben shooting at me. Jus like Id uppit bow at that black leader when I ben fealing humpy I think Durster ben kean to hit some thing after gettting flattent 1ce by me and 1ce by Fister. May be he thot coming suddn roun that ben he myt get his self a dog skin. Or may be he ben looking to miss the dog and hit me I dont know.

A nother asking in some peopls mynd and you cud see it in ther eyes wer why hadnt I done nothing. It lookit bad a nuff them dogs hadnt jumpt me but at leas I cudve got some blood on my spear when they ben pulling Durster down. Every body knowit how fas the dogs wer and how clevver but stil I cudve ben a littl qwickern I wer I knowit that. Fister said, 'No use moufing it over we cant make it be no other way. Theres blame on all of us but mos on me becaws Im 1stman nor I shuntve had no wandrers out in front.'

It snuck me a littl I dint have no fealings 1 way or a nother about Durster dying. It ben mor to me when that las boar come onto my spear or the old leader dog. I never had nothing agenst Durster that rumpa ben jus 1 of them things jumps up on its oan sholders all on a suddn. But then I never had nothing for him nyther. I wer jus as glad to have his space as to have him. Dead with his cock and balls toar off and his head near toar off his neck and his face gone grey and the wet leaves trampelt roun him and his eyes looking up to the grey sky over him.

Different 1s stanning roun him. This 1 and that 1 ben his frend and mummelt this or that but you cud see it drawt them same as flys to honey. It give us all jus that littl thril. Watching Durster do it with Aunty. She took him in stead of us and us what wernt dead felt that much more a live.

We wer closer to hoam nor we wer to Widders Dump. We cut a drag and put Durster on it and back we gone to fents and there gone the death wail yet agen. Littl Nimbel Potter he lookit at me and made the Bad Luck go a way syn. His mum and some others as seen him do it they lookit at me that cern way you dont want no crowd never to look at you. Col iron in that look and heads on poals.

That nite we done the berning and thinet hans and the res of it. Wording roun and it come to Jobber Easting he ben a frend of Dursters he said, 'Bye bye Durster theres some of uswl keap it in memberment how you got dog kilt nor no 1 to lif a han for you.' He ben in that same rota when Durster got kilt. He come roun that ben with the others when Durster ben all ready dead so he knowit there bint no 1 only me there to lif a han. Nex wordit Coxin Shoaring a nother frend of Dursters. He said, 'Bye bye Durster theres others may be shudve give you crowd on that long road you gone.'

Id tol Lorna Elswint how that black leader and me ben looking at each other before Durster lucet his arrer. She said, 'Wel did you get any 1st knowing this time?' Wel it bint til we ben coming in to fents with Durster on the drag when it come to me all on a suddn how I ben that close to a dog for the 2nd time and looking in them yeller eyes nor never even *thot* of 1st knowing. Hadnt ben thinking of nothing at all. Jus looking in them yeller eyes.

Now all on a suddn I wernt sure how it wer. I fealt like when youre sleapy on look out and trying to stay a wake and suddn you catch your self nodding you wunner if youve droppit off and mist some thing.

What with 1 thing and a nother I dint qwite feal like sleaping in my shelter that nite. Lorna had the same fealing so we slyd up on top of the gate house when the lookouts wernt looking. If the skyd ben clear it wudve ben the failing moon littling tords the las ¼ but it wer cloudit over solid. Looking at the candls and the nite fires in the divvy roof and littl glimmers here and there from candls in the shelters. Lissening to the crowd shutting down for the nite. Coffing and farting and belching and peeing 1 place and a nother.

Foot steps and mummering now and then thru the nite. Nothing else.

A Symposium on the British Novel

Lorna Sage
Invasion from Outsiders

It seems necessary to say at the outset that I find the English novel a problematic entity, difficult to be properly sensible about. The language now is so much larger than the culture, and somewhere between them is the literature: the sphere of influence—that sense of being at the centre—seems always to be shrinking. It shrinks but, importantly, hardly disappears: it is not a new centre but new centres which emerge. Wells saw this, and in the *War of the Worlds,* the martians, in a brilliant depiction of our smug, arrogant provincialism, do not invade London; they invade the home countries. And although Wells wanted his readers to see themselves dwarfed by this interplanetary point-of-view, colonized, naturally he also felt that suburban life in the home countries *was* the cosy plateau of human achievement. You were, there, at the centre of things, even for a hungry martian.

English writers are potentially experts in some of the great formal problems of contemporary fiction: the problem of removing yourself from, or confessing yourself at, the centre; the problem of the microcosm that no longer necessarily implies a macrocosm, but proclaims its own marginality. I say 'potentially', because adopting the alien viewpoint, seeing yourself in the long perspective, goes against the grain (Wells doesn't strike one as a fair example). John Fowles in *The French Lieutenant's Woman* identified the capacity to stand outside as one of Hardy's most prophetic achievements: in pasticheing his famous narrative awkwardness ('a person of curiosity could at once have deduced several strong probabilities about...'). Fowles was claiming kin, and acknowledging that a contemporary English novelist is standing on an island that has something uncomfortably in common with Wessex.

Explicitness on the matter, however, is still uncharacteristic. John Bayley in his *Essay* on Hardy, in defence of the implicit, found *The French Lieutenant's Woman* vulgar and exploitative. This isn't as much of a digression as it may seem: Iris Murdoch, married to Professor Bayley, remains the grandest and most teasing exemplar of continuity with what for brevity's sake I'll call the pre-martian past. She is an awesome shamateur, who uses or abuses or ignores the prestigious techniques of alienation (Beckett and Queneau were amongst her early mentors) with a gusto and fine carelessness that make self-doubt seem small minded. Worries about 'where next' recede when you produce a novel (almost) every year; her answer to such questions is as triumphantly and infuriatingly pragmatic as Dr Johnson kicking his famously unphilosophic stone, and indeed the inventiveness of her fiction and its deliberate impurity are buttressed by her conviction —reiterated in her book on Plato, *The Fire and the Sun*—that art is at best second-best. She is, as I want to argue English writers have tended to become, an allegorizer, a speculator, deeply aware of the bad faith involved in seeing yourself at the centre of things. But her fantasy monsters (*The Sea, The Sea*), her UFOs (*The Nice and the Good*), her aliens (Luca in *The Sacred and Profane Love Machine*) are never allowed to take over. She may, in the Plato book, contemplate almost enviously cultures that eschew complex and illusionist fictions, but she shamelessly relishes not belonging to one. Her doubts serve her: that her characters are all sustaining a more-or-less theatrical sense of their own importance must seem to her, I think, merely 'natural', the result of being cumbered with the particular set and wardrobe they were born into.

'Natural' here means something rather odd. And this sense of pervasive, *familiar* unreality—often expressed as theatre—is one of the main ways in which crucial changes in perspective have been, as it were, smuggled into English fiction. The climate *is* cloudy with reticence, anti-programmatic, and to that degree anti-experimental. Nonetheless it is possible (trying for the martian perspective on Wessex) to discern food for speculation. The theatre metaphor will take one some way: Angus Wilson's most recent novel, *Setting the World on Fire*, uses with much panache a lovingly described (and entirely fictional) English great house as the stage on which a baroque Lully opera and a right-wing terrorist happening are spectacularly and simultaneously enacted. Though the novel declares faith in art and artifice, the *kind* of art in use is significant: at once allegorically grand and thoroughly fragile. Wilson's characters are set now against a humanly-created, *made* backdrop.

Wilson's career, since *Late Call* (1964) has been describing a defiant course away from 'organic', rooted fiction (*The Middle Age of Mrs Eliot*). The scenarios of *No Laughing Matter*, and the ecological jet-setting of *As If By Magic* cultivate much more elaborate and desperate diagnoses of English society, and indeed, quite simply, set English characters in a widening world where influences from, say, George Eliot have to jostle bizarrely with orgies parodied from Petronius. It is clear that, for Angus Wilson, the question of what kind of novel comes next has become a real one, and reviewers have often treated this new uncertainty as itself a flaw. Even V.S.Pritchett, for instance, in an otherwise most appreciative piece on *No Laughing Matter*, tactfully regretted that 'He inclines to have too many ideas and his stress on The Game played by the family seems to me excessive.' In the same review, however, Pritchett described Wilson, very finely, as 'an anthropologist at work among the remnant of the upper middle class,' which catches exactly the change in perspective I've been trying to identify. It may be relevant here that, as Angus Wilson pointed out to me in a recent interview, his father was Scottish 'gentry', his mother South African 'business', and he spent his childhood largely in hotels: Englishness from such a vantage point may always have looked more hybrid and strange.

It certainly did for Doris Lessing, who grew up in Southern Rhodesia. She has undergone an extraordinary metamorphosis over the years, from the socialist realist of the early African fiction to, in her case, the *cosmic* anthropologist, who has relegated socio-personal concerns to perhaps 'five per cent' of the whole, the preference of an historically limited culture whose (probably suicidal) end is in sight. 'The Children of Violence' started in 1952 as a *bildungsroman* sequence and ended in 1969 (*The Four-Gated City*) with the utter dissolution of the progressive package (rationalism, materialism, optimism) that earlier sustained her. *The Golden Notebook* (1962) famously recorded, out of sequence, her exhaustive exploration of the traditionally mediating role of (especially) the woman novelist. Deliberately, traumatically (and now at last it seems serenely) she has mislaid her sense of humour, her sense of proportion, her 'English' personality. The science fiction and fantasy she's writing in her new 'Canopus in

Argos' sequence reveals a fragmented cosmos seen by a composite, coolly impersonal eye. She's drawing on western culture's own underground hermetic traditions, on eastern thought, on extra-sensory perception, and unconscious imperatives. If Iris Murdoch and Angus Wilson demonstrate— as I think they do—the English novel's capacity for de-naturing itself without breaking with the past, Lessing suggests much more apocalyptic possibilities.

She demonstrates what her generation otherwise has contained: the centrifugal, even explosive consequences of the unmaking of an English heritage. The traditional virtues (I've mentioned humour, proportion) have in her case lost their efficacy, their prestige, their power—as one of her star-travelled anthropologists might say—to isolate the organism and give it the illusion of coherence. When she talks of what is most living in the novel, she lists African writing, speculative fiction, and women's fiction; she sees 'realist' impulses still at work in a sense, but emanating from ex-colonies, sub-cultures, alternative worlds. And while her particular formula for planetary eavesdropping presents serious difficulties—a sometimes sinister, monolithic stress on universal patterns, a certain bleakness and amorphousness attendant on dissolving boundaries—her example does suggest, very persuasively, that the sub-genres can't be submerged any longer. And if Gothic, speculative writing, and fable, develop independent lives, it obviously gets harder to define the English novel 'proper'. The problems about its contemporary character, and where it's going, have to become explicit.

The most exciting writers now are those who have been 'invaded', and who are 'haunted' in the manner of Doris Lessing's mad ladies by voices from other continents and alternative worlds. Obviously, it's not merely a formal matter, but connected with what is known euphemistically as 'Britain's Changing Place in the World' (Britain, note, not England). Vengeful voices from (the novel's) colonies and subcultures? It's not so simple. However, Muriel Spark or John Fowles on this view reacquire a certain Englishness, not least in their analyses of power-relations between authors and characters, and—paradoxically—in their acute sense of the limits of English culture. But I'd want to consider the speculations on historical change in *The French Lieutenant's Woman* alongside, say, the overt treatment of imperialist themes in J.G.Farrell's *The Siege of Krishnapur* and *The Singapore Grip* (1978). Farrell, sometimes spoken of as a documentary writer, chooses events and images for their fictive quality, their capacity, for instance, to reveal the play-acting tendencies of colonial life. His presentation in *The Singapore Grip* of the gradual process by which the British *lose* their grip—of the way they can't get things into focus any longer, militarily, economically, or sexually—is splendidly vertiginous.

Women, of course, are another emergent nation, and perhaps precisely because English tonal decorum has especially 'suited' women, the effect is lively. The prevailing mode has to be called Gothic; and there are, I think, eerie analogies with the late eighteenth/early nineteenth century, when it must have looked as if women were taking over the novel: Duckworth's in the 1970s—with a fiction list that included Beryl Bainbridge and Caroline Blackwood—standing in for the Minerva Press. But though some of the women writers have produced literal Gothic (Fay Weldon's *Remember Me*, for instance, with its mobile, furious, dead divorcee; or Julia O'Faolain's *Women in the Wall*, set in the Dark Ages, in 'a world as fissile and fragmented as our own') it doesn't do to make them into a coven. It is a useful label because it suggests the subversive vitality of the writing, and the writers' malicious inventiveness in discovering monstrous cracks in English domestic architecture. For of course these novelists are very different. Fay Weldon has a blowsy, sarcastic hit-or-miss manner that in some ways relates her to American feminist writers; Beryl Bainbridge is dead-pan and shell-shocked, an expert in domestic claustrophobia (that ghetto of women, children, and animals where 'civilization' is regularly suspended); Caroline Blackwood is spare, stylish, and ruthless. All of them are very funny, though none has any sense of humour at all in the moderating, accomodating sense. Most self-conscious, versatile, and impressive is Angela Carter, who has launched, since *Heroes and Villains* (1969), into a full-scale anatomy of the codes and symbols of the sexual imagination. She is a truly speculative writer (or martian anthropologist) who relishes our deliquescent mythologies.

But it's not necessary to labour the point that women writers are currently very important to the novel's life. Under the 'speculative' banner I ought here to be enlisting Michael Moorcock, except that for all my talk of the spread of science fiction techniques I find his writing mysteriously, hermetically sealed off. J.G.Ballard, however, bridges with bleak efficiency the gulf between present and future tenses (*Concrete Island, High Rise*). More generally, my case for the importance of the alien perspective is, I think, served by the example of younger writers like Ian McEwan and Martin Amis, whose styles are hard-eyed, knowing, curious, utterly sceptical.... But here the map-making has to stop, and the listing begin. I always admired Anthony Burgess's *The Novel Now* for its cheerfulness and generosity and the excitement of its omnivorousness, which I'm not able to emulate. Burgess's own absence from my map, in fact, when he so clearly belongs on it as an unstoppable raider on new worlds and new languages, is a sample of the embarrassments of literary cartography. The absences of William Golding and David Storey are even more embarrassing. Perhaps I could fit them in to my 'end of empire' scenario for English fiction, but that, really, is not its point.

What I've wanted to stress is that if the English novel in the years after the war appeared to be strangling in its own decorous and unappetizing repressions—and I'm not sure it did—it's not that way now. Instead, the direction is centrifugal. (Another way of putting it is that the world the *language* colonized is breaking in: Nadine Gordimer's Africa, for instance, or Ruth Prawer Jhabvala's India, which are indeed in some ways English.) My line is that enormous changes have taken place in what it means to be English, and that you'd expect the novel to reflect on them, even if not comfortably or quickly or very directly. I have perhaps slightly dodged my brief in not talking about comparisons with writing elsewhere, but then I am arguing that much of what's significant in English fiction is written with 'elsewhere' very much in mind; is, in a sense, written *from* elsewhere.

Chris Bigsby
The Uneasy Middleground of British Fiction

The English novel has for far too long been regarded as a cosily provincial, deeply conservative, anti-experimental enterprise, resistant to innovation, rooted in mimesis, and dedicated to the preservation of a tradition of realism casually related to that of the nineteenth century. It is a view especially popular abroad, particularly in eastern Europe, which has a vested interest in the 1950s, and in the United States, which stakes an imperial claim to the contemporary. But it is a view also to be encountered in this country. Even John Fowles, speaking in 1979, remarked that 'a lot of contemporary English fiction is abysmally parochial and of no conceivable interest to anyone who is not English and middle class,' while the novel itself is easily 'the most despised of the contemporary major art forms in this country.'*

As Malcolm Bradbury has pointed out, most recently in *The Contemporary English Novel* (1979), whether or not this paradigm would be applicable to the hinterland of the English novel it would certainly have a hard time accommodating Beckett, Lowry, or, later, Burgess, Wilson, Golding, Spark, or Lessing, not to mention B.S. Johnson, Alan Burns, Christine Brooke-Rose, Ian McEwan, or Angela Carter.

In part this model is, indeed, the product of simple disregard and critical myopia. It offers a version of English writing as it appeared to be twenty years ago when the English novel discovered the midlands and the north of England and when Doris Lessing, Angus Wilson, John Fowles, and to some degree Iris Murdoch seemed more unambiguously committed to realism than their subsequent careers suggested. In part it is a product of an implied contrast with the 'deconstructive' art of the postmoderns who choose to stress the contingency of experience, the fictive nature of the self and of history, the problematics of writing, the relativity of experience and perception; who seemed, in other words, so

*All quotations are from interviews conducted over the last eighteen months

much to engage a contemporary vision of life as metatext as to condemn other kinds of writing to irrelevance, a kind of metaphysical parochialism. It is a view which does as much violence to the postmoderns as it does, say, to Saul Bellow who was never the simple realist which some critics chose to suggest and certainly, does not warrant the critical limbo into which they wish to project him. The same is equally true of a number of major English novelists.

The truth is that the English novel, at least as represented by writers such as Murdoch, Wilson, Lessing, and Fowles, occupies an interesting middle-ground, that it does respond in some degree to a sense of a fundamental shift in our perception of the real but that it reflects above all a sense of unease, of cultural dislocation, which leaves it negotiating some kind of rapproachment between humanist commitments and an increasing sense of relativism.

It is, of course, simply not adequate to characterize the Iris Murdoch of *Under the Net* (1954) and *The Black Prince* (1973) as reacting against experiment. As she herself has pointed out, her first novel actually anticipated concerns which later surfaced in the French and American novel and in criticism somewhat later still. What is true, however, is that beneath the level of play and parody, below the surface of textual instability, and behind the destabilized characters is a model of art and society which remains more secure, more wilfully structured than that of many contemporary American novelists. Her call for the novel to be a house fit for free characters to live in rests on a conception of character which would plainly not be displayed by Hawkes, Coover, Gass, or Barthelme. That is to say there remains an attachment to liberal values which requires some sense of the real, some faith in the idea of character, some sense of history which is not simply the unfolding of fiction or the deconstruction of the self against time. 'If you are writing novels you can't avoid morality,' and equally you can't avoid the constituents of morality, that is 'I think the average novel needs both plot and character.' Indeed she has, if anything, felt increasingly at odds with certain contemporary views of art, its function and its substance. A work of art, she insists, 'must have authority over its victim, or client or whatever you call the person who is meeting it. This is, of course, a principle which is now very much disputed and even attacked but in this sense I am an authoritarian. I want the work of art to stand and have authority and be able to endure. Again, the notion that it should endure is criticized by many now and a character in my first novel raised this question long before it was raised elsewhere....This was long before Barthes and Co had even appeared on the scene. But I don't hold this view.'

The narrative experiments of *The Black Prince* are not designed to destabilize the real. They constitute a series of games. Iris Murdoch resists the co-option of her novel to the postmodern aesthetic. 'It's made pretty clear,' she insists, 'how you should interpret the wanderings and maunderings of the narrator, where you should believe him and where you should not believe him....I think it is quite clear what you are supposed to think.' Reality is not offered as problematic and her observation that 'art must be connected with truth' clearly relates her to a liberal tradition invigorated by her own awareness of the reality and power of the contingent.

Iris Murdoch has also called for a renewed sense of the difficulty and complexity of the moral life and the opacity of persons. It seems to me that her work attempts this particular task by balancing a realist account of character, milieu, and social relations against a sense of the mysterious, the deforming power of the imagination, and a fascintation with the plots which people create for themselves as an analogue for the real.

Her first novel, *Under the Net,* which she herself is prone to undervalue, is concerned with the space which opens up between the world of tangible realities and the conceptualization of them. She has claimed that she is not a philosophical novelist despite her career as a teacher of philosophy, but the nature of reality and the means whereby it is apprehended remains a central concern of her work. Her characters are frequently shown to be trapped in a moral world from which they would willingly break free if only they could find the right mechanism, if only they did not grant some final authority to values which at times they effect to despise. And human relations are the agents both of moral demand and release; they are a clue to a necessary definition of reality, private and public. Love, confused, at times humiliating and entrapping, nevertheless remains a central fact and primary moral agency in her novels.

Iris Murdoch is fully aware of the ironies involved in the processes of writing, of spinning fictions in the name of truth, trapping thought in language, sculpting contingency. Indeed at times this becomes her subject, as it is, in a sense, in *Under the Net,* and as it clearly is in *The Black Prince* and to some degree in *The Sea, The Sea* (1978). And this is not simply an expression of contemporary self-doubt, a concern with acknowledging the degree to which art is implicated in the contingent world which it describes. It is because the making of fiction is coeval with the making of history, the elaboration of private meaning, and the invention of a self.

Iris Murdoch remains concerned with the struggle of her characters to deal with the dual problems of creating a life, constructing a coherent response to a world which presents itself in a series of tangible realities and moral dilemmas, while at the same time avoiding the facile consolations of simple fantasy and dream. The moral drive rests on her insistence of the primacy of the real and the obligation to distil its essence from the flux of events. In terms of personal identity it lies in the need to distinguish role from character. Sometimes the mechanism of release is humour, sometimes a commitment to values desperately invoked. The act of reconciliation may take place in the imagination, as in a sense it does in *A Word Child* (1975); sometimes in a gesture of resignation and self-abnegation. There is no single path to truth or the kind of integrity which on the whole her characters admire and long for. Their actions are hedged around with ironies, self-deceits, and betrayals but the will remains alert if not quite intact, determined to make some sense of random experience. And if this image is not untouched by absurdity there is a certain dignity and even courage in a responsibility which can never wholly be discharged, a commitment which is often defeated because it is not wholly acknowledge for what it is.

This is a recognizably liberal vision but her position is not a wholly rationalist one. In recent years she has become more and more interested in Buddhism and Christianity, though not in a dogmatic sense; that is, she has become increasingly concerned with a non-supernatural sense of spiritual life, with re-introducing a sense of the transcendent, and this is potentially at odds with a moral drive, or at least creates a tension which disturbs a simple realist reading of her work.

Something of a similar situation can perhaps be observed in the work of Angus Wilson. Seen first as social satirist, he subsequently revealed a range of style and approach which made it difficult to sustain the notion of him as essentially a provincial realist. At the beginning of his career he was identified as a brilliant if brittle social observer—a witty satirist with a skill for mimicry which was both precise and malicious. It took him some time to shake off this reputation which was built, essentially, on his early collections of short stories, *The Wrong Set* (1949) and *Such Darling Dodos* (1950). In fact, though he has never lost his incisive humour or his imitative capacity, his interest quickly broadened beyond a concern with placing his characters socially and morally with a precision which was part of the pleasure of writing.

The move from short story to novel invited a more engaged and humanist view of the human personality. And as many critics have observed there is a nineteenth century feel to his work. The plots are complex, dense with characters, events, and meaning. The social world is so important to the task of locating his characters and identifying the moral dilemmas which they face that he feels obliged to elaborate that world. That he is highly selective in the tradition which he is prepared to acknowledge and claim, however, is evidence both of his awareness of the nature and subtlety of that tradition and of his own sense of the literary quality of the world which he is constructing and thus in part validating. Thus he accepts descriptions of himself as heir to the nineteenth century tradition only in a very limited way. He accepts some relationship to Dickens but only if that writer is seen in his experimental and innovative aspects. The Dickens whom he admires is a writer aware of the constant threat of deconstruction which confronts the author and his characters.

There is also clearly a dimension on which Angus Wilson is a social realist who sees moral values as generated by the world which he describes. But he is also aware of the contingency of that world. The parodies of *No Laughing Matter* (1967) are a clear indication of his own awareness of the constraints which face the writer and the games which he plays in order to evade those constraints.

And a certain self-doubt circles around Wilson's own liberal commitments. Clearly *Hemlock and After* (1952) presents the obverse side of the humane commitment to individual freedom, to the liberation of the artist. The act of writing has a coercive quality which he suspects and which he exposes to view. And his liberalism is under pressure from another direction. The sheer density of his novels, the kaleidoscope of characters who parade before the reader, hint at a complexity of experience invulnerable to analysis, a perception of the real which, for all its apparernt 'realism', hints at levels of experience just beyond the line of vision of the observer. The point of rest tends to lie in a moment of moral balance deriving from an intimate connection between individuals, or, in a work like *The Old Men at the Zoo* (1967), a vital nexus between the individual and the natural world. The latter seems to offer a principle of continuity; it may also, however, be seen as evidence of a growing misanthropy, its social world being in a state of collapse. But against this must always be set his wit, his sense of the deep comedy of human affairs which, if it can move moral seriousness to the point of collapse, can equally redeem the bleak and the denatured.

Wilson rightly asserts the existence of an aesthetic pressure which distorts this persistent moralism; the significance of an experimental strain in his work is too often ignored because it relates to a tradition which is imperfectly perceived. 'I think that for lots of people especially those who have coined or used the word "modern" or "modernist", the tendency is to suppose that experiment can only be identified post-Jamesian and is in some way connected with the Jamesian view about the narrator and so on.' But, even within these terms, there are certain experimental novels which are absolutely vital for me. I suppose closer to me than any other novels in the twentieth century are *The Waves* and *Mrs Dalloway,* and they could be called experimental novels. But they do have this same thing I am concerned with: they tie onto the kind of novel I like to write.' And he has rightly insisted that 'both *No Laughing Matter* and *As If By Magic* have strongly experimental things in them.'

But fundamentally Angus Wilson is a humanist, though one who is deeply suspicious of the class presumptions and paternalism of British liberalism. It is the humanist dimension of Beckett to which he responds, though he regrets that he himself has never 'expressed in my novels the compassion that I think I can feel,' primarily because he is afraid of pressing that concern to the point of sentimentality. He describes himself as 'a romantic trying to make shapes because' he is aware that 'the romantic temperament is liable to go off the edge of the precipice.' This is the balancing act which is at the heart of his work and especially of his new novel *Setting the World on Fire* (1980).

Clearly he observes a society which is no longer homogeneous, as once it seemed to be, where barriers of class and sex are dissolving. And just as his early works observed individuals unable to rely on social position, money or a natural defence to find their way through life, so, in a book like *As If By Magic* (1973), he dramatizes the lives of other people trying to adjust to a sudden social viscosity, a world in which the rational and the irrational are no longer comfortably held apart. The homosexual fantasies which play a central role in the book constitute the release of energies formerly kept suppressed or expressed more obliquely. But there remains a sense of moral behaviour, the need to act as though values survived even if the evidence for them is not strong in a life which is so overtly lived through fictionalizing; in a life in which parody becomes a central strategy. 'I do believe in order and shape for books. I don't believe in happenings;' but Wilson also acknowledges the centrality of fantasy, the importance of imaginative refractions, a flight from literature as model and method which creates a vital tension in his work. And that combination is a crucial one for him and, I suspect, for a particular kind of English novelist.

Doris Lessing began her career by expressing her admiration for the climate of ethical judgment which the nineteenth century novelists generated and within which, for the most part, they operated. She even praised realism as the highest form of the novel. Her Children of Violence series began as a realist account of a young girl's movement towards personal and political maturity in Africa and London. Her primary concern lay in examining the nature of the relationship between the individual and the group, a crucial subject in the context of post-war left-wing politics. But this sequence was interrupted by *The Golden Notebook* (1962), informed by a personal and artistic crisis in the life of a woman writer, occasioning a radical reconsideration of the form of the novel and the direction of her own career. She moved away from realism 'because it's too narrow...because we have gone beyond...We now live with our head in the middle of exploding galaxies and thinking about quasars and quarks and black holes and alternative universes and so you cannot any more get comfort from old moral certainties because something new is happening. All our standards of values have been turned upside down....Everything is too relative.'

The shift from a realistic tradition of writing was vital for her career and the final volume of The Children of Violence series, *The*

Four-Gated City (1969), showed signs of a new interest in the possibilities represented by projecting the action into the future and in pressing the novel towards myth and prophecy. An increasingly apocalyptic tone typified works like *Briefing for a Descent Into Hell* (1971) and *The Summer Before the Dark* (1973). Breakdown and catastrophe were seen as preconditions of personal and social reconstruction. The nightmare vision was balanced, or at least mitigated, by a utopianism, a growing belief in the ability of man to regenerate through, if necessary, the violent agency of a cataclysm whose inevitability human imperfection ensured. Perhaps in some degree these ideas owed something to Sufi thought, which began to engage her attention, but Doris Lessing resists too mechanical a connection between her work and her spiritual and philosophical concerns.

Where Wilson has embraced Beckett for his humanism Doris Lessing once rejected him for his despairing statements of emotional anarchy, suggesting that his luxuriating in despair was a betrayal of the function of the writer. This is a position which she now rejects, as she does her assertion that a writer must become a humanist and an instrument for change, strengthening a vision that good will overcome evil. 'I wouldn't say that now because I don't know what good and evil is.'

Her recent work has taken a new direction. Always fascinated by space fiction she has come to feel that it offers her precisely that opportunity to combine experimentalism with tradition which has increasingly characterized the work of a number of major English novelists. 'It is by now commonplace to say that novelists everywhere are breaking the bonds of the realistic novel because what we all see around us becomes daily wilder, more fantastic, incredible.' She has turned to fable and myth.

And yet, for all that, the humanism remains. Her utopianism has changed its form but it remains. Her ex-patriation has always afforded her a perspective from which barriers of national identity, race, class, and even sex seem deeply suspect, destructive of a unity which she feels to have existed in a distant past and towards which she continues to look with some hope. She also feels that her ex-patriation is in some senses a modern condition, conferring an insight which is at the same time privileged and like that of the individual cut adrift from cultural, political, social, and moral traditions which have become suspect. It is an alienation which her early visionary communism had once been designed to neutralize and is now projected into a future, beyond the apocalypse. For all the transposition of the action into the future, however, the essential tenets of the realistic novel survive in her work. Though character shows signs of dissolving into an essential unity, the individual remains a primary agent and story an essential concern. The pressure of history, though displaced now into the future, operates as a central and informing fact. Angus Wilson's balancing act has its counterpart in Doris Lessing's work, though she rejects the kind of dualism which this implies.

This border territory is very much occupied by John Fowles. A writer whose formal experiments are accommodated to a liberal, almost a didactic, drive he sees a special virtue in treading what he regards as the social and aesthetic middle ground. 'My own preferred contract is in the middle ground, and I am not ashamed of being widely read....To the extent that liberalism is a teaching or converting belief, then I think realism must always hold a powerful attraction to "liberal" writers; conversely, the always lurking suspicion of elitism in experimental or highly intellectual writing...will repel them.'

Like Iris Murdoch he sees the novel as an instrument of freedom, while being equally uncertain as to the constituents and reality of that freedom: 'I am convinced there are degrees of being conditioned and that there is an area where many people...can achieve moments or periods of comparative freedom. I think it is very necessary to cling to that.' But he is all too aware of the paradox of propounding freedom through an art which can never be entirely drained of its totalitarian element. It is in this sense that a concern with art becomes simultaneously a concern with moral paradox without the one becoming simply a transposition of the other. This is the essence of *The French Lieutenant's Woman* (1969) and *The Magus* (1966) alike. This is border territory in another sense. '*The Magus* was of course a deliberately artificial, model-proposing novel, and a good deal more about fiction than any "real" situation, and I shouldn't go to the stake for Lily's morality (or her master's). Sarah, in *The French Lieutenant's Woman,* was always intended to be a sort of borderline case. I've long reached the conclusion that one principle function of the novel, or at least of my own novels, is to present such borderline cases. Daniel Martin was very intentionally conceived as such a one.'

Regarding the extremes of experimental writing (the box novel, the employment of chance procedure) as 'twentieth century rococo' which he would be happy to regard as 'amusing nonsense...if only its creators would,' he nonetheless acknowledges the force of the contingent in the natural world and accommodates it to his own work, though, like Iris Murdoch, again insisting that 'nine times out of ten' he does so 'purely for fun.' This is plainly not an entirely accurate account of his early work, the playful element being clearly subordinated to thematic concerns, but there is more than a little truth in his observation that he resists 'less and less' the pull of realism. It is perhaps not too fanciful to see this as an expression of his own political convictions which penetrate his work less as subject, except in *The Collector* (1958), than as a set of presumptions about the function of the novel, the nature of the relationship between writer and reader, and the centrality of narrative and moral stance. 'I soon lose interest in novelists who do not show their prejudices and their opinions, who do not try to sell me something beyond entertainment, wit, clever techniques, exquisite prose....Iam afraid I give good story tellers far more credit than they deserve by other literary standards, and devalue writers who depend more on stylistic gifts than narrative ones.'

The Collector is a study in power. A man imprisons a woman. The novel is generated by the struggle to impose their own models of reality on the other. The patent paranoia of the kidnapper is pitched against the social truculence of his victim, a woman whose class perspective deforms reality as powerfully as the deranged sensibility of her captor. The battle between them operates on various levels as the imprisonment exists in more than the immediate physical fact of the kidnaping. Both their worlds are placed under pressure. Her death is in some large degree her own fault. She fails morally. Challenged to find a point of contact with a being beyond herself she cannot do so. Indeed the novel stands, among other things, as a study of the pathology of a culture.

The Magus consists of an elaborate series of games and mystifications enacted on the Greek island of Phraxos. A model of the rational mind's attempt to penetrate mystery, *The Magus* probes the central question of power in its various guises. And out of this examination there grows a strongly assertive model of moral responsibility, an insistence that the self owes its shape and, finally, the justification for its being, to the acknowledgement of the rights of others: the acceptance of an automony which can be engaged but not violated. At the heart of this, as of *The French Lieutenant's Woman*, is the sexual relationship, loaded down with biological determinisms and social definitions of propriety and notions of sexual role. And though the chief manipulator, the conjurer, the magus, is a man, the agent of moral education is a woman. Masculine egotism, indeed, is presented as a principle barrier between the self and its acknowledgement of responsibilities. The novel is an assault on a hubris derived in part from rational assumptions about the precision of language and the world's propensity to void its meaning carelessly. Mystery remains a fact of the private and public world, an essential part of its reality.

The mysteries may be explained on one level. They are tricks, just as a novelist's gestures are tricks. But on another level the mystery remains. Why, after all, bother? Why the impulse to deceive, to corrupt in the direction of goodness? Conchis, the master magician, is Prospero, spinning worlds of mystery to protect something of value; but that something is a mystery located in the individual who is both his victim and his pupil.

Fowles clearly mistrusts trickery while necessarily practising it. Equally clearly he is wary of simple rationalism. He wishes to endorse neither as an adequate account of the real. He distrusts equally a world too completely contained by enigma and one in which meaning is too completely displayed through language or contained by social structures. There is a virtue in refusing to be contained by plots generated by others but there is equally a virtue in the moment of self-abnegation which is the essence of love.

The Magus plays with myth and is myth. On one occasion he was persuaded to say, 'I was trying to tell a fable about the relationship between man and his conception of God.' But in this world God, too, is suspect; the pleasure of manipulation is not without its moral implications. The conjurer relies on deceit and the process whereby the individual is moved in the direction of truth is not without its ironies and, more importantly, its hypocrisies.

These lessons are all hard-earned, particularly in *The French Lieutenant's Woman* in which the protagonist is pressed beyond the parameters of his experiences on a social no less than sexual level. As in *The Magus*, it is the woman who instructs, who draws him towards a world in which time collapses no less insistently than outmoded social models. An imitation nineteenth century novel, the book blossoms out of that moment in which the familiar structures and assumptions dissolve. The book presents the reader with a series of alternative endings, offering itself as primary evidence of the possibility of taking radically new directions, breaking free of contours assumed too easily to be defining boundaries.

Fowles is committed to story-telling. The process of invention is itself the source of values. But it is also the origin of coercion. And in this respect he identifies an ambivalence which equally affects the individual, part constrained, part free agent. His form reflects and contains this debate, as in some degree does Iris Murdoch's (more especially in *The Black Prince*). To some extent, of course, this freedom which he offers is factitious. The author unavoidably has his thumb on the scale, but his gestures of deconstruction, his offer to let the text go where it will, is not wholly unreal or deceptive. The reassuring patterns, once disrupted, can never entirely re-form. The spaces have been opened up and the mind cannot help but begin to fill them. The wound may not be primal but the imagination's power to people it suggests a level on which we evade control or at least determine the texture and tone of our existence if not its fundamentals.

Daniel Martin (1977) is a confessedly self-indulgent book. Passages and incidents are sustained too long, drained too completely of their meaning, too ruthlessly pursued for their metaphoric significance. Nonetheless, the scale of the book is important. It ranges from England to America, restlessly searching for the real source of moral collapse. There is a powerful sense that in some ways his characters here inhabit a social world not really hospitable to the moral being. And yet the central task remains to discover a mode of living which bypasses the distractions, the trivializing flood of experience, the ready-made worlds of Hollywood or fantasy for a purer world of genuine emotion and personal commitment. The real objective remains the moral self, a point not of stasis but of balance, of sustained tension, which is equally the aesthetic of Fowles' work. He is both a traditionalist and an experimentalist. His admiration for the natural world, exemplified in his book *The Tree*, is not a sentimentality or a simple piety. There is a value to be found in the very fact of a vital existence, in a Zen-like awareness of process which contains both growth and decay, the contradictory but complimentary elements of a world which, like his own work, operates by contrarities.

If all four of these writers remain in some sense realists, theirs is by no means an innocent realism. It is an enterprise suffused with an awareness of the suspect nature of language, the manipulative power of art, the fragility of character, the dubious nature of historicism, the relativity of value and perception, and the collapse of the absolute. It incorporates the parodic, shifting tenses, multiple narrative possibilities and fictive games, but does so in the context of an art drawn to moral imperatives, committed to the centrality of narrative, the survival of character, and the assertion of the significance, if no longer quite the centrality, of the individual located against a history whose logic cannot be easily evaded. The real which they engage has expanded to acknowledge a spiritual dimension (Murdoch and Lessing) and the significance of fantasy (Wilson) but the freedom which they assert is not limited to the imagination or the spinning of fictions. There are other urgencies, as there are for a writer like Bellow who also inhabits this border territory and who likewise resists the reduction of all experience to text. This, of course, is neither a virtue nor a vice. The postmodern writer, feeling the pressure of history, will assert playful release occasioned by apocalypse, or detail the collapse of axial literary and social forms. In contrast, the English writer is apt—like a number of American authors—to reflect the anxiety generated by such a vision, but does so by negotiating a territory where it is possible to sustain a commitment neither neutralized by irony nor rendered inoperative by relativism.

Frederick Bowers
An Irrelevant Parochialism

What strikes an ex-patriate most about the contemporary British novel is its conformity, its traditional sameness, and its realistically rendered provincialism. Shaped only by its contents, the British novel is the product of group mentality: local, quaint, and self-consciously xenophobic. Why is it that of the many able craftsmen writing in Britain so few have experimented with form, and, of those, experimented with such caution? There is no reason special to the novel genre itself. There are, however, properties about its form—an expression of a particular relation between art and life—which reveal the assumptions and beliefs underlying the characteristic narrowness of the British novel. The culture from which British fiction derives, and the culture insistently expressed in its writing, is clearly oriented towards fact, content, metonymy, empiricism, and the body.

It is a commonplace that British intellectual history since the seventeenth century has consistently evidenced support for the pragmatic and experiential at the expense of the formal. The Lockeian *tabula rasa* provided a paradigm for British thought. In philosophy, linguistics, psychology, and especially criticism, it is function and accountability that matter. Johnson, Arnold, and Leavis all saw literature as a moral instrument rather than as imaginative re-creation, and successfully disseminated their assumptions through generations of readers. The *reductio ad absurdam* must surely have been David Holbrook's complaint in the *Guardian* that the Profumo scandal could only have occurred because of a lapse in vigilance of contemporary literature.

The instrumental view of literature is especially evident in the novel, which from the start was concerned with the uplifting effect of the 'good read'. Bunyan, Defoe, Richardson, Fielding, and their journalist colleagues all worked toward establishing a static *lisible* novel genre whose function was to reinforce the values of the society the reader inhabited, entertaining him with sequenced gossip organized by a clear moral. This is not to deny, of course, that some writers played games, as evidenced by the fiction of Defoe (the unclear moral direction of *Moll Flanders,* for instance) or of Sterne, probably the only true British postmodernist. But generally, and as if by mutual agreement, the novelists of the nineteenth and even the twentieth century have experimented, if at all, only with the events 'out there'. Eccentric characters, strange (but rarely bizarre events) may from time to time relieve the sociological tedium; but even so, the distance between *The Cement Garden* and *This Sporting Life* is not so great.

The preoccupation with real-world experience and the distaste for experience-distant reflection characteristic of contemporary British fiction are representative of a more general contemporary spirit. Two instances recently attracted my attention. One was the obituary for Roland Barthes in the *Times*, attacking him for 'errors of abstraction which besides being particularly uncongenial to the Anglo-Saxon spirit, were often simply wrong-headed.' The statement requires little comment, expressing far better than I can the lazy, provincial authoritarianism of twentieth century Britain. The second was the publication of Ian Robinson's *The New Grammarians' Funeral*, combining a consistently superficial reading of Chomsky with a non-nonsense, down-to-earth, common sense denunciation of a theory because it *is* a theory (and, moreover, a rationalist one) rather than what is presumably preferable: a collection of anecdotes, more congenial to the Anglo-Saxon spirit. These examples, unfortunately, are not isolated cases.

The underlying principle informing the distaste for theory and the referential narrowness of the British novel is a confusion about the relation between fact and fiction, between the world and the word. A thoroughgoing empiricist, true to his principles, must find fiction difficult to accommodate. If objects and events 'outside' wholly constitute reality, then there is no reality left to rearrange. And fiction is, among other things, a rearrangement of perceived reality: there is something in the human mind as real as the reality on the outside that permits reaction and rearrangement.

Man as a fiction-making animal is a datum that the empiricist cannot at last account for. The behavioural psychologist, confronted by similar data, must erect a system of mediation between stimulus and response, as any step towards mind is impossible for him on logical grounds. The literary critic, of course, is excused the formal explicitness that the psychologist must achieve, and so can dismiss notions of mind and form without addressing them seriously enough to upset his referential principles. In turn, the writer of fiction permits himself only the slightest rearrangement of reality (thus becoming almost as passive as the reader) and the reader happily dons his cardigan of local colours to have his received notions about the world once more reinforced.

The empiricist view of fiction is that it is a special and awkward case of fact. However, the contrary view may be asserted with more confidence and evidence, that fact is a special case of fiction. Certainly recent semantic investigation supports this assertion. The common words of our utterances do not indicate real objects in the world but merely summarize sets of semantic features whose combinations may or may not be matched by some real object or event. *Tree* is a meaningful word, but so also is *elf;* we can define both words despite the fact that there are trees but not elves. The point is that words, as opposed to names, are fictional constructs: they can be matched by objects and events in the real world; but they can also map out objects and events not in the real world. To interpret discourse as though it were strictly referential excludes metaphor, and denies the human imagination. To interpret all words referentially ignores their independent status as fictional forms and structures.

The fictionality of words is matched by the fictionality of utterances in general. An utterance does not become a speech act unless conditions of sincerity, capacity, and uptake are met. 'Hand over your wallet!' is only real in the right circumstances; the same utterance in the 'as if' context of a novel does not bring the reader out in cold sweat and make him drop his book. Again, we have to acknowledge the potential use of utterances in real life while at the same time denying their exclusive use as real life tokens. The constant state of words and utterances is their form not their function: formal properties are present regardless of function. Because words and utterances have formal properties, they are eminently suitable for all kinds of games and play, with or without concomitant rearrangements of reported actions or events. In many respects, the degree of abstraction called on to permit games of verbal rearrangement is less than that required to view them only as tokens of reality. Literature may be seen as the final stage of language acquisition in its play with linguistic forms: perhaps

British children are forbidden to riddle once they have reached eleven.

Referential fictions inevitably encourage specific, referential interpretations, inviting a reader to approach what he reads like a complex puzzle with an isolated solution. Apart from that this assumption logically leads to dismantling libraries and replacing them by a short-list of themes, it urgently underestimates the writer's craft, first by readers and ultimately by writers themselves. In Britain, such a process of underestimation is, like a disease, far advanced, accelerated during the past thirty years by the reference-based criticism so aggressively preached by F.R. Leavis and his disciples.

Recall Leavis's criteria of greatness in the novel: the 'awareness of the possibilities of life', 'marked moral intensity', form 'appreciated only in terms of the moral preoccupations that characterize the novelist's peculiar interest in life.' Leavis was the strongest critical influence on those growing up in the fifties and sixties, and his insistence on reading fiction for fact and evaluating it in terms of morality firmly authorized a wholly non-formal mode of interpretation. From this date and distance Leavis's work looks parochial and insignificant; but his apparent insignificance must not distort the real and profound sway he had over several generations of writers and readers. Leavis trivialized imaginative literature to a moral tract, encouraging a generation to deny their innate appreciation of form to the degree that they are no longer able to recognize or respond to it. Moreover, in establishing an autonomy of literary interpretation, critics of the Leavis school have managed to demonstrate a wilful ignorance of the nature of language and meaning by rejecting or ignoring what philosophers like Austin, Ryle and Strawson, and linguists like Firth and Halliday had to say, preferring to remain loftily distant from issues which might have had significance for literary interpretation.

Thus, the original thrust towards empiricism, once technologically liberating, has ultimately fossilized into a rigid, blinkered orthodoxy, one of the expressions of which is the modern British novel. Nor do there seem to be many signs of change. The exchange of ideas and methodologies among philosophers of language, linguists, and critical theorists that has enlivened and informed writers and critics in, for example, France and the United States seems to be unknown in Britain. Even as sympathetic and generally open-minded a critic as David Lodge finds the 'great formal brilliance and indeterminable purport' of postmodernism ultimately only absurd, because he too maintains the tradition of referential interpretation, restricting literary meaning to relevance for the human condition. The medium of postmodernism may be different, but the message, he insists, must be the same. His list of postmodernist characteristics—contradiction, permutation, discontinuity, randomness, excess and short circuit—leads him to see postmodernism as 'essentially a rule-breaking kind of art' parasitically depending on conventional works that keep to the rules. This is, of course, to get things quite upside down, imposing a wholly prescriptive meaning on 'rule'. Postmodernist writers assume that fiction is ultimately rule-governed in the way that all language is, so they use the (generative, predictive) rules freely. Like the last of Bluebeard's wives they insist on opening the forbidden door and living to tell the tale. To a culture which has suppressed many of these rules and prescribed a code of usage instead, the free exploration of rules might well look like rebellion. However, if we make analogy with language, exploring possibilities is natural, suppressing them unnatural. When John Barth refers to postmodernist fiction as 'the literature of exhaustion', he surely means a determination to explore the rules of language and form as far as they extend.

Postmodernist writers, then, are asserting the freedom to explore the possibilities of fiction; in doing so they reject reference and moral message as the limits of the novel's meaning, seeing them instead as merely parts of the novel's possibilities. However, the British empirical tradition acknowledges one authorized form only. The modes of traditional realism and postmodernism are not a dichotomy but an implication whereby the latter includes the former. Mid-century British criticism, by presenting a false either-or picture has, I believe, brought about a failure of creative nerve. Perhaps if critics and reviewers started to address the novel with the same openness with which they have addressed poetry the unnatural fetters which at present bind the British novel might dissolve.

James Gindin
Taking Risks

Transatlantic literary critical lenses are no more immune from distortion than are any others. Recently, these lenses have been more often compounded with generosity than with insularity, a fairly typical example of which is evident in David Lodge's review in the *Guardian* of *Granta's* issue on American writing; Lodge concludes:

> So, is contemporary American fiction more challenging, adventurous than ours? Well, yes. It seems less constrained by respect for realism, and less fearful of seeming pretentious. The American writer is apt to dare more, not only in form, but also in subject matter.

The terms of this praise are no more convincing, for me, than the comparative conclusion. I am not sure that daring is a measure of good writing, but, more significantly, I suspect that many of the novels Lodge means to praise, novels that work through fantasy or through a formal indictment or reversal of what they stipulate as the conventional novel form, in fact dare considerably less than do many British novels.

What is often called the anti-novel, characterized by its conspicuous rejection of the 'traditional' novel and its insistence on the disjunction between literature and life, seems only to avoid risk in name of innovation, fleeing to the safety of formal preoccupations. The fiction of Donald Barthelme and John Hawkes, for example, are, in different ways closed off, removed, self-satisfied in the intricacies of their formal concerns. Although they contain a kind of fascination, they expose a fear of engagement, reposing in the closet of a safe structure. I do not mean to attack all formal experimentation in contemporary fiction, or all novels that implicitly question their own forms. Thomas Pynchon's *Gravity's Rainbow*, for example, is probably the best, most probing and comprehensive novel written in English during the last decade. But Pynchon's experimental form organizes experience, as, within the novel, paranoia organizes the chains of cause and effect we invent, as rocketry organizes aggression, as gravity and colour give texture to the changes of history, in a way that is far from self-enclosed. Pynchon, in other words, uses his formal paraphernalia to create a world that is both a metaphor for human experience (as science creates metaphors to describe experience) and a thoughtful, dense commentary on the world we inhabit. Other anti-novels, however, come closer simply to fabricating the 'anti' as a refuge from the novel itself.

Formal innovation is not in itself a standard for judgment of the novel; the standard is the use or function of the formal innovation, in form *and* content. Perhaps the fact that the literary and the academic cultures have become so much closer in recent years has led to the increasing concentration on formal elements in fiction. Discoveries about form make dependable seminars, and 'innovation' in academic circles now approaches the sanctity once accorded 'truth' and 'beauty'. Yet attention to form alone restricts the range of considerations of the novel, and becomes its own form of easy evasion. In a similar way, many British novelists, otherwise talented and engaging, have diluted their recent work by excessive or disproportionate attention to form, deferring to the critical idea (which we know already) that this is only fiction, not life, after all.

Doris Lessing's fiction, for example, has always demonstrated an interest in the nature of fiction. At its best, in the interlocking notebooks of *The Golden Notebook* or the consciously changing perspectives that provide self-definition in *The Summer before the Dark,* this interest centres on the function of fiction, fabricated schemes for organising complex experience. At times, as in *The Four-Gated City,* the consciousness of fictionality seems disproportionate, or, if not disproportionate, strangely suggestive of a sudden leap into an extended and apocalyptically produced future world. But, more recently, the obtrusive consciousness of fictionality seems less a gesture of apocalpyse than an obligatory sign of deference to current critical fashion. *The Marriages between Zones Three, Four, and Five (as Announced by the Chronicles of Zone Three),* the second novel of an intended trilogy, establishes a cosmos of fantasy, creating different zones of experience like the panels of a large medieval tapestry. Through the metaphors of tapestry, Lessing presents dense and fascinating observation on human relationships, on childbirth, and on the resentments of women in different societies. Yet, at several points the novel breaks off to concentrate on the voice of narration, a disembodied communal voice that is 'storyteller, ballad-maker, Chronicler', and to speculate for pages that add little about the nature and problems of communal voices. The narration is self-indulgent.

Margaret Drabble's two most recent novels are infected by a similar virus, in this instance a more specifically academic strain. In *The Realms of Gold*, the heroine is carefully and sensitively described. But other characters, who, in the initial scheme, seem equally important, are shunted aside because, as the suddenly emergent authorial voice announces, 'Omniscience has its limits'. Here, the contemporary critical truism seems an apology for a partial failure of imagination or an unwillingness to work out all the issues the novel poses—a matter that also affects the judgments the novel delivers. A similar dislocation is even more destructive in *The Ice Age* which ends in a sudden and elaborately casual gesture of futuristic fantasy (after all, it's only a novel—why not?) simply, it appears, to sustain the metaphor of the title that was too rigid for the characters and the life depicted. David Lodge's *Changing Places* is a funny and acutely

David Lodge's *Changing Places* is a funny and acutely sensitive novel about an American/British academic exchange. In switching from one visit to another, the novel can also accommodate an insertion of the epistolary novel (each professor has left his wife at home) in which the epistolary novel is referred to as a quaint, irrelevant tradition. But the novel cannot accommodate its own ending. When all four principals finally meet in New York because wives as well as jobs have to be exchanged, Lodge switches to a film scenario, saying novels have to end and films don't, and the relationships between the four cannot really be worked out. My objection is not that the relationships should have been worked out in any particular way, not even that they should have been resolved. Not all novels resolve their premises. Rather, the switch to another art form appears as only a flippant rejection of the interesting and intractable material the novel itself generated and an evasion of its own comic terms. Even in fiction more pedestrian that that of Lessing, Drabble, and Lodge, the ending that emphasizes another perspective, another fictive view on the fiction that has been the novel, is, as in Paul Bailey's *Peter Smart's Confessions,* commonplace. In each of these instances, something vital, something potentially probing or amusing, or both, is lost or shunted aside by the author's insistence on emphasizing his or her consciousness of the fictionality of fiction. It is, at a crucial moment, a safe retreat to form at the expense of content.

In arguing against excessive formal experimentation, I am not advocating 'realism' as a necessary criterion. 'Realism' is a false issue. By its nature, all fiction is selected, shaped, edited, created—none of it is a transcription of a 'real' world, whatever that may be. At the same time, all fiction is someone's version of what experience is significant or unusual or interesting, someone's version of what really matters. What I am advocating, however, is a confrontation with content, a realization that the experience transmitted in fiction connects in some way with human experience. And in spite of the qualifications I mentioned earlier (and within a good deal of the work of those novelists I mentioned earlier as well), British fiction over the last thirty years has significantly confronted the content of contemporary experience. In many ways, British fiction has confronted content more directly than American fiction, has settled less often and less centrally for the evasion of excessive formal intricacy and the self-indulgence of reiterated fictionality. In the terms of Lodge's contrast in the *Guardian* British fiction has, if the contrast is meaningful at all, taken more risks.

Admittedly, the confrontations with content in British fiction have often been limited. Malcolm Bradbury's novels are, for the most part, confined to expositions of university life. Taken together, *Eating People is Wrong, Stepping Westward,* and *The History Man* provide a chronicle of the changes in the institution over the last quarter of a century. Martin Amis, in *The Rachel Papers,* develops a lively texture of contemporary reference, full of familiar elements like anatomies of seduction. His range of concern is limited to a sense that life is an 'empirical or *tactical* business', yet, unlike that of some of his elders, his stance never hardens into slogan or dogma. In both authors, a sense of comedy that establishes and undercuts its own premises allows the referential statement about the contemporary world to stand in spite of its limitation. Other contemporary writers, with considerable skill, exploit the dimensions of other kinds of narrowness. Beryl Bainbridge, in novels as different as *Harriet Said, The Bottle Factory Outing, Injury Time,* and *Young Adolf* brilliantly depicts the sense of menace and violence lurking within mundane experience in a variety of dingy urban and suburban surroundings. David Cook creates the world of the economically or mentally indigent as they wander, often in escape, around contemporary Britain. In *Albert's Memorial, Happy Endings,*

Walter, and *Winter Dove,* Cook's stark and particular porse establishes a world that is both internally, self-referentially coherent and socially significant. It, like Beryl Bainbridge's world, creates metaphor without preening itself on its metaphorical status. Similarly, contemporary taste has helped to resurrect interest in some valuable and risk-taking novelists from the past, the late Jean Rhys and the late Barbara Pym for example. Each writer's fictional world is different—none of them is the 'real' world—and each is a coherent statement about experience.

With its development coinciding in so many ways with the growth of classes, the novel form has always seemed generically suited to accommodate issues of class. This seems particularly true of the British novel, not because class is necessarily more visible in British society or more restrictive, but rather because, to some extent, American fiction has always exhibited a relatively greater concern with the mechanics of its own metaphors, has always been relatively more hesitant confronting the society to which its fictions refer. The focus on the relationship between individuals and the world outside them, the influence of political changes, and the authority of social myths are all familiar elements of British fiction, involving considerable risk because they refer to a world partially known and knowable for the reader. This particular kind of confrontation often takes considerable time and practice for a novelist to develop. A number of writers, first recognized and praised in the fifties, have done their best work a good deal later, published when critics had begun to carp, complaining about a falling off or a repetitive pattern (again, criticism, both popular and academic, is most likely to reward the innovative). John Wain needed to purge his moral perspective of insularity, of a pride in localism that, although always handled comically, restricted understanding before he could write his best novel, *A Winter in the Hills* (1970). None of Angus Wilson's early, comprehensive fables of English society had quite the range, the depth, or the complexity of *No Laughing Matter* (1967). David Storey ventured his capacious social novel several times, in varying degrees of abstraction, before managing the complicated intensity of *Saville* (1976). And Frederic Raphael seemed to require a considerable apprenticeship before achieving the social range and density of *The Glittering Prizes* (1976). A novel like *Glittering Prizes,* in which each element is superficially familiar, almost every character in some way recognizable from the composite of fiction and experience that most of us carry around with us, is easily underrated as insufficiently distinctive, yet its distinction inheres in the unusual probity and intelligence with which its familiarity comes to life, in the depth, the strength, and the originality of its art.

The issue that I have tried to describe, with some hesitation and some realization that the alternatives attach themselves to British as against American fiction only partially and imperfectly, is finally a statement about how one builds and applies his fictions in worlds (both literary critical and actual) that provide no certainties. Some prefer multiple re-inventions of the wheel, recognizing that each wheel can be intriguingly different in design and construction. But, if that wheel is, as it must be in a world without certainty, one without a paradigmatic model, a wheel of chance, then spinning it and seeing where it accidentally stops, involves me more than does the construction of the wheel itself. The interest in construction, like an interest in ever more elaborate fictional forms, is surely one kind of legitimate interest. Still, so is an interest in the patterns of the numbers or the colours or the textures on which the wheel stops over a period of time. The second alternative seems to me to reflect experience more often and more closely, with more involvement, although I know that any wheel is only metaphorical. This interest in the changing patterns of colour and texture on the wheel is, for me, often imperfectly and occasionally enthusiastically gratified by the diversity, the range, and the challenges of contemporary British fiction.

Christine Brooke-Rose
Where Do We Go from Here?

The 'postmodern' phenomenon has been much written about lately, and some high claims are being made for it, notably by Ihab Hassan and Mas'ud Zavarzadeh, though both Susan Sontag and David Lodge in their work have been more cautious, each ending on a qualifying note.

Ihab Hassan's *Paracriticisms—Seven Speculations on the Times* (1975) is a highly stimulating if disorderly study, itself a new type of 'postmodernist' criticism, using typographic juxtapositions, digressions, and so on, and ending in a vision of a 'new gnosticism' (see end of this essay). Some of his modernist categories as developed by 'postmodernism' seem over-generalized and purely thematic: Urbanism, Technologism, Dehumanization, Primitivism, Eroticism, Antinomianism, Experimentalism (the only non-thematic one, which of course applies to all new art forms of any period).

Mas'ud Zavarzadeh's *The Mythopoeic Reality—the Postwar American Nonfiction Novel* (1976) is naturally mainly about the nonfiction novel as a 'postmodern' phenomenon, which he calls 'supramodern' and which covers nonfiction and 'transfiction'. The latter he divides into *metafiction, surfiction*, and *science fiction* (that is, the 'new' SF), thus bringing a little more precision into the discussion. All 'supramodern' novels are united by what he calls a 'nontotalizing' sensibility or resistance to interpretation. In 'transfiction' this is achieved by means of a 'baroque over-interpretation of the human situation.' *Metafiction* (with which I am mainly concerned here) is 'ultimately a narrational metatheorem whose subject matter is fictional systems themselves [...It] exults over its own fictitiousness, and its main counter-techniques are flat characterization, contrived plots, antilinear sequences of events, all fore-grounded as part of an extravagant over-totalization, a parody of interpretation which shows up the multiplicity of the real and the naîveté of trying 'to reach a total synthesis of life within narrative.' Over-totalization thus 'creates a work with low-message-value at the zero-degree of interpretation, thus freeing the narrative from an anthropomorphic order-hunting and insuring that, as Barthelme says, there is nothing between the lines but white spaces,' echoing 'Witold Gombrowicz's concept of the mocking of meaning and his advice to readers (in *Ferdydurke*) to "start dancing with the book instead of asking for a meaning."' None of which of course has prevented critics from interpreting these works.

Susan Sontag's essay 'The Aesthetics of Silence' in *Against Interpretation* (1966) is too well-known to summarize, but she was one of the first to sound the 'postmodern' note, without using that now current but meaningless term. David Lodge's *The Modes of Modern Writing—Metaphor, Metonymy, and the Typology of Modern Literature* (1977) uses Jackobson's fundamental distinction between the syntagmatic and paradigmatic axes of language to discuss 'postmodernist' fiction in a brilliant last chapter.

On this occasion, I would like to look at the work of a few of the 'postmodern' writers, giving, I hope, a clearer picture of their achievement, and I will conduct my analysis in the light of a broad but useful formal division, that between parody and stylization.

Most of the novels commonly regarded as 'postmodernist' are characteristically implausible but (technically) realistic representations of the modern human situation: they dramatize, that is, the *theme* of the world's non-interpretability. John Barth's long novels, *The Sot-Weed Factor* (1961) and *Giles Goat-Boy* (1966), would be the first manifestation of this, though perhaps only retrospectively, for at the time they were appreciated as uproarious satires. And of course *The Sot-Weed Factor* also stylizes, in the sense that it parodies seventeenth-century English, but I shall define stylization more precisely later.

Similarly, John Fowles' *The Magus* (1966) is 'about' the

individual's construction of reality. Nicholas is lured into the rich magnate Conchis's property on a Greek island, and at first does not know that his experiences are artificially concocted. Slowly he loses all his certainties, but each time he thinks he has understood what is real and what is illusion, the real is revealed as another illusion. This is Conchis's 'godgame', so named because it is not 'really a game and there is no God' (except Conchis). David Lodge has called this a maze without exit, the plot of which we cannot unravel, but this is not so: there are explanations throughout and a final explanation, when Nicholas is told that *all* was organized, and how. His resulting rage, self-pity, and despair result not so much at having been tricked as at realizing that the godgame has ended; that Conchis and his 'assistants' have loaded the dice and quit the game; that he is back where he started but now lost, unwatched by them, stripped of significance, of spectators; that life is not a performance.

In a thoughtful article, Ernst Von Glaserfeld points out that as long as man acts for spectators he is neither free nor human.[1] Further, that it is not the Magus who has loaded the dice that drove Nicholas nearly out of his mind, but the way Nicholas himself interpreted the events around him: he had loaded the dice long ago by accepting a commonplace and naive view of the world, thinking he knew what the world was like. 'Fowles comes to the core of constructivist epistemology when he lets Conchis explain the idea of coincidence when he tells the two stories, of the rich collector in Paris and the farmer in Norway: "There was no connection between the events. No connection is possible. Or rather, I am the connection, I am whatever meaning the coincidence has."' As Glaserfeld notes, this amounts to an everyday paraphrase of Einstein's revolutionary insight that in the physical world there is no simultaneity without an observer to create it. In the modern constructivist theory of knowledge, 'not only coincidence are seen as arising out of the experiencer's own activity, but also the events that are coinciding, the notions of space and time, of motion and causality, and even those experiential compounds that we call objects—they all come about through the experiencer who relates, who institutes differences, similarities and identities, and thus creates for himself a stable world of sorts' (see Piaget, *La Construction du réel chez l'enfant* (1967), or, in physics, Heisenberg, *Physics and Philosophy*, (1958)). Fowles is concerned with the pragmatic and ethical aspects of this.

Von Glaserfeld admits that *The Magus* is 'in many ways an old-fashioned novel', and compares it to Fournier's *Le Grand Meaulnes* or to Pirandello; but he also insists that 'seen in the framework of the history of ideas, it belongs to the front of constructivist thought.' The 'theme' is new (though a *de*constructionist 'theme' would be 'newer'), but the form is old-fashioned.

So there we have it, the old split between form and content. There is indeed not a line, not a formal device (or represented speech, thought, action, or scene) in the book that does not belong to the traditional realistic novel—which is why of course, it is so 'readable' despite its plot's complexities. And many of the 'postmodernist' novels or, to use Zavarzadeh's more precise term, metafictions, are of this type. Robert Coover's *The Origin of the Brunists* (1966) is an ironic investigation of mystical sects in America; a local newspaper editor provides the ironic authorial eye, with all the paraphernalia of detailed description, description openers, narrator explanation in pluperfect analepse, lengthy free indirect discourse of the most fatigued kind, narrator comment to dialogue of the 'participial phrase', variety parodied by Barth, and so forth. *The Universal Baseball Association Inc* (1968) has a lighter, more slangy modern tone, but technically does not differ from the mainstream novels of the thirties, forties, fifties (etc.). *The Public Burning* (1976) is more 'outrageous' in subject matter: it imaginatively dramatizes a well-known contemporary political figure, Vice-President Nixon, during the week just before the execution of the Rosenbergs; in odd visionary moments Uncle Sam appears (who protects, scolds and guides him). But it is also dead-pan realistic, and that is of course the point: all Nixon's thoughts, worries, ambitions, and ludicrous moments are imaginary, but set forth in what reviewers call 'utterly convincing', 'forcefully realized' terms. Only the 'intermedia' *Intermezzo*, in dramatic form (*The Clemency Appeals—A Dramatic Dialogue by Ethel Rosenberg and Dwight Eisenhower*) between President and Prisoner (Pres/Pris), is given full parodic treatment.

Coover is concerned with history and our constant reinterpretation of it (though of course his over-interpretation is yet another interpretation), just as Fowles is concerned with man's interpretation of the world. One can see Coover moving from both traditional and parodic dramatizations of contemporary problems to 'stylization'. But in *The Public Burning*, the parody is intermittent; although it pervades the whole, there is no manifest difference between what I call 'dead-pan' realism and realism, except where the topic (e.g. the meetings with Uncle Sam) make it clear. In a sense of course, parodic dramatization is one long stylization of realism, but the balance between parody and stylization is delicate. I shall return to this problem in a moment.

Similarly, Thomas Pynchon's *V* (1963) and *Gravity's Rainbow* (1973) are quests for meaning in a man-centered world where the multiplicity of interpretive systems makes it impossible to envisage a whole.[2] Both novels draw on science-fiction motifs (anti-utopia, the talking computer, radio-controlled characters, loss of identity, and dehumanization generally). *V*, moreover, heavily parodies the spy-story in all sections of the past 'recovered' by the main quester Stencil; while *Gravity's Rainbow*, by making all the characters paranoiac, drugged, and hallucination-prone, cancels even provisional realities: as Tony Tanner has said, 'it is not always clear whether we are in a bombed out building or a bombed-out mind'.[3]

Unlike *The Magus* and Coover's or Barth's books, *V* and *Gravity's Rainbow* are not (and presumably not meant to be) 'readable' in the book industry's sense of 'entertaining', chiefly because the 'theme' is considerably more blured than in Barth's social satire or Fowles' 'constructivist' theme or Coover's non-interpretability of history. It is blurred, first in itself: the object (or non-object) of the quest (or anti-quest) is couched in old-fashioned symbolic terms such as the phallus/rocket business in *Gravity's Rainbow* and the 'scratching the surface' notion that pervades *V*, as for instance in the Vheissu motif paradigmatic of the whole work (Vheissu as a lost civilization but also a constantly changing surface, an aesthetic pleasure, a luxury). Symbolism of this kind is notoriously over-exploited in modern realistic fiction. Second, it is blurred in the over-interpretation which Zavarzadeh speaks of, which 'creates a work of low-message value at the zero-degree of interpretation.' And, lastly, it is blurred in the clogging traditional mechanisms of the realistic novel that inevitably go with interpretation, and, *a fortiori*, with over-interpretation.

One such blurring would have been enough, but the heaviest is the third. Even the present tense and the present participles used in *Gravity's Rainbow* seem a mere pointless substitution for the past and pluperfects of other sections: the present is a historic present (as in the nineteenth-century novel), and the past would do just as well; despite the time-shifts (clearly marked), it does not have the eerie effect we get from its atemporal use by Robbe-Grillet. Apart from the occasional present tense (occasional only in *V*, and used in a traditional way for generalization), and some 'intermedia' bad verse and songs (but one finds songs in realistic fiction) we get the whole realistic machinery, including the defocalized heroes and the constant shifts of viewpoint, parodied (within the parody of the novelist writing a novel) by Barth in 'Life-Story' (*Lost in the Funhouse* (1968)), with his letter-characters: 'D comes to suspect that the world is a novel, himself a fictional personage....Moreover E, hero of D's account...called upon a literary acquaintance....C comes to suspect that the world is a novel....If I'm going to be a fictional character G declared to himself....How revolutionary J appears to be....If he can only get K through his story I reflected grimly' (I being both a letter and a pronoun). Of course here the letter represents the author's various versions (versions of himself and versions born up), but it also accurately reflects the formula of modern realistic fiction, whereby A is introduced, then B in the next section, then C, then back to A, then D and so forth in infinite permutations. In *V* for instance this technique apparently amounts to parody (new place/new person plus explanatory description, or vice versa):

> As the afternoon progressed, yellow clouds began to gather over Place Mohammed Ali, from the direction of the Libyan Desert. A wind with no sound at all swept up rue Ibrahim and across the square, bringing a desert chill into the city.
> For one P. Afeul, cafe waiter and amateur libertine, the clouds signalled rain. (52)

> The bierhalle north of Ezbekiyich Garden had been created by North European tourists in their own image ...but so German as to be ultimately a parody of home.
> Hanna had held on to the job only because she was stout and blond. A smaller brunette from the south had stayed for a time but.... (76)

> Dudley Eigenvalue, D.D.S., browsed among treasures in his Park Avenue office/residence. Mounted on black velvet

in a locked mahogany case, showpiece of the office, was a set of false dentures, each tooth of a different precious metal. (138)

In April of 1899 young Evan Godolphin, daft with the spring and sporting a costume too Esthetic for such a fat boy, pranced into Florence. (141)

Miss Victoria Wren, late of Lardwick-in-the-Fen, Yorks., recently self-proclaimed citizen of the world, knelt devoutly in the front pew of a church just off Via dello Studio. (151)

But when a parody of such a clumsy method is repeated throughout, almost as a tick, one starts taking it at face-value, which is particularly unfortunate when one of the 'counter-techniques' (Zavarzadeh) is flat characterization.[5] The defocalization is pushed to extremes to prevent us from identifying with any of the characters by staying too long with them, so that when we return to them and their supposedly absurd but flatly, realistically told activities (hunting alligators in New York sewers, having a nose altered by a plastic surgeon, getting drunk, having sex, stealing supplies from ship, etc.), we hardly care, as we hardly care in 'real life', with its 'meaningless' millions and their 'meaningless' activities; indeed we would, as in real life, have trouble remembering them were it not for their often highly motivated names (Profane the 'schlemihl', Stencil, McClintic Sphere, Schoenmaker the plastic surgeon, Eigenvalve, Pig, The Whole Sick Crew, etc).

This in theory does not happen with the model parodied, which tries (and sometimes fails) to make us identify and care, and it is a moot point whether parody of a model for its failures, in dead earnest and at such length, is true parody or simply the model in its fatigued aspect. For if we roughly summarize the determination of the Barthes codes in Pynchon, we find that the Action and the Hermeneutic Codes are underdetermined (as in realistic fiction), the Referential and the Symbolic over-determined (as in realistic fiction) and only the Semic (character) *supposedly* underdetermined (flat characters) yet in fact using the same techniques, parodied. Thus the one element of realistic fiction generally regarded as its crowning achievement (though essentially fantasmatic) is the only one supposedly parodied, but in a way which borders on (equally fantasmatic) imitation.

Sukenick also plays with defocalization in *Out* (1973), in which the hero changes names in each chapter (and the chapters are numbered backwards, starting with 10; and, from 9 down, consist of paragraphs of 9, then 8, then 7 (etc.) lines. It is possible also that Sukenick may be parodying the mystery of *V* in *98.6* when the central character vomits in the bathroom and feels jerked up by the neck: 'Something is holding him by the neck shaking him like a doll something huge but invisible. It has long v-striped fingernails many parallel stripes red and white and blue surprisingly Hallmark with horizontal continuations out from the top to the v....V why v what is is is the question. What does it want he wants it to leave him alone he can't take any more of this.' And later in Israel a specific character has v-striped fingernails. If this does refer to Pynchon then the whole parody business is becoming ultra-incestuous.

Zavarzadeh defines writing of this sort (parodies of interpretation) as metafiction, and the writing frequently poses some serious problems: is it really achieving everything it sets out to do? If *only* the topic distinguishes Coover's dead-pan realism from realism; and if, as in Pynchon, the very topic is drowned in a parody of realism that fuses with traditional realism, just where or how does the reader feel the difference between interpretation and over-interpretation (or parody of interpretation), between realism and the parody of realism? If the parody so fuses with its model as to become the model, the parody must cease.

For Bakhtin who has done much to clarify the various types of dialogical utterance (the degree to which the 'other' discourse is heard in the first), parody appropriates an existing discourse as object, but introduces into it an orientation diametrically opposed to its own. In contrast, imitation appropriates and takes seriously another discourse. Between the two he places stylization, that 'slight shadow of objectivization' thrown upon the series of procedures used by the other's discourse. The stylizer is careful not to confuse the other's voice with his own (as does the imitator), nor does he set off a clash between the two voices (as does the parodist). He simply lets the presence of another voice (another style) be heard beneath his own. Stylization however can tip over into imitation 'if the stylizer's enthusiasm for his model breaks down the distance between them and weakens the deliberate sensation that the reproduced style is indeed that of *another person*.[4]

But why then do we experience this tipping over into realism in these parodic dramatizations of a modern theme? Why does the distance continually collapse? This is partly because of certain difficulties inherent in the novel as genre and partly because of the nature of the ambition. There *is* parody of interpretation: that is, over-interpretation. But over-interpretation is not, as *technique*, sufficiently opposed to 'interpretation' to stop the discourse from tipping over into imitation, although the basic *thematic* orientation (the non-interpretability of the world) is diametrically opposed to that of the model.

It is all very well to talk of the 'zero-degree of interpretation...freeing the narrative from an anthropomorphic order-hunting and insuring that, as Barthelme says, "there is nothing between the lines but white space."' But this hardly differs, as view, from the New Criticism notion that, in Macleish's words, 'a poem should not mean, but be'. A huge novel is unfortunately not a poem, and the concrete result, with its sheer weight of realistic techniques and over-interpretation in Pynchon's case, is that one cannot, in fact, follow Gombrowicz's advice and 'start dancing with the book instead of asking for meaning': the book is too clumsy; it keeps treading on one's toes.

There is of course no reason why we should not appreciate these novels 'straight', that is, not as metafiction but as realistic and/or satirical dramatizations of serious contemporary problems. But in that case there is no essential difference (except, precisely, the 'counter-techniques: flat characterization, contrived plots') between them and earlier such novels (and the best): Musil and Mann also dramatized problems that were highly contemporary, so did Lawrence, or for that matter Tolstoy or Balzac (*The Magus* is then a modern version of *A la recherche de l'absolu* or *Les illusions perdues* and its sequel, *Splendeurs et misères des courtisanes*). And there is only the power of the controlling intelligence, the abiding interest of the central idea, to distinguish *these* from more popular versions (Galsworthy down). To take the difference between dramatization of a theme and stylization further back, it is like the difference between Langland and Chaucer, or between the second part of *Le roman de la rose* (by Jean de Meung, who didacticized and philosophized it) and the first part (by Guillaume de Lorris, who used the allegorical 'style'); or, more extreme both ways, between Bunyan, who used the by then moribund allegorical form to dramatize the Christian ideal, and Lyly, who in *Euphues* stylized *á outrance*; or, to raise the level again both ways and to show that this is not an issue of 'realism' vs. 'fantasy', between Swift or the philosophical novel generally, and Defoe, who 'stylized' documentary style for fictional purposes and thus laid the basis for the rise of the realistic novel.

Lodge calls *The Magus* (wrongly), Pynchon's *The Crying of Lot 49*, and Robbe-Grillet's *Le Voyeur* 'labyrinths without exits', and certainly the labyrinth is a powerful image in modern writing (Borges's library in 'The Tower of Babel', Robbe-Grillet's *Dans le Labyrinthe*, Butor's mysterious itineraries, Lacan's Moebius bands and other puzzles). But the important qualification is 'without exits'. As Clement Rosset points out, the labyrinth is not at all a place of non-significance, one exit, however hidden and hard to find.[5] To this he opposes, as paradigm of the modern situation, the confusion of paths in the famously ambiguous line in Sophocles's *Antigone* (1.360) which, although it 'means' *having all paths, pathless he walks towards nothing*, a situation which is not only that of Oedipus (that enigma on two feet; that deluded man; that self-styled detective who uncovers the true murderer, himself; that double man whose double vanishes progressively, at first certain, then probable, then improbable but still possible, then impossible), but also that of modern man. Thus one can hardly 'dance' through or with a labyrinth, but one must get out of it or die. But pathless at the forking of many paths one can but 'stand and stare'. But, in the end, Oedipus is blind. And Pynchon's reader is blinded by his own attempt to play detective.

Interestingly enough, modern attempts at stylization are remarkably short (often short stories), while the parodies, or parodic dramatizations, are all remarkably long. This may be a coincidence of my reading, but I think that the type of stylization I have in mind is difficult to sustain (Pynchon's new place/new person, for instance, is simply repetitive). As I said, the novels which take the theme of the world's non-interpretability and dramatize it are in a sense long stylizations of the realistic novels which interpreted the world; there is, however, a fragile frontier between that stylization and the literary model. Parodic dramatization of a theme works on the principle of expansion. Stylization, on that of reduction.

Pure stylization, when successful, is always clear as stylization of a model. I have already spoken of Barth's *Lost in the Funhouse* and its variations of tone, and Coover's stories are similarly varied, rather like experiments in the true sense, which may or may not come off. 'The Magic Poker' in *Pricksongs and Descants* (1969) is perhaps the most obvious (and so the most discussed) stylization of the writer's creative act, and also visibly influenced by Robbe-Grillet in its present tense time-shifts and incidents repeated but changed (here explicitly by the writer's creative act), and has the same uncanny poetry. Others are more concerned with the illusion/reality shift and the games people play, with themselves, with each other; but 'The Gingerbread House' and 'Seven Exemplary Fictions' are clear stylization of literary models.

Olga Scherer, who has most closely studied the Bakhtinian 'voices', has recently turned her attention to William Gass in a remarkable essay ('William Gass: Instances de la stylisation').[6] Without taking up her detailed typology, I shall merely recall a few points, the first being that there are of course innumerable models, 'prototexts' being infinite; secondly that the semantic value of the reiterable sign in the chosen model must be infallible, that is, limited and coherent, not containing another value, from another model (though there can be several models), nor contain just any old value, which would weaken the distance either by introducing a potential contradiction or by reducing the value to irrelevance.

In *Omensetter's Luck* (1966), we find the idyllic model, 'one of the most tenacious in American literary tradition', for instance in the descriptive introduction of Omensetter:

> Brackett Omensetter was a wide and happy man. He could whistle like the cardinal whistles in the deep snow, or whirr like the shy 'white rising from its cover, or be the lark a chuckle at the sky. He knew the earth. He put his hands in water. He smelled the clean fir smell. He listened to the bees. And he laughed his deep, loud, wide and happy laugh whenever he could—which was often, long, and joyfully.

And, later: 'A bee flew by his face. Omensetter was a wide and happy man. Fact.' Similarly the minister Furber's 'secret polemic' (Bakhtin's term) is itself very Dostoevskian, but also contains an imaginary interlocutor called Horatio. This does not, as Scherer points out, refer back to any actual dialogue between Hamlet and Horatio, 'but to a more abstract notion of Hamletism', or a literary model of hesitation and tragic conflict, 'of which Horatio is one of the infallible and reiterable signs'.

Another model in Gass is that of the narrator. In 'The Pedersen Kid' (*In the Heart of the Heart of the Country,* 1968) the stylization of the 'naive' or 'unconscious' narrator tends to fuse into imitation of the model, whereas in 'Mrs. Mean' the opposite happens, the omniscient narrator is stylized almost to the point of parody. Thus, although clearly only an outside observer of Mrs. Mean (he knows what towels and doylies she has only because he has seen them on the line or through the windows, etc.), he is an over-informed *voyeur*, sure of his conclusions about the mentality of his neighbours ('I rest my stories on their backs. They cannot feel them') and boasts of his superiority. He even intensifies his authority by giving himself an assistant-narrator, his wife—('My wife and I find it strange that they should'....)—an impossible procedure for a serious omniscient narrator who, even if he burdened himself with a wife, could hardly invoke her to affirm himself as true interpreter of the world' (Scherer). I should add, however, that the wife does not merely affirm or duplicate him, for, insofar as she is given any role, she is the one who has the 'nice', the 'charitable' interpretations; she is as it were the 'ordinary' man in him, not the transcendent omnisicient one:

> My wife maintains that Mrs Mean is an immaculate housekeeper and that her home is always cool and dry and airy. She's very likely correct as far as mere appearance goes but my description is emotionally right, metaphysically appropriate. My wife would strike up friendship, too and so, as she says, find out: but that must be blocked. It would destroy my transcendence. It would entangle me mortally in illusion.

Gass fluctuates between parody and a stylization so undistanced that it fuses with the model. In the long central part of *Omensetter's Luck*, entitled 'The Reverend Jethro Furber's Change of Heart', the model is the stream of consciousness, and through this the 'secret polemic'; but ultimately both refer back to an original single and total model, that of 'puritan hypocrisy' (Scherer). The familiarity of these models, together with the serious tone, tend to make the entire section (the main part of the book) tip over into a secret discourse taken seriously (i.e. the same problem we found in parody). As Scherer observes, Gass, in his war against genres (see interview in the same number of *Delta*,) is aware that all forms, and even the polyphonic discourse discovered by Dostoevsky, however revolutionary at the time, degenerate. Hence the present strong impulse towards parody and stylization is a form of regeneration via self-consciousness. The remedy, according to Scherer, would be 'either to inject the model with new strength by abandoning'....'the more or less deterministic philosophical positions and rediscover the original inspiration of polyphonic discourse; or to avoid the infallible and reiterable marks of the model that are most tired, by reducing them to the conventional. Gass has opted for this second solution, with unequal success.' And obviously the second solution is more liable to the danger of tipping over into imitation, since the marks are 'reduced to the conventional'. But at its best it is particularly subtle.

This can be seen in 'Icicles', the hero of which, Fender, is a real-estate salesman, from the start crossed by two primary models: the first a contemporary, socio-economic one (publicity discourse), where the relation between being (a man) and having (a property) is reversed into possession of the man by the property; the second, a literary model, goes all the way back to the early nineteenth-century: the inefficient office-clerk whose living is nevertheless his job (see Scherer for examples). The fusion of these two models is particularly rich, and well demonstrated by her. But personally I feel that the 'narrator' model is *also* lurking in the boss Pearson's admonitions to Fender: 'Keep your ears to the ground, Fender. Listen. Listen with all you've got, with the whole business—hard—with your eyes, with your nose—with the soul, Fender'....'That's how you get on in this business.' And later: 'People pass on....but property, property endures. That's why it's called real, see?...People are property. Does that seem like a hard saying, people are property? Not even real?' Pearson (a person), the boss (a figure for a narrator), runs a 'business' which involves listening hard, with all his being (itself a business, 'the whole business', i.e. the narrator's being, which is listening, is his business); but being is having, possessing (being possessed by), and his 'business' is 'real' property (reality/represented reality), which will survive (a literary work). In contrast, are people who are unreal, mere Fenders, who fend off reality or defend themselves badly in the system but get owned by the 'real' property, or rather by the melting aspect of it, the icicles that 'go with the house', and who become characters in a work that survives. The paradoxical complexity is much richer than that of 'Mrs. Mean' ('to see, to feel, to know, to possess'), but it would take too long to demonstrate here. In any case, if this third model is also present, it is subtly, almost surreptitiously introduced, and would add to the already subtle crossing of the other two.

Brautigan and Barthelme are much more overt stylizers. Brautigan's *The Hawkline Monster* (1974) is subtitled *A Gothic Western*, thus declaring its two models. *The Abortion* (1971) is subtitled *An Historical Romance 1966*, and *Willard and his Bowling Trophies* (1975) is a hilarious take-off of pointless Mafia murder. The Gothic, the Western, the Gangster film have of course often been parodied, even by the same medium as the model, but Brautigan's take-offs are not parodies in the usual sense of *exaggerating* the features of the model for an opposite purpose. On the contrary, there is rare reduction, in simple, factual sentences (statement for utterance, *éconcé* for *éconciation*) expressed by a dead-pan, omniscient narrator (who has made a big come-back in both metafiction and surfiction), who 'dips' into every character's mind in a way that would shock the post-Jamesian school. The minds into which he dips, however, are almost empty:

> During supper Greer and Cameron casually watched the Hawkline Monster about the throats and in the hair of the Hawkline sisters.
>
> The monster was very informal during the meal. Its light diminished in the necklaces and the shadowy moving colour in the sisters' hair was motionless, fading almost into the natural colour of their hair.
>
> The meal was steaks and potatoes and biscuits and gravy. It was a typical Eastern Oregon meal and eaten with a lot of gusto by Greer and Cameron.
>
> Greer sat thinking about the monster and thinking how this was still the same day they had awakened in a barn in Billy....
>
> Cameron counted random things in the room. He counted the things on the table: dishes, silverware, plates, etc... 28,

29, 30, etc.
It was something to do.
Then he counted the pearls that the Hawkline Monster was hiding in: ... 5, 6, etc.

The chapter (28 lines) is called 'Counting the Hawkline Monster'. The tone throughout is casual, inconsequential. Similarly in *Willard and his Bowling Trophies* we follow the sex-life of two separate couples in two separate apartments of the same house in San Francisco, one couple playing (badly) at sadism, the other having a room full of bowling trophies under the watchful eye of a huge papier-mâché bird, Willard. Elsewhere, the Logan brothers have had their bowling trophies stolen. They set out to find them, for three years, from one state to another, living on filling-stations hold-ups and in dingy hotel rooms, one drinking beer, one reading comics, the other waiting for a phone-call with information about the bowling trophies. Eventually, the Logan brothers locate the house and kill the wrong couple, shouting 'BOWLING TROPHY THIEVES DIE!' We never know how the trophies got to that room or whether the Logans find out their mistake or get the trophies back. The stylization is one of tone (the dead-pan Bogart style) and reversal: the unreal world of the cinema, which has spread to and is being overtaken by 'real life', is treated, not with the whipped up and quickly forgotten sensationalism of the media, but with arbitrary images of buying cornflakes or opening a can of peas. As in *Trout Fishing in America* (1967), *In Watermelon Sugar* (1964) (idyllic models), and *A Confederate General from Big Sur* (1965) (idyllic drop-out model), the extravagant is stylized into the norm.

Barthelme also uses reduction to bare, factual sentences, statement for utterance, but his stylization is much more mysterious. *The Dead Father* (1975) for instance is a mythic, heroic quest, but treated with consummate irony: the giant quester is 'dead' and eventually buried in a quarry-sized hole dug by bulldozers; that is, as R. Davis has pointed out, he is psychoanalytically dead but in fact, (during the mythic journey) alternately comatose and frenetic.[7] His fits of slaying (e.g. 'in a grove of music and musicians') are both biblical in tone and wildly implausible:

> First he slew a harpist and then a performer upon the serpent and also a banger upon the rattle and also a blower of the Persian trumpet.... The Dead Father slew a cittern plucker and five lyresmiters (long list of more and more

absurd instruments). The dead Father resting with his two hands on the hilt of his sword, which was planted in the red and steaming earth.

My anger, he said proudly.

Then the Dead Father sheathing his sword pulled from his trousers his ancient prick and pissed upon the dead artists, severally and together, to the best of his ability—four minutes, one pint.

Moreover, the Dead Father is drawn by a cable (chained, like Prometheus) and his assistant-quester-son is highly suspect in his attitude. The son's story of his 'imitiation' is also treated with irony, and of course the 'father' is itself both a literary and a psychoanalytical model. The point is, however, that the mythic quest and the mythical elements are not the 'key' to the meaning (as in 'modernist' writing and as R. Davis appears to think), but are stylized *as in themselves meaningless*, or rather as meaning no more than what the text literally says, nothing 'in between the lines'.

Another model is the fairy-tale glass mountain ('The Glass Mountain', in *City Life,* 1976), which 'stands at the corner of Thirteenth Street and Eighth Avenue', climbed by the narrator as crowds watch. The climb is told in one hundred numbered paragraphs, ranging from one word ('11. "Shithead". /12. "Asshole" ') to eighteen lines (80), but more often one simple sentence, and ends: '100. Nor are eagles plausible, not at all, not for a moment.' *City Life* also plays with visual models in a most intriguing way (e.g. 'At the Tolstoy Museum'). Similarly the Jamesian and post-Jamesian complexities are stripped bare: 'Where is the figure in the carpet? Or is it just ... carpet?' (*Snow White*, 1968). Meaning is itself one of our many fictions.

Barthelme's stylization is not only more mysterious than Brautigan's or Gass' but also more varied, and so, inevitably, a hit-or-miss affair, to use Lodge's term about postmodernism in general. Some of his pieces have a certain *New Yorker* smartness that leaves one with the emptiness, not of the 'stare' but of disappointment (relative to his other texts).

Finally I have chosen as illustrations of postmodern stylization two books by writers whom Zavarzadeh mentions under *Surfiction*, Ishmael Reed and Ronald Sukenick. They are utterly different from each. Zavarzadeh says that surfiction lays bare the conventions of narrative but less incestuously that metafiction, and prefers to 'engage' the reality outside (rather than inside) the fictional 'discourse', refusing 'to make any claim to interpreting reality' (not even in the parody of 'over-interpretation'). But since Surfiction also stylizes (as opposed to dramatizing the theme of non-interpretability in basically realistic form), I prefer my broad division, (stylization and parody) for surfiction is not essentially very different from the stylization considered here: Reed is as whacky as Barth and as zany as Brautigan, while Sukenick is as directly engaged with 'the reality outside' as Gass, and only the stylization in each is individual.

Reed's *Yellow Back Radio Broke-Down* (1969) is a strongly stylized send-up of the Wild West, to the point of parody in Bakhtin's sense of an orientation diametrically opposed to that of the model. The hero, for one thing, the Loop Garoo Kid, is the baddy, and he is black, a black cowboy being inconceivable in the racist model. The only Indian is one solitary left-over, Chief Showcase, who flies in his private plane to and from Paris to pick up the latest Cardin 'jacket with fur in the hood', dropping off in mid-desert to save the Loop Garoo at one point, or in Washington to talk to Field Marshall Theda Doompussy Blackwell, an elderly queer in a wig, and Pete the Peke, Congressman. There is complete anachrony since the President (Frenchy) is Thomas Jefferson, who 'likes niggers a whole lot' and appropriates $2,500 to add to his collection of mammoth bones at Monticello. Loop's enemy is Drag Gibson, who has close-circuit television in his room to spy on his own gang, and who is more and more defeated by Loop's voodoo, although a last minute visit from the Pope slightly restores his prestige. The Pope (dropping his American Italian accent) tells Drag how to catch the Loop Garoo, by bribing his stray artist supporters to steal the mad dog's tooth around his neck, which Loop, pretending to sleep, allows them to do. The Pope visits Loop in jail and has a very funny pope-to-devil dialogue with him ('You're his Son too, Loop'), Loop refusing to 'end this foolishness and come on home', for 'even martyrdom can be an art form, don't you think?' And when the Pope says, 'So you think by allowing yourself to be humiliated by mortals he'll respect you too, huh?,' Loop answers, 'No, I just wanted to show the world what they were really up to. I'm always with the avant-garde.' Loop's execution is inevitably stopped at the last minute by the Field Marshall, 'dressed like a Dresden doll'; Drag falls into the swinepit he used for punishing others (the pigs later discuss this unexpected dessert); and almost everyone is massacred by the sudden spears from the children who have survived an earlier massacre and formed their own community ('We decided to create our own fiction'). 'They all ignored the Loop Garoo Kid left standing and cheated out of his own martyrdom.' He rides off on his green horse and rushes after the Pope, reaching the coast to see the ship on the horizon and plunging in after it. 'Well I'll be damned, and hallelujah, here comes the Loop, the Pontiff smiled. Thomas Jefferson was out of a job but that was O.K. too' (last sentence).

The story is told in a racy 'western' vernacular and brief paragraphs with spaces in between (even in dialogue) like separate film-shots. Almost every page is a parody of cultural archetypes, Europeans, African, and American, but chiefly the latter: and, as we have seen above, there are also 'art' models. When Loop wakes to find himself surrounded by 'a shabby crew' of horsemen: 'It was Bo Shmo and the neo-realist gang.'

So Sympathetic Americans sent funds to Bo Shmo which he used to build one huge neo-realist institution in the Mountains. Wagon trains of neo-social realist composers writers and painters could be seen winding up its path.

Ronald Sukenick seems almost neo-realist in contrast, but again in such a stylized way that the effect can be unreal. *Up* (1968)—despite a couple of tales with the tale (Strop Banally), a mock review of *The Adventures of Strop Banally, by Ronald Sukenick* (a self-indulgently and implausibly long review), and the author appearing as Ron or Ronnie or 'our hero later called Suchanitch Subanitch Sockenack Bookenack Sackanook and so on'—is straight-faced narrative of scenes and dialogue between people, with a lot of sex, mildly funny but no more interesting than many reportage-of-daily-life novels. *Out* (1973) has diminishing paragraphs and changing names; ultimately, however, the deadpan stylization of reportage is in constant danger of fusing with the model, and unless one is particularly fascinated with sex and violence, the model is uninteresting.

In *98.6* however (1975), Sukenick seems to find the more subtle balance between realism and its stylization that the 'slight shadow' requires. The first part, 'Frankenstein' (a place which could be San Fransisco, but which later acquires the sense of America during 'the Dynasty of the Million Lies' and 'the Slaughter' and, on another level, monster building modern civilization) is told in the third person, present tense, and unpunctuated sentences: as a reportage-collage of sex scenes, dialogues, poetic moments, and frank narrator comment which (being in the present tense) tends to fuse with free indirect discourse. Each chapter starts with a double figure (times or American style dates, it doesn't matter which, the precise but arbitrary notation being itself a stylization of diary writing): 12/25 the blond comes in two parts. One part comes in a red Triumph 500.... 1/7 the blond comes in two parts here comes the second part she falls in love with him' (30,32). Or:

> 10/23 he has a thing and that is that he's only interested in the extraordinary. He thinks that the extraordinary is the answer to The Problem. For example he'd rather sit at home and watch the hummingbird at the feeder outside his window than go through the motions of a common seduction with nothing special about it.... He believes in powers meaning the extension of the ordinary to the point of the incredible and he believes that these powers are real though they can't be willed and they belong to everyone who isn't blinded by the negative hallucination of our culture. A negative hallucination is when you don't see something that's really there.

And there is a very funny 'chapter' in which his car, first called a canoe, then a boat, 'sailing down 7th Avenue', having lost its brakes, metamorphoses sentence by sentence, as does the place:

> The car hurtles down the street... turning off the ignition he finds he can slow the careening motorcycle in fact he manages to stop the Harley pretty fast for such a heavy machine. He gets off tinkers with the mechanism isn't able to fix it luckily a motorbike like that is just light enough to carry though it's no bag of feathers especially when you're not even sure which direction to take in a city like this. It's discouraging but still he can think of worse situations than carrying a broken ten speed bike through the streets of Paris. In fact he feels it's a good thing that all he has to lug around with him is his pogo stick even though it's sadly wilted and he feels terribly deserted being so completely lost in a city whose name he even forgets.

Similarly the notion that nothing visible is real or unique but a spectacle, a duplication which is the mask of the unreal, was the basic philosophy of Surrealism, of which American 'postmodernism' often seems a late and diluted version. The lateness, then is itself a naîveté,

But these are occasional moments, and mostly we're in the reportage style of *Up*. In the second and longest part, 'The Children of Frankenstein', the 'he' at first seems to have become Paul, one of many in a settlement, who try to reinvent life, to become 'mutants', among whom is Ron, the original 'he', a writer. The third person shifts to anyone of them: 'Ron is writing a book. He has a novel idea as a matter of fact it's an idea for a novel. His idea is to write a novel by recording whatever happens to their group so that they're all characters in his book including himself.' But later: 'Hi Ron. How's the novel about us going says Paul. I'm not writing it.' And later still: 'What chaos. Cloud (as Ron has become clutches his head. Cloud no longers believes any of this is happening. This is not real life. What was happening is now all over. It lacks credibility. Cloud is writing a novel again. It's almost finished.' That is, when things lack credibility, he can start writing again. Or, more self-reflexively still, and as rather an in-joke: 'Cloud has tried up and he has tried out. Neither of them works. Maybe nothing works,' which refers within the fiction to one of his many philosophies ('all the horizontal things are interchangeable, the vertical ones unique') and outside the fiction to his previous fictions. The whole style in fact is partly an imitation, partly a stylization and further extension of Gertrude Stein's, without the repetitive aspects of what she called the 'continuous present', not in fact a present tense but constant minute variations of repetitions to insist on the uniqueness of each episode.

The characters as we can see decide to change their names after a potlatch or other sexual or ritual experiences. Ron becomes Cloud, Evelyn his girl-friend becomes Eucalyptus (and when she leaves him for a rival community, Eve), Joan becomes Valley, Paul becomes Wind, Ralph (after resisting) becomes Quasar (but it doesn't stick), etc. The settlement is Earth, a neighbouring one is Trypton (The Superman Planet), etc. Ron's settlement, like all utopias, disintegrates, Cloud eventually 'bursts' and becomes 'he' again, and even 'I', and even (once) 'Someone'. The poetic idyll is interrupted brutally by the third part, 'Palestine', where 'I' takes over, in a curiously shifting way, in an unreal conversation with Bobby Kennedy, who is both assassinated and still alive, at the White House and apparently at the same time on a beach or with a rabbinic figure of a sage. In fact all the figures in the novel, but particularly Ron, 'filter' a general commentary on life, so that the 'narrator-filter' problem, apparently resolved by the style, is as much present as in the realistic novel.

Cloud for instance has invented 'psychosynthesis', as opposed to psychoanalysis, and psychosynthesis is based on the Mosaic Law (parts in the absence of wholes), an absurd contradiction since synthesis means making a whole out of parts. But the contradiction seems not to be a joke, for the context continues apparently in earnest. Eucalyptus has 'dropped psychoanalysis not because it did no good but because she didn't want to spend the rest of her life preparing for the rest of her life.' 'Cloud feels that life is a lot like a novel you have to make it up,' while Blossom
> no longer has to filter events through the particular distortions of her psychology psychology was the mark of a previous era. What we have instead of psychology is imagination. In any case psychology was always the science of the imagination but as a medical science was obliged to treat it like a sickness. For Bud and Branch imagination is a cure what does it cure why itself of course. It cures psychology. Which is to say it cures nothing it's just a beginning but a beginning has one great advantage it allows us to proceed.

This somewhat Beckettian last sentence inverts the whole notion as expressed in Todorov that the themes of the fantastic left literature because they were taken over by psycho-analysis, and Sukenick is obviously serious here, filtering his own ideas through the characters, as indeed the narrator-voice does throughout.[8] But unfortunately his ideas are often more naive. The imagination is much less rich than Brautigan, Barthelme, or Reed, closer to fancy in the Wordsworthian distinction.

Yet the book is much more than 'slice-of-life'. For what Sukenick is ultimately concerned with is the uniqueness of the real, the uniqueness of the 'ordinary made extraordinary', of the real made unreal. And if he doesn't always succeed, that is part of the 'hit-or-miss' character of the task, which is quite unusually difficult, and is being tackled in many ways.

If we imagine a circle, the upper half representing parodic dramatization, the lower half stylization, with a fluctuating dividing line and the content of the circle representing the 'task', then the writers I have discussed could be noted round the circumferences, representing various segments or slices of the circle: at the top of the upper half (parody of realism), Fowles (almost straight dramatization); to the left, Barth (pure parody, towards stylization, but satirical, light of touch); to the right, Pynchon (ostensible parody, towards stylization, but less so, and still heavily realistic in manner; then Coover (further towards stylization). Beneath Coover, in the lower half (stylization), Gass (still tipping back into realism), then Brautigan (stylization), then Barthelme (pure stylization); moving up to the right, back towards parody, Reed; then almost realistic dramatization again but in a highly individual style, bordering on imitation rather than stylization of a specific (Steinian) model, Sukenick. But such imaginings are 'schemas', anathema to these writers, which is why I don't dare draw it, but give it discursively, that it might get lost.

Where Do We Go from Here?

Towards silence, exhaustion? Or a new beginning? A good 'theory' should be able to 'predict', not in the futurological sense, but in accounting for all the theoretical possibilities. But I am not a pure theorist, and even less a prophet, and critical prophecies have a way of being undone by artists. Apocalyptic prophets can be pessimistic (total destruction) or optimistic (death and renewal).

One absurd fallacy should perhaps be got out of the way: the 'death of the novel' has been announced for half a century or more, and journalistic critics always mock this and point out that thousands of novels go on getting published and read, because people will always want 'stories'. That is entirely beside the point. Stories of one kind or another (even stories about stories) will indeed always continue, but they have always found and will continue to find their home in different forms. When the medieval verse romance got exhausted it became prose romance, and when that got exhausted, roughly in the fourteenth century, romances went on being written for at least a hundred years, and even well (Malory), just as Chaucer wrote an excellent verse romance (but in stanza form) a century after its heyday. But stories eventually found a more vivid form in the theatre, which regalvanized story-telling later into epic, then satire and the novel. The great nineteenth-century novel has continued, in both diluted and revivified forms, right through the twentieth, but it has for a long time shown signs of exhaustion in its turn, so that stories have escaped into the new media, film and its younger, as yet babbling offspring, television. Hence the 'elitist' wave of experiment and iconoclastic deconstructionism and stylization of various kinds. The new wave itself, in its concern about non-interpretation and its self-reflexive ways of dealing with it, is a sign of decadence and apocalyptic premonitions, like the multiplication of rhetorics and their concern for systems of meaning.

It is true however that iconoclasm as such cannot last (I mean the individual works may last but not the deconstruction). As Lodge says in a more specific context, 'it would truly abolish itself, by destroying the norms against which we perceive its deviations.' Similarly Susan Sontag:

> The present prospect is that artists will go on abolishing art, only to resurrect it in a more retracted version. As long as art bears up under the pressure of chronic interrogation, it would seem desirable that some of the questions have a certain playful quality. But this prospect depends, perhaps, on the viability of irony itself.

I have postponed the problem of irony, and clearly I shall not solve it here, it would require a book in itself, and has had, from others. Barthes dismisses it as just another code that merely shows the superiority of one voice over another, which closes off the plurality of codes; and he insists that it has disappeared from modern writing, thanks to the degree zero of tone, already nascent (as *uncertainty* of irony) in Flaubert—for the idol must be disculpated.[9] Sontag also casts doubt on irony, for although it has been valued from Socrates on as a serious method of seeking and holding one's truth and saving one's sanity, 'as it becomes the good taste of what is, after all, an essentially collective activity—the making of art—it may prove less serviceable.' She adds that we need not judge it as categorically as Nietzsche, who equated the spread of irony throughout a culture with decadence and the approaching end of that culture's vitality, but

> There still remains a question as to how far the resources of irony can be stretched. It seems unlikely that the possibilities of continually undermining one's

assumptions can go on unfolding indefinitely into the future, without being checked by despair or by a laughter that leaves one without any breath at all.

Similarly Ihab Hassan talks of a self consuming irony.

As we have seen, the writers I have surveyed here depend a great deal on irony, on more than a humdrum collusion with the reader (for collusion there must be). Some of the irony is naive, curiously mingled with earnestness and sometimes (if it is irony) astonishingly regressive in character, for instance in the treatment of sex, which is often ludicrously, limitedly, and it seems unconsciously phallocratic in most of the writers examined here (with the exception of Barthelme and Brautigan). But the healthy signs are surely the very element of naîveté I have here and there commented on, not by way of carping but to bring them out as such. If Northrop Frye is right, an exhausted literature turns to more popular forms either directly, in the sense that they are themselves taken more seriously by the 'central' tradition, or indirectly in the sense of parody and stylization by the 'serious' artists of that 'central' tradition.[10] The fact that this is happening so late, so long after the forms have become stereotypes, oft-parodied, and even declared moribund, is one of the paradoxes of American literature: its naîveté, its vigour, as well as the undeniable fact that it is now sometimes over-rated simply because it is American, and the culture of a great power always has more sway (for itself, for others) than that of a minor country, especially if its language becomes quasi-universal. But perhaps European experiments against realistic fiction, in the early part of the century (Gide, Pirandello, Surrealism on) were themselves part of an exhausted tradition. Sukenick has pleaded for an even more radical break-away of American literature from its European roots, since America, with its many and enriching non-European elements, is culturally far wider than Europe, and certainly *all* dead and dying models are grist to its parody-mill: Westerns are no longer made, the Gothic is over a century old, the gangster film long overtaken by life, SF weighed down by clichés and only here and there renewed, the realistic novel, by now a popular form, long declared dead, and only its most tired and nineteenth-century features parodied or stylized, etc.[11]

Similarly the notion that nothing visible is real or unique but a spectacle, a duplication which is the mask of the unreal, was the basic philosophy of Surrealism, of which American 'postmodernism' often seems a late and diluted version. The lateness, then, is itself a naîveté, which should regalvanize procedures, more vigorously perhaps than their more sophisticated European antecedents. Just as *Don Quixote*, a mock-romance long after the romance had died, was the beginning of modern fiction, or *Tristram Shandy* the end and the beginning of the modern novel, so the result now should be a new strength, new forms, *even* realistic ones, stripped of their tired formulas and interpretive mania, merely showing the real, in its unique 'idiocy', as the fantastic which it is. For ultimately *all* fiction is realistic, whether it mimes a mythic idea of heroic deeds or a progressive idea of society, or inner psychology or, as now, the non-interpretability of the world, which is our reality as its interpretability once was (and may return). A fantastic realism. A new classicism perhaps: 'nous vivons peut-être un pré-classicisme' , as Gaetan Picon said of Robbe-Grillet.

But not, I think, the romantic 'New Gnosticism' Ihan Hassan rhapsodizes, whereby, according to McLuhan, Buckminster Fuller and others including of course Teilhard de Chardin who sparked it all off, the old gnostic dream and the new technological dream, after the present period of transition or disjunction, would converge toward a universal consciousness, the consciousness of God in Susan Sontag's terms, or the noossphere in Chardin's. Hassan admits that the radical insufficiency of the human condition still offers intractable resistance to the old gnostic dream; and this resistance, he says, whether we call it evil (ananke) or The System, must be acknowledged, without assent.

At the risk of siding with ananke or The System, I am less optimistic about the gnostic dream. This consciousness that is to wrap the planet seems to me dangerously like the pollution that may stifle it. For every work of incomparable genius in all fields there are millions of tons of paper wasted in garbage, in the same way as that every benefit of civilization is paid for not only in entropy but in pollution and extremely ugly politics to get hold of raw materials—what's left of them, not to mention the thousands of children's brains atrophied from lack of protein. The gnostic dream of the best scientific, technological, and artistic brainstuff enveloping the earth seems to me essentially an elitist dream, akin to J.D. Bernal's (ironic, SF) suggestion that mankind may eventually divide into two species, the scientists and the others, the scientists colonizing the heaven but reverencing the earth as a sort of zoo (*The World, the Flesh, and the Devil*, 1929), or else not far removed from Wells' collective mind or world-wide information service

(*World Brain,* 1938), which presupposes an unprecedented harmony of minds: a mad and perhaps naive fusion of oblivion and utopia one could call oblitopia. Let the artists dream their gnostic or other dreams and produce verbal or other structures of them, but why, if art is to be regarded as 'no more nor less than anything else in life' (Hassan's words), should these dreams at the same time be given the supreme power of enveloping the planet (conquering the world), when neither those dreams nor man have shown the slightest capacity for solving the world's real problems, only a brilliant capacity for displacing them? At any rate, that envelope of brainstuff, more and more words and formulas and forms, continuous or discontinuous, theoretical or intuitive, not only seems to me yet another displacement, but also has me dead scared, even if like everyone else and in my infinitesimal way I am contributing to it, or to the garbage.

I prefer to struggle more humbly inside that paradox, which to me is nevertheless the fundamental one today and the true symptom of mutation: the paradox of the liar who says he is a liar, the paradox of using words to say meaninglessness, the paradox of letting everyone *prendre la parole* when everyone knows that real power, whether political, economic, social, psychological or even mystical, functions silently and has no need of the semblance of speech, even though it never ceases to use that semblance to persuade that we participate. If art can cope with that kind of terror and humour, it has a long future yet.

Notes

1. Ernst von Glaserfeld, 'Reflections on John Fowles' *The Magus* and the Construction of Reality,' *Georgia Review* (Summer, 1977,) pp. 444-48.
2. See Melvyn New, 'Profaned and Stenciled Texts: In Search of Pynchon's *V*', *Georgia Review* (Summer, 1979), pp. 395-412.
3. *City of Words: American Fiction 1950-1970* (1974), p.51
4. *Problems of Dostoevsky's Poetics*, R. W. Rotsel trans. (1973), p. 157.
5. *La réel: Traîté de l'idiocie* (1977).
   Rosset's general thesis in this short but remarkable book is that all reality is both necessarily determined (in virtue of the identity principle that A = A) and necessarily fortuituous in the sense that it is not necessarily this or that, but cannot escape the necessity of being something (i.e. anything). This property inherent to all reality he calls the non-significance of the real, and what makes reality tip over into non-sense is precisely the necessity we impose on it of being always significant. There are however privileged moments in which we have access to the real, when an occurence or object seems to us both necessary and fortuitous, but these are isolated perceptions, at once sanctioned by laughter (in certain types of humour) or by irritation (as when losing a game of chess, the moves of which are both necessary and fortuitous), or when drunk (the drunk's seeing double is a superficial optic phenomenon; he in fact see things in their prodigious ontological singularity—or 'idiocy'—and it is we who see double) or when suddenly bereft of love (coffee exists, washbasins exist) or through a work of art. Or finally through philosophy, which sums up the last three in the sense that the philosophic state, in Plato's words, is a state of being perpetually drunk, in love, and an artist. All other perceptions pass through the Double, the 'value-added' of significance.

6. In *Delta* (May, 1979), 8, pp. 65-86.
7. 'Barthelme: Post-Modern Paternity', *Delta* (May, 1979), 8, pp. 127-140.
8. *The Fantastic: A Structuralist Approach to a Literary Genre* Richard Howard trans. (1975).
9. *S/Z*, Richard Miller trans. (1970).
10. In *The Secular Scripture: A Study of the Structure of Romance*.
11. In 'Eight Digressions on the Politics of Language', *New Literary History* (1979), X, 3.

J.K. Klavans
God, He Was Good

'I wish I could do it to myself.'
She plunged.
'When you love somebody, Sal, are you constantly afraid of losing him?'
'I guess so,' she said poising the needle over Dolores's lip. Dolores flinched, the needle jutting into her thick skin. 'That hurt, didn't it? Sal smiled. 'Gotta be a big girl and take it.'
'Gotta keep smiling all the time. Right, Sal?' Dolores tightened from the electric shock. 'This hurts like hell.'
'It all hurts like hell, Babe,' Sal laughed taking a sip of her Tab, swallowing it quickly and placing it carefully back on top of the black metal electric box. 'Don't let go of that sponge, Okay?'
'What happens if I let go of it? I get electrocuted and die here on the table?'
'You'd like that, wouldn't you?' She placed the needle in the fleshy smile line and pressed the button on the side of the pencil-like holder. 'You ain't gonna die. You might kill everyone around you, but you ain't gonna die.'
'Thanks,' Dolores said noticing that the feet of her stockings were already dirty at eight twenty-five in the morning from walking around the salon barefoot. She rubbed her toes together and made a static noise, a noise like great thighs rubbing together in the heat, she thought. 'It's just that there ain't a whole lot to talk about before I start talking about him again, you know?' She squeezed the sponge. 'Oh, God, Sal. Salllll.' The needle drew a long dark hair from under the nose area, tender, the skin now red and paunchy, the root in the mouth of a tweezer. 'I thought only old ladies were supposed to have hairs like that.'
'Well, you got 'em.'

'Shit,' Dolores said, pulling herself up from the table, her eyes filled with fluid as an involuntary response to the electrolysis, 'tomorrow we'll work a little bit on the eyebrows. Okay?'

'You sure you can stand the pain?'

'Yea,' she laughed. 'What've I ever done in my whole life that wasn't painful anyway?'

'You got a four year old who isn't all bad.' Sal straightened out the needle by running her index finger over the edge, a bit of spit on the tip of the finger. 'Looks like you got it pretty good to me.'

'If I fear I'm losing you, it's just no good,' she sang with the stereo. 'Seemed like the real thing.'

'Better shake it this morning, Dolores,' Sal said swinging around on her stool to face the tall blond. 'You ain't got it any worse or any better than the rest of us. You remember that.'

'How can I forget?' She bent down and combed out her fringe with the tips of her fingers. 'Love is so confusing there's no piece of mind,' she whispered, closing her eyes slightly and running a long sculptured nail over the puffy lip area.

How come, after all this time, Jude, I still wake up afraid that I'm going to lose him. I mean, he's already gone. What am I so afraid of?' The medicinal smell of the glassed in black and red combs in alcohol wafted up into Dolores's face.

'You want a love story.'

'It's a little late for a love story, don't you think?'

'I think so, but you must not think so or you wouldn't walk around daydreaming about something that happened so long ago, would you?'

'Guess not.' She swished a hard plastic bristled brush through the solution. 'But, I just can't help it. I mean.'

'Sure, Hon. I know what you mean. It's not easy to go home and look at a kid and not remember where it came from. I mean, it came from your gut. You gotta remember. The kid won't let you forget.'

'Yea,' Dolores said looking at the picture of Rosemary she had taken last Easter, tiny blue dress, clean white patent leather shoes, plastered in her mirror with cement glue, 'sometimes you just don't even want to forget though.'

'What's that smell?'

'I threw up.'

'What do you mean you threw up, Sheila? Are you sick?' Jude asked.

'I don't know.' The bottom of her jawline began to expand with the tears. Her hair, so recently cut short above her ears, hung limply in her face. 'I don't know. Maybe I have the flu or something but I don't think so. I don't know.'

'What's wrong?'

'I don't know, Dolores,' Jude said. 'Sheila thinks she's pregnant.'

'I don't know,' Sheila said wiping her face with the back of her dried out hand.

'Well, don't worry,' Dolores said, 'you can still work pregnant.'

'But I don't want it. I don't want to be fat. I don't want to get married fat.'

'But you do want to get married?'

'I don't want to get married fat,' she argued.

Dolores shrugged. 'I don't see what your problem is, Sheila.' She looked into the bathroom and winced at the odour. 'If you want to marry Jeff and have a baby, then tell him about it.'

'And if you don't,' Jude said taking a hand and pushing the stringy hair out of the girl's face, 'pee in a bottle and take it over to the bank building, upstairs on the third floor, and they'll tell you if it's really there and when you can get rid of it.'

'Where would I get the money?' Sheila's shoulders shook like coat hangers in the back of a dusty closet. 'I haven't got the money.'

'Hasn't Jeff got any money? He's a policeman. They make good money, don't they?' Dolores and Jude looked at each other. They'd learned their lesson on this kind of thing before. Katie Michaels had left them in the lurch when she worked at Betsy's Hairlines and needed bail money for her boyfriend. Then Katie and her boyfriend had just forgotten all about the loan. Tough luck, Sugar.

'He won't let me,' Sheila said. There was water dripping down through the soft fuzz of her upper lip. 'He'll say I'm a horrible person and he won't let me. I know it.'

'But if you're going to marry him anyway?'

'I don't know,' Sheila shook. 'I don't know.'

'Sheila,' Betsy called in the back, 'you've got a lady that needs to be washed.'

'If you need us, let us know,' Jude said locking her teeth together. 'We can't help you moneywise, but, anything else.'

Sheila looked at the dark tiled floor beneath her feet. Her shoes, dark, low heeled lace-ups, looked old and matronly. She wished she were the type who could wear those high-heeled Candies all day and never feel the pain. She wished she were sophisticated like Dolores, or tough like Jude. She wished she were blond, not dirty blond but white blond like Claudine, fresh and seductive with clean white tits that bubbled out from behind cool looking fabrics. And she couldn't wear the sculptured nails because they'd break off from all the hair detergent. And she couldn't walk down the aisle fat because she'd be embarrassed. And because Jeff was nice but she'd seen others she'd a-rather had. And because she wouldn't feel right being in church.

'Isn't she something out of another century?' Jude smiled.

'I guess so,' Dolores leaned against the bowl and flushed.

Jude diluted shampoos into plastic bottles, the pink liquid meshing inconsistently with water. 'So where is he now?' she asked shaking the bottle with the force of a mad woman. 'Some *wonderful* when you were pregnant routine.'

'Yea, well, he was really great when he was there. I can't hardly blame him for leaving either.'

'Oh, bullshit, Dolores. It must have been hell having Rosie alone.'

'Yea, but, while he was there it was wonderful.' Dolores studied the Mr Coffee Maker grains. So dark, so brown, like a handful of seeds just waiting to be planted. 'One morning I got up, you know, and I was taking a real long hot soaky bath while he was shaving. I'd just relax and watch him slide the razor over his face. God, he was a novice even at that. He'd always knick, well,' Dolores counted ten Maxwell Houses into a clean paper filter, 'I stood up too quickly I guess and I almost fainted. I mean, I just blacked out. I don't know. It was probably the heat or something together with being pregnant. But we didn't know I was pregnant then. I'd just get a sick feeling in my stomach, you know, and I'd walk around feeling like my jeans were riding up my crotch.'

'God, Hon, I've got that feeling now,' she shook. The third plastic container was full and frothing over with pink.

'Yea, well, I stood up too fast to dry off and I lost my balance and collapsed half in and half out of the tub. Thank God he was standing right there to catch me. Thank God. God, he was good.'

'Uh huh. Sure sounds like it.' Jude finished the fourth container and started screwing on the spurt tops.

'Well, he was, Jude. He made me sit on the toilet with my head between my knees and I threw up all over the goddamned place and I didn't even have to clean it up. He did all that for me. I didn't have to touch the stuff. He put me to bed and he cleaned it up.'

'I guess I know sort of what you mean,' Jude said as she screwed in the last top. 'Like when I was pregnant with my Tonie I remember Rick and I together. I'd get a sick feeling in the bottom of my stomach like I was gonna throw up.'

'Yea, and it was kind of nice when you think about it now, wasn't it?'

'Dolores,' Jude smiled, wiping the necks of the bottles down with a ragged pink and white Handy-Towel, 'I'm not crazy, Honey. I know it. That was a bad feeling then, and now, when I look at my Tonie, such a big boy and married with his own babies, the feeling hurts even more.' She placed three of the bottles on the lower shelf and pulled one side of her mouth to the corner of her face, her age becoming apparent even in the dim light, the glossiness of her dyed 'Black As Night' hair flat against her complexion. 'But you are right in one way. Sometimes, even now, when I'm not sleeping, but just very lonely, peaceful in my bed, I think of my Rick and that sick feeling I used to get when I was having one of his babies and he had to get up in the morning and go to work. And it is then, that I am glad that I'm alone.'

Dolores watched the coffee drip into the pot, just drip, and she felt sorry for Jude. 'Don't you ever want him back?'

'I'm sane now.'

'If that's sanity, then I'm glad I'm crazy.'

'I wish you were crazy, Honey. Then they could lock you away and make it all a lot easier for you.'

'He's gonna die,' Claudine said. 'I'm writing a book.'

The woman placed three gold rings, one carefully after the other, into a cup full of cleaning solution and rolled up the sleeves of her dark red blouse, silk.

'Pretty,' said Claudine sweetly, smiling up from under blue tinted lashes.

'Thanks,' the woman said, looking away, looking away anywhere,

Claudine folding each hand lightly onto a clean white towel. 'This the little boy?' the woman asked. She couldn't help it. The photograph was taped to the white wall right above Claudine's table.

'Uh huh.' Claudine chewed her gum with a sucking motion as if trying to extract all the flavour before having to toss it into the bin. She couldn't stand the smell of polish remover to get in her mouth. 'He's ten and she's eight, but he only comes up to her hip. Can you believe it? I'm gonna write a book about it. He was supposed to be dead seven years ago.' The woman groaned in uncomfortable sympathy, a patient on an operating table. Claudine felt her fingers tighten. 'Loosen up,' she tugged at the hand, strong healthy bones used to pare apples, slice and dice. 'Yea, can you believe it? Seven years ago and still livin.' The lady smiled and watched Claudine intensely as she swabbed her pinky and removed the leftover 'Honeysuckle' polish. 'Yea, but it's not so bad.' The hand was placed limply in a shallow dish of green soapy liquid. Claudine worked on removing the polish from her customer's other hand. 'Bad break here, Lydia,' she said. 'How'd you do this?'

'Car door,' the woman spoke. It was like words being pulled from the dead, or a radio annoucer on Easy Listening.

'Yea, like I said,' Claudine continued, pulling the first hand out of the soap and laying it flat on the towel, placing the other hand into the same dish, 'I got to meet John Glenn, you know. You know, the astronaut? He came into the children's hospital one day and right into Johnny's room. Yea. He came into the room and Johnny was just laying there like he does and you know, John Glenn the astronaut starts to talk to me about Johnny's ailment and I told him, well, I told him just what I told you...that I was gonna write a book about it, specially cause I had met him, John Glenn the astronaut and all, and he was really flattered.' Claudine clipped back the acrylic with a metal utensil, the false nails flying across the room getting lost in heaps of dead hair in piles across the floor.

'Do you know what's wrong with him?' the customer asked, watching Claudine at work closely.

'Nope.' Claudine mixed the pink solution in the white powder with a thin paint brush, tapped it against the side of the plastic carrying box. She looked up into her customer's face and let out a long breath, 'Nobody knows. He's just been dying since he was born, you know.' She continued painting her lady's hand in acrylic, smooth, white, like dressing paper dolls. 'If I'd only realized he was gonna be a dwarf I'd

never had Michelle, that's all. I mean, he acted real normal when he was a baby.'
'That's funny, isn't it?'
'Nope. Don't think so. The doctors say he's smart enough. He just doesn't grow and he can't get used to his body or something. He's a freak, that's all. He's reallllll fucked up.'
The metal tips of the shaping cut into the woman's fingers under her own nails. The acrylic, heavy in weight, clung around the bones of her finger tips.
'I'm sorry,' the woman said. 'I didn't realize things were so bad. I knew your little boy was sick, but...'
'Oh, that's Okay,' Claudine smiled, 'I just gotta wait until he dies.'

Dolores kept her face turned into the recording list, the titles typed in red ink under rows of Country Western, Pop, and Rock-N-Roll. She placed her palms against the glass trying to feel the vibrations from a remake of an old Frankie Valli single. It just wasn't there anymore. Dolores let her hands slide across the glass, sweat marks smearing titles, her hips grinding into the metal of the machine. She felt her body moving in small circles to the beat. She couldn't help herself. She moved. Her lips mouthed the words.
'Dance for us, Lady,' the three young sailors behind her yelled. She tried not to look at them, at the crowd. The Blue Garter was always crowded on Sunday nights. The muscle men, the big brawny sailors, the little pipsqueaks who thought they could get ass just because they were shipping off or stuck in port. They always had some sympathetic excuse and, of course, they always wanted to get married afterwards. Only the very young girls fell for it. Usually, the young were the ones with the diseases anyway. Only the very young fell. Love substituted for infection. They were too stupid or scared to know they were infected. Dolores, at twenty four, wasn't very young anymore.
Dolores looked across the bar, small with smoke and Brute aftershave. The smell was unnerving, the men so clean and shaven looking...so young, most of them. She spotted a table where Sal stood talking to a serviceman, not much over eighteen, she thought. He didn't even have a beard to shave yet, probably not a hair on his chest. His adam's apple stuck out, jutted forward almost into Sal's large breasts. He looked as if his mother had just sent him an apple pie. Sal must be

crazy, she thought. They pull in and they pull out. And Sal had a hard time remembering her husband who had pulled out only a year ago last May. He'd been a fool to ask half the men on the Base to watch out for her. After all, she had had to leave Base housing, and with him out to sea, it was just as if having been divorced.

'Dance.' 'Dance.' 'Dance.' 'Dance.' 'Dance.' 'Dance.' 'Dance.' They stomped like hordes of hungry animals searching for something that would relieve the pressure. Sheila's Jeff, out of uniform, walked over and pulled the plug to the juke box. From Thursday to Monday, he worked at The Blue Garter undercover, as if everyone didn't already know him.

The lights flashed off, a Dolly Parton recording of 'It's All Wrong But It's Alright' slurred into the holocaust of men and women on rampage for Loretta Sweat and her daughter Louise Little Feet Sweat. Loretta ran out first, her spare rolls bouncing with the heartiness of dark beer against stained teeth. Her face a pancaked whiteness that only called to be ignored. It was the topless show she was selling, her large abdomen and prickly thighs covered by a tiny black danskin skirt. 'DANCE.' 'DANCE.' 'DANCE.' 'DANCE.' They got louder and louder, monsters in a movie theatre. Dolores stood against the darkened juke box and watched. Jeff, in the background, helped Rod bring bright pink and green lights out onto the bar, the smoke rising slowly to the roof of the building. Desire. Dolores watched Sal's young sailor lay his head against her black polyestered rear. And Loretta Sweat danced to 'Bad Girls', loud thumping noises on the wooden floorboards that made the whole scene ridiculous. The thumping continued, the men stomping their feet in perfect rhythm, the music being up louder and then louder again as Little Feet appeared, her chest flat as a paddle racket, rubbing herself up against her mother's large hanging boobs. Together they stood, mother and daughter, naked from the waist up in front of an audience, the music blaring. Dolores watched Sal and her sailor, felt as if simply a bystander as Loretta and Louise bent over hard backed chairs and challenged each other to lifting dances. Of course, Little Feet didn't have the flab needed. There, too, was where age fell. Still, some sailor would take her cunt home and make it worth something. It had only been last year that Rod had told her Loretta had held a private cherry popping party for Little Feet. Admission had been nine dollars at the door.

On Mondays Dolores dressed Rosemary and drove down to Ocean View. Her heart pounded excitedly as she looked at the spot. Rosemary, in a yellow gingham dress, sat very still, used to these trips.

'Where again, Mommy?' she asked, looking out the windscreen of the Mustang onto the dark sand. There was no sun. There were no waves rushing onto the beach. Maybe it had all been a dream. It had been too long ago. The only proof was her little girl, the child who sat beside her and needed her.

'There,' she pointed. Rosemary lifted her chin. It was true. The child moved. She was real and honey coloured with an oversized nose for a four year old, freckled and dappled with large spots over her shoulders and one very large one near her left eye. Dolores could look at her and believe in him. It was her love story and, God, she loved the melodramatics of it. All that gushing sincerity when it came to love, she had found the key to keeping it with her even after its death. All the lyrics that she had memorized, had sung by the hour while standing on her feet in the shop, those lyrics which had helped her to pass the time and feel the half-witted emotion that she reveled in, they were still there in Rosemary. They turned on the radio and looked at the beach again, backed the car up out of the empty parking lot and drove onto the highway.

'Baby, Baby, don't get hooked on me...'

I've got mine,' Dolores whispered in Sal's ear, 'so no bikini line today.'

'Oh, Hon,' Sal laughed through slackened nose tissue, 'thank God mine tapered off. But, you know,' she cleaned the edge of the needle, 'pussy smells when it don't bleed anymore. Funny thing. It's like it rots away or something. I'm thinking about getting a dusting and cleaning just so the damn odour won't keep me awake at night.'

'Oh, Sal,' she heard herself say, 'it's all in your imagination.'

'It's not.' Sal looked pitiful, as if she had a disease that was incurable and contagious. 'I had a man tell me the other night that I smelled. And that was after a vinegar douche and a dab of Madame Rouch.'

Dolores's eyes teared, the eyebrows being one of the most sensitive spots and her lids beginning to itch. 'Sally,' she mumbled, 'does this ever stop hurting?' The loud whining noise of the machine went through her body, the cold air chilling her, and the sponge wet and sweaty in her hand.

'You should be used to it by now,' Sal frowned. 'Still, it really depends on how you're doing physically.' She positioned the needle and the tweezer just so. 'Some weeks you're better able to accept the pain than others.'

'Oh, Jesus. Maybe I should start taking B Vitamin again.'

Sally laughed. 'Know one for twat odour?'

Claudine sat at her mirrored dressing table carefully applying white-out stick to the black circles under her eyes. Then, with her finger, drawing the whiteness up into the corner of her eye and across the yellowness of her lid. Johnny stood fingering the edge of a lace hanky anchored by a box of dried rose leaves she kept next to her perfumes. He watched her in the mirror, fascinated, his entire body only reaching Claudine's slender elbow, greased and smelling sweet. Chuck sat on the bed in the background, his hands clasped between strong ample thighs. He also watched, fascinated.

She ran a small plastic spatula in circles through a bottle of thick moisturizing cream and placed five dots on her face: each cheek, the nose, the chin, the forehead, and a dot on her neck to keep it from growing old and wrinkled. 'Fifty-four nails today,' she nodded to Chuck in the mirror, 'fifty-four. Sal and I figured out that if I do fifty-four nails a day I'll be doing over three hundred a week.'

'Will you get a raise then?' Chuck ran large hands through thick brown curls. He had the arms of a wrestler, wide, large boned, almost too big to even think about eating. Sometimes, with Hal, it made her mouth water just to look at his wrists, slender, like he could play the violin or the piano or something and be cultured if he had to dress up like the men on TV that wore tuxedoes and stuff. But not Chuck, he was just big...a big man who could smother her and her kids and keep them all warm at night.

Johnny gurgled. 'Deeeayeee.' No one knew what it meant. 'Deeeayeee.' Claudine just hoped he wouldn't follow anyone to the garage down the street and drink gasoline like he'd done when he was five. Hal should have watched him. Damn Hal. He probably offered it to the kid. She spread a brownish tone into the palm of her hand. Had to make it seem like a real suntan.

'More tips,' she sighed.

'Mom.' Her name was called from the living room. 'Mom, Blondie's on T.V. Come quick.'

'I can't, Michelle. Chuck and I are supposed to meet Dolores and Sal at eight-thirty and I'm right in the middle of putting on my make-up. Call Johnny for me, will ya?'

She looked straight into the boy's face, his reddish tint making her grimace, the powder in her worry lines caking into permanent features of the evening. 'Go to Michelle,' she spoke softly. 'Michelle wants you.'

He looked as if he understood, as if he took it as insult that she didn't want to allow him to see her go any farther with her make-up. A clown. She watched his arms and legs, the size of doll's appendages, toddle the midsection of a normal size boy out of her bedroom. He hated to leave the smell of fragrances behind on her vanity table. His nose was perfect, she thought, placed in the centre of a peanut face, small and raw with slats of coal blue eyes peering out from underneath slack folds of skin.

'Here, Johnny,' Michelle patted the floor, never taking her eyes away from the set. She had given up looking at him. He sat uncomfortably, dutifully at her side.

'It's the flip side to that American Gigolo song,' Claudine explained to Chuck. 'Don't touch me while I'm putting this on. It makes me nervous. Okay?'

> *Having fun in Puerto Rico! Wish everyone was here! The sun is shining and I am really black! Shines even when it rains! Bobby is a living doll! No more room—missing you and loving it! Dixie*

Said she was gonna get a real brick house when she got back from her honeymoon.'

'It's The Good Life,' Jude sang. 'Sinatra.' The girls nodded and recognized it, but only the early customers knew all the words. The early ones on Fridays were always the oldest. Somehow they knew that the best work was done before ten on Fridays and Saturdays. After ten everyone just rolled and set in some kind of blistered haze.

'Think she'll come back?'

'Ummm,' Dolores answered. 'I suspect so. She'll probably want to. It can get awfully lonely being locked up in an ivory tower all day ironing sheets.'

Jude snipped the back of her customer's neck. 'Well, Puerto Rico can't last forever and a brick house isn't exactly my idea of an ivory tower if you want to know the truth of the matter.'

'What is?' Sheila asked, setting the aqua rollers on the first and second tiers of the roller holder between Dolores's and Jude's chairs.

'Looks like Dixie hit jackpot to me.' Dolores teased out the soft grey hair of the woman sitting in front of her. She noticed the scalp pores seemed to be closing.

'Yea, she's good and happy now.'

'What's Bobby do?' Sheila asked. 'Sounds like he's got loads of cash.'

'Used car salesman. We can probably get a good deal.'

'Yea. She'll probably have a baby right away. Used car salesmen are always horny. They stand on that lot all day trying to sell their sex appeal and then come home and give it to their wives.'

'Or whoever,' Jude smiled. 'Remember, he was married when he met her at the Sixth National.'

'Maybe we oughta go up there sometime,' Sheila blurted out. Jude gave her an ugly glance. They didn't like their early customers to know they hung out at bars.

'The bars are only for the young,' Jude said. 'I'd rather stay home and watch Happy Days.'

'Besides,' Dolores said, 'we know a lot of people up at The Blue Garter.'

'Yea, like Jeff,' Sheila said. She averted her eyes from Dolores and continued placing the smaller green rollers on the stand.

'Well.' Dolores swallowed. 'Like it?' She handed her customer a mirror and swung the chair around to get the full view magnified off the back wall mirror.

'You can't run away from things, you know, Sheila.'

'How about a little more on this side?' the customer asked. It was really aggravating. You worked on them for forty-five minutes and it was hardly ever perfect. She brought the teasing comb around to the woman's left ear and softly pulled the hair out and then upward.

'Really,' Jude answered taking a drag off a cigarette and looking in the mirror for Betsy. Betsy didn't like them to smoke on the floor. Especially with the early customers. Of course, the customers were allowed to do whatever they wanted. More often than not Jude just couldn't stand it when one of her ladies smoked. She just had to have

one. 'Nicotine fits,' she explained to Betsy.
'I'm not runnin' away from anything,' Sheila assured them. 'I'm just tired of going there.'
Jude's customer kept her eyes plastered to the mirror in front of her and the postcard from Dixie Painter taped to the glass. 'She sure makes it sound nice, doesn't she?' the woman smiled.
'Yea. Got the message memorized. But, you know,' Jude said, 'I wouldn't want to be in her shoes. She's young. She can go through it. But if I had to start all over again with a man coming home from work every night and settling down on top of me, well, I just couldn't do it now.'
Dolores thanked her customer for the dollar tip, the black handbag snapping, the gold clasp catching the light from the electric overheads.
'I thank the Lord for divorce. And I hope to God that my Rick is out there cattin' about finding him some young woman to sleep with.'
The customer smiled, anxious to get out of Jude's chair.
'I thought it would stop working after five or ten years, but twenty years later he was still rearin to go. It just about killed me.'
'Everyone's marriage isn't like that,' Dolores joked. 'Some men settle down.'
'Sure,' Jude answered, combing her lady's hair just so perfectly down in the back. 'Dye job looks good today, Elsie.... Sure, some guys die down. But they're the ones you're never attracted to in the first place. And who needs them?'
'They pay the rent and don't mind if you spend a little to pamper yourself,' the customer answered. Her Calvin Klein jeans pulled tightly over her stomach. 'And that one's got a trip to Puerto Rico out of it to boot,' she nodded toward the postcard.
'She's lucky,' Dolores said. She sat in her chair and crossed her legs. Her next customer was still being washed by the new girl.
'For now,' Jude added.
'Seems lucky to me,' Sheila said, the last few tiny pink rollers being placed on the tray. 'Not a worry in the world.'
Jude gave her lady the hand-mirror, swung her around to the right angle. The woman, in a hurry, agreed that the styling was fine, and left to pay the bill up front at Betsy's desk.
'Postcard doesn't do much for tips,' Jude said, 'but it sure is a pretty picture.'

Claudine liked rolling over in bed and finding herself straddled against Chuck's overformed body, the muscles bulging from behind his neck, the rippled tonnage of his thick arms and legs and simply his overall weight excited her in the morning. She would run her fingers over his back and chest with her eyes closed, feeling, touching, sensing the magnificence of the out of proportioned body. Chuck would crawl on top of her in half sleep, forcefully spreading her skinny limbs apart with one strong foot, and then enter her. A long groan later, like a tremendous shift of pressure, her whole body would stiffen and she would find herself stretching her arms down over his torso, trying to squeeze the solidly tight muscles out of his ass with her sculptured nails. She did it with hatred, with disgust, and partly because Chuck was only nineteen years old. What kind of future was in that? She was prepared for him to get up one morning, go over to Old Dominion and buy his books and never come back. And when he would leave, he'd just leave. She had been left before, and she had never expected this one to stay any longer than just one night.

Somehow, she thought, the people lingered that she didn't love. And those that she had loved had slipped away. Well, she acted foolishly. Frank had lasted a year after Michelle was born, even with the baby crying all through the night and him not being the father. Hell, if only she hadn't lost the ability to speak. But, she loved him so much she just couldn't talk anymore. Only at work. Only when she went in to talk to the women could it all pour out. But, with Frank, it was if her tongue had grown thick or something. He began to call her stupid. She had just been so much in love. And she couldn't move correctly. It was as if his just being there made her overly nervous, as if she wanted everything to look and sound perfect. She had had her hair cut for the first time, short under her ears. He hadn't liked it, calling her a bitch for changing her looks. She told him it would grow back. But, in the meantime she began to stumble a lot, knocking things over around the house. One morning she got up early and put away everything that had been breakable. She hid the candy dishes from herself, moved the blue bud vase to a closet shelf, carefully placed the flower pots on the back step. Then she'd made him breakfast in bed. Spilled the cornflakes all in the sheets. What a white mess they'd made. And he'd screamed so loud because of the cold. She had wanted to die. Die. Die. Die. Die. I am going to stay deformed forever, she had thought. Please God, don't let him leave me. I am going to stay deformed and I need him.

Johnny hadn't been too bad then. Sure, she had known he was dying, but at two, he just stayed in his crib and didn't bother anyone. Sometimes she even forgot he was dying. Then, all she had to do was look at him, grotesque baby monster behind bars. Where had he come from? Frank had wanted to give him to Social Services. They'll know what to do with a freak like that, he'd said. Give him up. He's ruining your life. But the children didn't mean much to him, She knew. Even her precious newborn little girl. Frank would have given her up to Social Services too. But what he didn't realize was that she loved them; she really loved them. When she looked into Johnny's face she saw someone she knew, someone she had forgotten and yet, could not forget. She couldn't put him away.

'Deeeayeee,' he called. She rolled over. It was too early on a Sunday morning. Chuck stretched out against her back.

It was as if having one justified loving the other. She felt no loss loving Johnny. He, in fact, made Michelle all the more beautiful. She had fed them together and bathed them together and brushed their hair together. She had love for them both. She had all the love for them that she had had for Mike Downings, for Mike's dirty socks and his mechanic's tools. And when he left her he left her in peace with her babies. He had not left her alone. She thanked him for that.

They didn't need a father. She hung their pictures over her manicurist table, always new pictures to show how one had grown and one hadn't. And she was making more money than anybody in the shop, except Betsy, of course. And the babies didn't want much, they didn't eat much, and Michelle watched over Johnny and had good common sense. She was glad Mike had left. Glad Frank had left for sure. Didn't mind where they lived. Robin Hood was good and cheap and then, there was Dolores, she lived right down the street if anything was ever needed. She didn't have to report her full earnings to the State of Virginia and that was good. She could get away with affording luxuries. She even had a colour TV. The three of them were just like everyone else. And she didn't mind the coloureds living around her. They were just like everyone else too. Why were they any different? They had babies and worked and sweated and slept just like her. Jude was crazy. Who the hell did she think she was?

Frank had screamed, knocking over a plant she had missed, a plant given to her by one of her customers for Christmas, 'I don't know how you can live this way!' And she had pretended she didn't know what he was talking about. 'Here in this shit hole with two whiney kids—one who ain't even a kid. God knows what the hell that is.' He had opened his hand toward the middle of the floor where Johnny sprawled on his backside, a three year old's body, a newborn's arms, legs and head. Deformed.

'I love him,' she had cried, trying to sweep the dirt from the plant's roots into the broken pieces of ceramic. 'If you don't like it, get out.'

He pulled her face up by the thin pointy chin, such strong fingers from such a slim wrist.

'What do you want me to do?' She spoke softly.

'You're picking the freak over me?' he had asked. 'Baby,' he said getting down on his knees beside her. He ran his hands over the smooth whiteness of her cheeks.

'I can't kill him, Frank,' she had snivelled. 'He's my baby and I love him.'

'I'm not telling you to kill it.' He was gentle, like the TV violinist, used his greasy tools like an artist. She had loved him. 'There are places for things like that.'

'I know,' she had said.

'We'll take him up to Williamsburg and if you don't like the looks of the place you don't have to leave him there, Okay?'

'Okay,' she had said. Later, when he was leaving, she remembered his fragile outline and his wide baby like eyes.

'You're a low class broad, you know that, Claudine?' he had said. 'Don't never want to live any better.'

'Deeeayee.' She rolled over. She had to remind Chuck to call his mother.

Notes on Contributors

Salman Rushdie's 'Midnight Children' is taken from a novel of the same title to be published in February by Jonathan Cape. He is the author of one other novel, *Grimus*, and is currently living in north London. **Angela Carter** won the Somerset Maugham Award for her first collection of short stories and has since published a number of books including the *Sadian Woman* and, most recently, *The Bloody Chamber*. **Desmond Hogan**'s next collection of short stories is entitled *Children of Lir* and will be published by Hamish Hamilton next spring. He is the recent winner of the John Llewelyn Rhys Memorial Prize for *Diamonds at the Bottom of the Sea*. **Alan Sillitoe** is the author of many novels, short stories, and poetry. He is married to the poet Ruth Fainlight, has two children, and lives in London. Jonathan Cape will be publishing his next book, *Second Chance*, this January. **Emma Tennant** is the founding editor of *Bananas*, and most recently Next Editions and a new series on British regional poetry. 'Alice fell' is from her sixth novel of the same title, to be published this November by Jonathan Cape. **Russell Hoban** has written over forty children's books and three adult novels, including *Kleinzeit* and *Turtle Diary*. *Riddley Walker* appears on October 16th. **Lorna Sage** is a reviewer and a Senior Lecturer in the School of English and American Studies at the University of East Anglia. **Chris Bigsby** is the author of a number of books on popular culture, fiction and the British and American theatre, and is co-editor of a new series he is organising with Malcolm Bradbury of books on contemporary authors. The Greenwood Press has just published his study of black writing of the last forty years entitled *A Second Black Renaissance*. **Frederick Bowers** lectures at the University of British Columbia. **James Gindin** is the author of a number of works including *Postwar British Fiction: New Accents and Attitudes*. He is Professor of English at the University of Michigan at Ann Arbor.

Christine Brooke-Rose is the author of novels, short stories, and criticism. She is currently a visiting lecturer at Brandeis University in Massachusetts. **J.K. Klavans** was a student of the Creative Writing Programme at the University of East Anglia and has two short stories in Faber's *Introduction 7*, to be published this February at £5.50. 'God, He was Good' is her first published work. **John Blanche** is a professional illustrator living in Liverpool.

Emma Tennant will be reading from *Alice fell* at the ICA, on Thursday, December 4 at 1 p.m.

Granta

Most magazines do pretty much the same thing, issue after issue. They have *continuity* and a *house style* and a *voice*. That is, after all, the sign of a good editor. That kind of magazine is a lot like your favourite arm chair, familiar and cosy: it keeps your thoughts, like your haunches, comfortably in one place.

The *new* GRANTA is doing something very different: we intend to be anything but the same. We want to surprise and stimulate, keeping your mind exactly as it should be: active and alert.

GRANTA 1: William Gass, Susan Sontag, Stanley Elkin, John Hawkes, Tillie Olsen, Joyce Carol Oates, Donald Barthelme, James Purdy, Leonard Michaels, Ronald Sukenick, plus Tony Tanner and Theodore Solotaroff.

GRANTA 2: George Steiner, Jerome Klinkowitz and Thomas Remington, Robert Coover, Walter Abish, Robert Boyers, Tony Tanner, John Barth, and many others.

Subscribe, while prices are still low: £5.50 for four issues (for foreign subscriptions, add £3.00 for postage).

Box 666, King's College, Cambridge CB2 1ST